THE POLITICAL ECONOMY
OF GLOBAL RESTRUCTURING

VOLUME I

New Dimensions in Political Economy
General Editor: Ingrid H. Rima, Professor of Economics, Temple University, US

This ambitious new series is designed to bridge the gap between received economic theory and the real world that it seeks to explain. The dramatic events in Eastern Europe, the resurgence of an invigorated market capitalism and the prospects of integrated trading and financial communities have created new interest in the term political economy, which will be a dominant theme of titles included in this series.

The Political Economy of Global Restructuring

Volume I   Economic Organization and Production

Edited by

Ingrid H. Rima

Professor of Economics
Temple University, US

Edward Elgar

Published by
Edward Elgar Publishing Limited
Gower House
Croft Road
Aldershot
Hants GU11 3HR
England

Edward Elgar Publishing Company
Old Post Road
Brookfield
Vermont 05036
USA

A CIP catalogue record for this book is available from the British Library

ISBN 1 85278 638 8 (Volume I)
     1 85278 808 9 (Volume II)
     1 85278 817 8 (2-volume set)

Printed and bound in Great Britain by
Hartnolls Limited, Bodmin, Cornwall.

For Adolph Lowe as a tribute to his pioneering and inspirational intellectual leadership in understanding political economy.

Contents

Figures

Tables

Contributors

Zoltan J. Acs	University of Baltimore, Baltimore, Maryland, USA.
Nicholas W. Balabkins	Lehigh University, Bethlehem, Pennsylvania, USA.
Volodimir N. Bandera	Temple University, Philadelphia, Pennsylvania, USA.
Stanley Bober	Duquesne University, Pittsburgh, Pennsylvania, USA.
Anindya Datta	Plymouth State College, Plymouth, New Hampshire, USA.
Bruce Elmslie	University of New Hampshire, Durham, New Hampshire, USA.
Felix R. FitzRoy	University of St Andrews, Scotland
Linwood T. Geiger	Eastern College, St Davids, Pennsylvania, USA.
Harald Hagemann	Universität Hohenheim, Stuttgart, Germany
Walter W. Jermakowicz	University of Southern Indiana, Evansville, Indiana, USA.
Mark Knell	Middlebury College, Middlebury, Vermont, USA.
Heinz D. Kurz	University of Graz, Austria.
Eva Marikova Leeds	Franklin and Marshall College, Lancaster, Pennsylvania, USA.
William Milberg	The New School for Social Research, New York, New York USA.
Christine Rider	St Johns University, Jamaica, New York, USA.
Ingrid H. Rima	Temple University, Philadelphia, Pennsylvania, USA.
Stephan Seiter	Universität Hohenheim, Stuttgart, Germany

Preface

The concept for this volume of collected papers and its companion volume, *Trade and Finance*, and the idea of offering them to the community of scholars worldwide who are concerned with the political economy of global restructuring, was developed in tandem with the idea for an international Workshop to be sponsored jointly by 'La Sapienza', the University of Rome, Italy, and Temple University in Philadelphia, Pennsylvania, US. In the division of labour agreed upon, Giancarlo Gandolfo and Ferruccio Marzano planned the local arrangements and secured the financing necessary to host forty scholars at a Workshop convened at the Hotel Jolly in Rome 29–30 May 1991. Ingrid Rima undertook the responsibility for editing those papers that were made available for publication, joining them with others that were commissioned for inclusion in these volumes, though their authors were not able to participate in the Workshop.

Special thanks are due to Ernesto Chiacchierini, Dean of the Faculty of Economics and Commerce, University of Rome, 'La Sapienza' and the members of his distinguished faculty, and to Banca Nazionale del Lavoro, which provided generous financial support.

Ingrid H. Rima
Philadelphia, Pennsylvania

An introduction to a political economy perspective of economic organization, production and prices

Ingrid H. Rima

While the orientation of mainstream economists towards positivism and model building has rendered the term *political economy* old-fashioned and even irrelevant (except perhaps among Chicago libertarians and public choice advocates), the recent dramatic events in the global economy suggest that both the term and its classical perspective will become newly relevant as we approach the 21st century. It is part of the folk wisdom of the economics profession that the term fell into disuse when Alfred Marshall chose the title *Principles of Economics* for his 1890 publication, ostensibly to enhance the scientific status of his 'engine of analysis'. Marshall's focus on the problem of exchange value and price and his extension of the principles of demand and supply to explain the prices of factors of production paved the way towards the later definition of economics as the science for allocating scarce resources among alternative uses (Robbins, 1932). From here it was but a relatively small intellectual step towards static 'maximizing' and equilibration models.

Such models have become increasingly irrelevant to the substantially restructured global economy. Whether we contemplate the events in Eastern and Central Europe, which presage a transition towards private property and a market welfare system, or the organization of the European Economic Community (with its counterpart in the making in the Canada–United States–Mexico trading bloc, no doubt to be followed by a Pacific Rim coalition with Japan at its centre) or the G-7 pledge of support to shore up the ailing economies of the Commonwealth of Independent States, these institutional changes are likely to alter for all time the rules by which most of the economies of the world function. By the same token these events offer a unique opportunity for rethinking, and so reshaping, the task of economic science and the method for arriving at economic knowledge and policy.

The political restructuring of Eastern and Central Europe signifies first, that the market system has triumphed over collectivism as the *modus operandi* for guiding production, exchange and income distribution in virtually the whole of Europe. The several revolutions of 1989 are a particularly dramatic example that the presence of a gross incompatibility between a desired

1

macro-goal and the system of social relations over a substantial period invariably makes it necessary to abandon either the goal or the existing social order. In the case of the Central and Eastern European economies, popular discontent with decades of low levels of consumption under collectivism were the prelude to a 'Velvet' Revolution, a substantially peaceful political overthrow of economic institutions that is without parallel in modern history.

The fact that the restructuring of the Eastern and Central European economies will involve a transformation for which there is no precedent, and for which traditional mainstream economics cannot provide informed guidance, prompts a search for an historical counterpart. The post reform experiences of China and some Latin American economies offer a degree of insight about the transitions of predominantly agricultural economies towards industrialization. However, the analogies break down because their reforms did not involve an attempt to shift towards a market-directed economy. Thus, the only case study that history offers of an emerging market economy (if, indeed, any exists) is the primary stage of capitalism that developed in England between the mid-18th and mid-19th centuries in tandem with the Industrial Revolution. This period is, of course, also the era of classical economics that was ushered in by Adam Smith's *Wealth of Nations* (1776), whose chief concern was to explain the 'progress of opulence among the various nations'.

It was precisely the failure of the planned economies to achieve even a modicum of opulence that provoked the recent populist revolt. The objective of their uprising (to overthrow collectivism and establish market economies and private property) is embedded in traditional (that is, neoclassical) economics: specifically, to achieve the largest possible output of goods (together with a 'preferred mix') given the human and physical resources available domestically or that can be traded for or acquired on credit. Neoclassical economics concludes that if artificial impediments are eliminated or avoided, this optimal outcome will automatically come into existence via the feedback relationship among market participants and the economic environment.

Leaving aside the dubious relevance of that vision for mature market economies, it is manifestly clear that the reforms of the East and Central European economies are likely to entail a level of supervision and guidance which may well rival the production planning that preceded it. The establishment of a market economy requires a comprehensive new infrastructure along with new laws, in particular, laws to govern the ownership of property and contractual relationships. The definition of property rights is basic to privatization in all its aspects and is pivotal to the way in which new market economies are likely to function. It is, of course, a prerequisite that if reconstruction is to proceed there must be a social consensus in favour of reform, along with political authority to proceed. Given these prerequisites, there are at least three legitimate tasks for economists to perform. The first is to identify the societal dangers that are likely to accompany reprivatization and deregulation. The second is to enlighten the public about the alternative economic states that are feasible, given the available resource base and the level of technological knowledge, and the third is to identify the set of alternative measures that is likely to be suitable for attaining the terminal state society desires.

The social dangers that are inherent in economic *laissez-faire* are essentially the same in the formerly socialist economies of Eastern and Central Europe as they are in the United States, Canada, the UK and Western Europe. The recent experiences of these economies in terms of high levels of unemployment, inequitable income distribution, environmental pollution and other problems make it all too clear that private enterprise economies are, in fact, *not* endowed with self-regulating mechanisms that can reliably be counted on to ameliorate negative outcomes.

It is for this reason that *instrumental analysis* as a means of achieving the economic goals which society desires is among the proper concerns of economists. Conceptually, both the problem of social control and the idea of developing instrumental analysis as a science are part of the legacy of the Keynesian revolution.[1] Keynesian anti-depression policy is an historical example of the kind of instrumental analysis towards which capitalist countries appear to be driving. The histories of macroeconomic management in market economies that undertook to put Keynesian measures into place are likely to become invaluable information sources for facilitating the transition through which centrally planned economies must pass as they become nonsocialist. It is likely that formerly planned economies will articulate their macro-goals for more efficient resource use and higher growth rates with increasing clarity and specificity as they proceed towards their objective of privatization and marketization. But it is relevant to note that the political restructuring initiated by the 1989 revolutions in Eastern and Central Europe are not ushering in *laissez-faire* systems of uncontrolled capitalism. Their form of capitalism may thus have much to learn from the 1930's experiences of those Western economies which undertook macroeconomic measures of Keynesian inspiration to restore stability after the Great Depression. A system of *laissez-faire* capitalism is as patently unrealistic an outcome in the East as it is in the West.

Adam Smith's *Wealth of Nations* identified the goals of political economy as being, 'first to provide a plentiful revenue or subsistence for the people...' and, secondly, 'to supply the state or commonwealth with a revenue sufficient for public services' (p. 397). It was among Adam Smith's concerns to develop a bill of particulars to guide the allocation of some inputs and outputs from the private to the public sector to correct the failings of mercantilism and the agricultural system, both of which he regarded as 'subversive of the great purpose which it means to promote' (pp. 650–51). Although Smith's system is predicated on a vision of a self-regulating economy in which policy intervention is either unnecessary or harmful, he thought the ideal of self-regulation via market processes to be realizable only subsequent to suitable institutional changes to control the system. It is thus clear that there is an instrumental premise in Smith's system of natural liberty, the determinism of the invisible hand notwithstanding.

Smith's caveats about the market system of exchange in his day are not without relevance in the context of the 20th century and the present phase of capitalist evolution. Just as the propitious outcome of the invisible hand would be realized only by the removal of features of the economy that were 'subversive', so there are equally destructive aspects inherent in modern capitalism. Smith's conception of political economy is thus fully compatible with the development of a science that studies problems in which neoclassicals are only peripherally interested, such as the distribution of income and the development of instruments of social control that nurture behavioural patterns that are compatible with socially desirable actions. Keynes's focus in his *General Theory* on the role of expectations as it relates to the investment and business sectors of the economy made us appreciate some of the possibilities. Studies that aimed at the control of inflation by means of 'incomes policies' are of the same genre in the sense that they aimed at utilizing the vehicle of the market mechanism to effect a policy of social control.[2] If the automatic feedback mechanism thought to be inherent in Smith's 'invisible hand' had shown itself capable of producing outcomes that are as socially beneficial as they are profitable to individual market participants, there would be no need, either in the West or in the newly privatized economies of Central and Eastern Europe, for political economists to develop instrumental analysis as a technique for achieving socially desired outcomes.[3]

Smith envisioned a science which would enable the statesman or legislator to propel the society towards a plentiful sustenance for its inhabitants and also to 'supply the commonwealth with a revenue sufficient for the (requisite) public services'. The obvious criticism of giving too much credence to Smith's analysis as a basis for contemporary study is that it is 'time bound' in the sense of relating chiefly to the early stage of market capitalism. It is certainly true, given the specifics of Smith's scenario, that the 'economic laws' of the classical school have little contemporary relevance.

Classical political economy is best conceived as offering a model. It represents linkages among the processes of production, income distribution, accumulation (investment) and growth in an economic system characterized by classes of persons whose claims to income derive either from their status as wage earners or as earners of property income. When classical political economy is conceived in this context, it is seen to have relevance to economies that are in different stages of development. Thus one can envision at one end of the spectrum the newly emerging market systems, several of which are predominantly agrarian and most akin to the England of Smith's day. At the other end of the spectrum are the highly industrialized economies of Western Europe and the United States. In between are the governmentally subsidized capitalist economies of the Pacific region and the Third World economies of Asia, South America and Africa that still languish far behind. Each can be explained in terms of a suitably modified model. The common point of departure for all is their vision of a market economy as having the potential for moving them forward towards greater opulence. With the constraints of scarcity loosened by technical progress, the potential for growth in many of them is probably no less dramatic than that envisioned by Smith when mercantilist restrictions were driven out or fell into disuse. Thus Smith's perspective was that of an order that was in the process of 'becoming', and his focus was on policy measures that would contribute towards realizing 'the natural order' in which the invisible hand could function to move the system towards the macro-objective of 'opulence'.

It is, of course, not possible to 'bring back pure competition' to realize its welfare maximizing potential. Indeed, many of the social changes that are today identified as 'rigidities' and 'immobilities' that impede the workings of an otherwise 'self-regulating system' were intended to modify the harshness of the system by helping to 'stabilize' it by reducing the pressure of competition.

What is possible is the development of political economy as a science to reshape the outcome of uncontrolled market processes.[4] It is society's task to identify the macroeconomic goals that it wishes to achieve, and electorates in the Western democracies appear to be expressing themselves more forcefully as their economies deteriorate. It then becomes the task of the economist to identify what kinds of policy measures will facilitate the ends society has determined it wishes to have realized.[5]

A vision of a system of *laissez-faire* capitalism is patently unrealistic either in the West or in the East. Without exception traditional market economies have incorporated 'safety net' measures with a view to limiting the hardships which unlimited competition so often imposes on the poor and near-poor members of society. Analogously, the populist uprisings of 1989 in Central and Eastern Europe signal a desire for the efficiency aspects of a market system, but they are by no means inclined to give up social provision of what they consider essential goods and services. Political economy as a discipline thus has the potential for becoming a universally relevant instru-

ment for reshaping the outcome of uncontrolled market processes. Both the
economies of the West and the new market economies of Central and Eastern Europe confront the challenge of articulating policies that will work
towards altering the way in which microeconomic units respond to market
incentives. The papers in this volume are offered as a contribution towards
this effort.

Our inquiry begins with Stanley Bober's paper, 'The Triumph of Democratic Welfare Capitalism' (Chapter 1). It offers, in a very real sense, an
essential first step towards providing perspective about the entire spectrum
of the more specific topics that will concern us as we proceed. Bober's
central insight is that the counterpart of the political restructuring inherent in
the transition of formerly planned economies to privatization and market-
directed production and income-sharing is the likely rejection of the neoclassical tradition of economic theorizing. In particular, he envisions that
political restructuring will encourage a rejection of the equilibrium approach
that has been so closely linked with analyses predicated on the assumption
that the economy is inherently constrained by the existence of scarce resources. This assumption directed economic inquiry towards the problem of
resource allocation as the economist's central topic from which a theory of
income distribution was derived by extending the marginal principle to
explain factor prices. Bober infers that political restructuring may well encourage economists to direct their thinking along lines reminiscent of the
classical tradition of Smith, Ricardo and Marx.

Eva Marikova Leeds pursues an analogous theme with her focus on the
essential relatedness of political structures and the theoretical fundamentals
which undergird them. Her argument is that central planning failed, at least
in part, as a consequence of its reliance on static economic theory and its
misperceptions about human nature. In 'The Birth and Death of Central
Planning' (Chapter 2), she recalls the famous paper by Ludwig von Mises
and the Lange–Hayek exchange that followed about the untenability of
rational resource allocation in the absence of a price system. The recent
demise of central planning thus validates, some 50 years after von Mises's
initial assault, the essential correctness of his theoretical argument that central planning was destined to fail because of its inability to allocate resources
rationally.

While the newly privatized economies of Central and Eastern Europe are
relatively backward in the state of their development *vis-à-vis* other European countries and Japan, they understandably aspire towards the achievement of comparable productivity levels. Hypotheses that relate to the advantages of relative backwardness suggest that the productivity convergence
experienced by industrialized countries since the late 19th century may well
foretell that they can, indeed, anticipate that this will be their future experience

as well. Whether convergence will be realized in actuality is, in principle, an *empirical* question which will require a suitable methodology for measuring productivity growth.

The paper 'The Advantage of Relative Backwardness: An Input–Output Approach' (Chapter 3) by William Milberg and Bruce Elmslie thus undertakes to test Gershenkron's well-known convergence hypothesis empirically. Their input–output approach can also be used to evaluate alternative theories about productivity growth.

The Milberg–Elmslie analysis is complemented by Nicholas W. Balabkins's insightful inquiry into the fundamental role of the identification of property rights as the necessary corollary of privatization. In 'Defining Property Rights After the Velvet Revolution' (Chapter 4), he notes that the transformation of the former state-owned firms into private firms modelled on those of the West is compromised by the absence of a legal and judicial infrastructure. Essential Western-style property rights are only beginning to be put into place in the countries comprising the Commonwealth of Independent States. The property rights theorem so clearly articulated by Western property rights theorists is not directly transferable to the newly privatized economies which will be burdened by a host of externalities which Balabkins identifies.

Chapter 5, 'A Critical Analysis of the Change to a Market Economy' by Linwood T. Geiger, notes that the trend towards establishing market economies is historically older than the revolutions of 1989.

While earlier reforms cannot match the drama of the dissolution of the Soviet Union and reunification of Germany, it deserves to be recognized that Yugoslavia, Czechoslovakia, Hungary and East Germany (the former German Democratic Republic) were among the Eastern bloc countries that had already experimented with reform programmes in the 1950s and 1960s. These reforms were harbingers of *perestroika* and *glasnost* in the Soviet Union in 1985 which signalled the end of the Cold War, the fall of the Berlin Wall and the declaration of independence by seven former members of the Soviet Union. Despite the euphoria which accompanied the severance, Geiger notes there are several reasons why 'the express train to a market system may become derailed'. Attitudes, of course, vary from country to country, but the only industry in which the preference for a private sector and a market economy is overwhelming is the agricultural sector. State control over heavy industries, banking institutions and the transportation and communications industries is preferred. Geiger thus anticipates that the government sector will continue to be significant in Eastern and Central Europe, much as it has long been in the Scandinavian countries and in such successful East Asian economies as Japan, Taiwan, South Korea and Singapore. The experiences of the latter bolster the expectation that the newly privatized economies will, indeed, improve their standards of living. In particular, Geiger argues, their pursuit of export expansion is likely to prove itself an effective strategy for encouraging economic development, especially if manufactured goods come to comprise a larger share of exports.

Yet, there remains the need to recognize that there are inherent weaknesses in the market system that will plague the transitional economies in much the same way as they have detracted from the economic performance of the more developed economies.

Thus, Christine Rider's paper, 'The Pricing Problems of Eastern Europe' (Chapter 6), extends Geiger's closing argument by making the essential point that it behooves those engaged in the formerly planned economies to recognize that wholesale transference of market economy characteristics is neither practical nor appropriate for solving the problems that accompanied central planning. Like Balabkins, she underscores the absence of a valuation system for establishing the worth of properties that are to become privatized. It is impossible to use existing prices to value enterprises and, in principle, more appropriate prices will not emerge until there is market competition among economically viable enterprises. Because it is by no means certain that consumer welfare will necessarily be maximized once a price mechanism is introduced, Rider emphasizes that the objective of restructuring should be *improvement* rather than maximization.

Simply to focus on the 'right' prices is too restrictive; it is necessary to determine what it is that markets do best. Meanwhile, the potential offered by tools and mechanisms other than the price system for achieving efficiency improvements must not be neglected. In particular Rider emphasizes the need for social control of investment. Intervention is also relevant in areas where markets fail, specifically in the provision of public goods, and in addressing the problem of externalities.

Walter Jermakowicz focuses more specifically on the macroeconomic aspects of reform in his paper, 'The Transition to a Free Market: The Case of the Polish Economy' (Chapter 7). His approach is to analyse the results of Poland's 1990 'shock reform', comparing it with Germany's 1948 currency reform. These dramatic and radical reform measures were designed to address the problems inherent in excess demand under conditions of severe resource constraint coupled with excess money supplies.

While the reforms undertaken by the Solidarity government of Poland in 1990 took place in a substantially different political milieu than the German currency reform of 1948, which proceeded under the supervision of US military authorities, it was similarly directed at accomplishing a radical reduction in the money supply. These were a prelude to the deregulation of most commodity markets and the liberalization of domestic and foreign trade. Suppression of inflation was a critical objective of the Polish authorities, though to a lesser degree than in Germany, which had learned from the 1920s that inflation is a phenomenon to be feared. The reform of 1948 revitalized German industry, whereas the Polish reforms of 1990 resulted in double-digit declines in employment and crises in centres that were particularly hard-hit by reductions in production.

Several insights emerge from German and Polish experiences: first, reform only seems capable of producing a slow recovery mechanism because the high propensity of consumers to save in times of uncertainty is a basic response. Secondly, monetary reform does not automatically 'cure' inflation. 'Corrective' inflation may be needed to achieve a healthy price structure. Nor can the political aspects of reform be overlooked. Reform movements must be sensitive to public perceptions and attitudes, and they cannot be successful without strong social support, frequently both at home and from abroad.

Mark Knell offers the observation that the austere monetary, fiscal and exchange rate policies favoured by the International Monetary Fund and the World Bank may in fact not facilitate the creation of an appropriate enabling environment to accomplish a successful transformation towards market economies. His paper, 'The Political Economy of Transitions to Market Economies' (Chapter 8), interprets the measures these international institutions are advocating as derivatives of the monetarist view that market economies are characterized by continuous market-clearing capabilities. He argues that the relevance of the assumptions underlying this view of the economy are especially suspect in transition economies, which are more likely to respond positively to policies that recognize that the kind of unemployment which plagues them is likely to be involuntary rather than structural.

The changing structure of unemployment is chiefly the result of consumption patterns that reflect declining real wages. Knell thus argues that the problem of enabling an economy to proceed from a centrally planned economy to a market economy is appropriately viewed as identifying the traverse from one growth path to another. Thus the role of instrumental analysis is to design 'goal-adequate' public controls. That is, controls that are consistent with macro goals that are democratically established.

Harald Hagemann's joint paper with Stephan Seiter, 'Structural Change, Productivity and Employment: Perspectives from a Unified Germany' (Chapter 9), emphasizes the critical role of a country's public consciousness in promoting reform. This is, perhaps, nowhere more dramatically in evidence in recent times than in the powerful demonstrations that brought down the Stalinist regime in the German Democratic Republic (GDR) in November 1989. The demolition of the Berlin Wall and the democratic elections that followed were the prelude towards an economic and monetary union with the Federal Republic of Germany (FRG) which envisioned one economy, one currency and one social system.

The vision of a smooth reunification was (and remains) complicated by substantial differences between East and West in their respective production capabilities and income levels. Thus the opening of East German markets to Western competition has produced substantial product substitution that East German companies have found disruptive. The introduction of the Deutschmark (DM) into East Germany is an added complication that is exacerbated by the decline in the export opportunities for East German goods. These developments have contributed substantially to the loss of jobs in East Germany. Hagemann and Seiter report that the 'real' level of unemployment at the end of 1991 exceeded 30 per cent, which is a level comparable to that of the Great Depression in the 1930s. Further, labour productivity in East Germany remains some 40 per cent less efficient than it is in West Germany, which has encouraged such a substantial increase in imports that it probably could not be supported if East Germany were a separate state.

These problems are at least partially attributable to the sectoral pattern of East German industry, which is heavily concentrated in agriculture. This contrasts with the West German sectoral pattern in which some 65 per cent are employed in the service sector, along with 31.5 per cent who are employed in the industrial sector and 3.7 per cent in agriculture.

The substantially larger service sector of the West suggests to Hagemann and Seiter that the expansion of the service sector holds great potential for the East German economy. Social services and child care are quite well developed, but other service production remains underdeveloped, which is partly attributable to the problem of ownership identification along with the inadequacy of the East German infrastructure. Transportation and communication services are conspicuously poor which has, in turn, compromised the development of an adequate material supply system. However, Hagemann and Seiter are of the opinion that even with restructuring there will probably be of the order of 9.5 million fewer jobs in the GDR than are needed; that is, the first phase of the transition process from the formerly centrally planned economy to a private market economy can be represented by a 'J' curve which traces out a fall in output and employment, with an expansion occurring only later, *perhaps* by 1993 but possibly not until afterwards. With modernization of the infrastructure and improved training for displaced workers there is a long-term prospect for improvement in a united Germany. However, in the short run the problem of substantial productivity and wage differentials remains. This suggests that Germany must direct a substantial share of its investment towards East Germany in the years ahead, which is likely to result in a loss of international competitiveness *vis-à-vis* Japan.

There are also 'distributive' problems relating to income and wealth that are inherent in German reunification. These are examined by Heinz Kurz in his paper 'Paradise Gained, Paradise Lost?' (Chapter 10). In particular, the currency conversion that accompanied monetary union involved severe purchasing power losses for the East German population. Even more serious is the apparent expropriation of East Germans by West Germans, either under the law requiring that property be returned to its original owner, or because the West Germans have savings with which to buy the capital stock that is becoming privatized by sale. Both routes towards privatization pose obstacles to East Germany's rapid 'economic recovery', besides posing problems of distributive justice. Thus Kurz proposes that privatization policy be amended to encourage private investment in East Germany by guaranteeing that the remaining property be given to the people, for example, through shares of stock. There is also a wide expectation that rapid wage increases and transfers are appropriate vehicles for compensating East Germans for the losses they have experienced.

Kurz also notes that the sheer magnitude of the capital needs of East Germany is putting upward pressure on interest rates. Given the financial requirements for rebuilding the East German economy, it is quite likely that Germany, once the world's major capital exporting nation, will become a major capital importer. Whether Germany confronts the long-run prospect of becoming a debtor nation depends, of course, on the success of German unification. Kurz urges the critical necessity of reversing present policies relating to privatization as the key to avoiding the deleterious consequences his analysis reveals.

The dissolution of the mighty USSR into separate republics brought with it another group of country specific problems. None is more urgent or difficult than that of redefining the economic relationships among the newly independent republics. While official Soviet policy has historically been to equalize living standards and the pace of economic growth among the 15 separate republics, if necessary by means of interregional shifts of labour and capital resources, these measures were vehemently protested as both burdensome and ineffective. Moscow's unwillingness to share its powers in this regard and make itself accountable to the republics was a catalyst to the forces that led to dissolution. Now that dissolution is a reality the problem appears in another guise: the republics must, perforce, trade with one another in order to maximize individual potentials for achieving higher living standards. Evaluation of their potential for doing so is handicapped not only by limited data availability, but also by the absence of an established technique for quantifying individual potentials.

Volodimir N. Bandera's paper, 'Accountability and Interregional Income Transfers in the USSR' (Chapter 11), uses the fortuitously available 1988 data for Ukraine to estimate its balance-of-payments account and interpret this in relation to its budgetary and national income accounts. Bandera establishes that the export surplus of Ukraine with the other Soviet republics and its trade surplus with Third World countries imposed a net loss in Ukraine's absorption, which represented 3 per cent of the gross social product of the republic. This experience is, in essence, the reason why income transfers among the republics were perceived as vehicles of exploitation that emanated from Moscow, and so led to demands for accountability. Bandera's utilization of contemporary balance of payments and income absorption analysis has made it possible to identify the magnitudes of interrepublic income transfers more concretely. Since these transfers can no longer be mandated, the prospect is that trade will enable Ukraine to earn hard currencies. This bodes well for the stability of the *hryvna*, its newly established currency, providing, of course, that the pent-up demand for imports is held in check.

Zoltan J. Acs and Felix R. FitzRoy inject an important microeconomic perspective into the debate about the nature of the problems that are likely to accompany the privatization of production units. Their paper, 'The Role of the Firm in the Transition to a Free Market: Lessons from the Japanese and American Models' (Chapter 12), maintains that the effectiveness of privatization can, and should, be evaluated against the standards of 'good management', regardless of whether ownership is public or private. They make the often missed point that simply transferring ownership from public to private hands will not invariably reduce the cost or enhance the quality of output. Nor is it the case that the American model of the firm invariably has the most to offer the managers of the newly privatized firms of the East. The Japanese firm is an equally useful model. A particularly advantageous feature of Japanese firms is their encouragement of team-work and career development for blue collar as well as managerial employees. The tradition of long-term employment encourages firm-specific training and work-sharing, while also contributing to a lower ratio of administrative and supervisory employees than is typical in American firms. Japanese firms have also concentrated on 'process' development, which encourages incremental changes which have cumulatively enabled them to achieve comparative advantages in manufacturing industries that require sophisticated skills and technology.

This *modus operandi* assigns a more prominent role to engineering departments than do American firms and encourages small-scale production which generates cost reductions. By contrast, East European firms, like American firms, favour large firms based on the belief that there are significant economies of scale. But this is sometimes an ill-founded belief. Thus, Acs and FitzRoy maintain that Eastern Europe must re-examine the large firm bias of its economic policies. What is needed is to recast the debate about privatization into the issue of greater managerial efficiency.

While the growth prospects of the newly privatized economies of Central and Eastern Europe are reasonably optimistic, the foreseeable future does not appear equally promising for Third World economies. Anindya Datta argues that the entry of Eastern and Central European exports into the world's market economy is likely to have negative implications for the developing countries of the Third World. His paper, 'Third World Development: Global Structure' (Chapter 13), examines the disparate experiences in the post-World War II period. The economic success stories of Japan, Taiwan and South Korea have been unique in ways that have set them apart from other Third World countries, India and China in particular.

The key to these differences is chiefly to be found in the initial conditions in agriculture. Where the agricultural sector developed in ways that encouraged 'land saving' rather than 'labour saving' technology, import substitution generally impeded 'premature migration' from the rural sector. This process paved the way towards the development of a more labour-absorptive industrial sector during the import substitution phase of development.

Because this was not the case in India, it rendered her import substitution phase relatively ineffectual. As a large, densely populated country with a moribund agricultural sector, India is unlikely to enjoy the success of South Korea or Taiwan. Nor is it likely to be able to avail itself of the opportunities that globalized finance has offered in Taiwan and Korea to make a transition from labour-intensive to capital-intensive production. Foreign finance, together with import liberalization, has expanded luxury industries with high import components. This has compromised India's potential for comparative advantage in some basic industries. India thus has only a limited export capacity, which competition from Eastern and Central European economies is certain to compromise even further. The likely experience of the LDCs *vis-à-vis* the newly privatized market economies of East and Central Europe is thus closely related to the global development of financial markets and world-wide markets for trade. These considerations are more specifically the subject matter of Volume II of the *Political Economy of Global Restructuring*.

Notes

1. No one has made the case for using instrumental analysis to establish political economy more eloquently or with greater depth of insight than Adolph Lowe. See in particular his *'On Economic Knowledge: Toward a Science of Political Economics'*, 1965, Armonk, New York: ME Sharpe.
2. See, for example, Henry Wallich, 'A Tax Based Incomes Policy', *Journal of Economic Issues*, June 1971.
3. Instrumental analysis is also in the tradition of recent American institutionalists, in particular Clarence Ayers. See, for example, *Towards a Reasonable Society: The Values of Industrial Civilization*, 1961, Austin: The University of Texas Press.
4. Lowe prefers the term 'political economics'. It is relevant to distinguish Lowe's political economics from political economy in the sense of Lionel Robbins, who draws the distinction between economic science as relating to the technical apparatus of the discipline and political economy as covering that part of our sphere of interest which essentially

involves judgements of value. Political economy thus conceived is quite unashamedly concerned with the assumptions of policy and the results flowing from them (Robbins, 1981, pp. 1–10).

5. Economists familiar with such modern techniques as activity analysis, input–output analysis and Tinbergen's 'Theory of Economic Policy and Operations Research' are conversant with the methodology of instrumental analyses that are concerned with achieving postulated goals and evaluating the compatibility of multiple goals. The focal point of these procedures is to identify the cost-minimizing way of achieving the end in view. In principle, activity analysis is a familiar example of instrumental analysis.

References

Ayers, Clarence (1961), *Towards a Reasonable Society: The Values of Industrial Civilization*, Austin: The University of Texas Press.

Heibroner, Robert (1990), 'Analysis and Vision in the History of Modern Economic Thought', *Journal of Economic Literature*, **28**, September, 1097–1114.

Lowe, Adolph (1961), *Towards a Reasonable Society: The Values of Industrial Civilization*, Austin: The University of Texas Press.

Lowe, Adolph (1976), *The Path of Economic Growth*, Cambridge: Cambridge University Press.

Lowe, Adolph (1977), *On Economic Knowledge: Toward a Science of Political Economics*, White Plains: ME Sharpe, 2nd edn.

Lowe, Adolph (1987), *Essays in Political Economics: Public Control in a Democratic Society*, New York: New York University Press.

Robbins, Lionel (1932), *Essay On The Nature and Significance of Economic Science*, London: MacMillan, revised edn. 1935.

Robbins, Lionel (1981), 'Economics and Political Economy', *Papers and Proceedings of the American Economics Association*, **71**, (2), May, 1–10.

Smith, Adam 1776 [1937], *The Wealth of Nations*, New York: Modern Library Edition. Book I, chapters 2, 3, 8, 9, 11 and Book II, chapters 3–5.

Tinbergen, Jan (1952), *On the Theory of Economic Policy*, Amsterdam: Kluwer Academic Publishers.

1 The triumph of democratic welfare capitalism

Stanley Bober

'Political economy after global reconstruction' may perhaps be better put as the 'state of political economy in the bright light of the triumph of democratic welfare capitalism'. For it is a fact that of the three great systematic ideas of the 20th century – fascism, communism and democratic welfare capitalism, only the last is vigorous and growing. The others have collapsed in many cases in terms of practical institutional settings, but more importantly as ideas that grip the imagination and drive society towards a way of organizing the shape of human life. What we see is a universal movement, away from such ideas as the supposed security of 'The worker's paradise' or the grandeur of rule by the superior being, as was inherent in 'the Thousand Year Reich', towards their very antithesis; towards what may seem by comparison to be a pedestrian ideology, that of a society based on a democratic polity and a capitalist economy.

We can use the term 'pedestrian' because it is felt by some that, as advantageous as this development is for mankind, its general achievement removes the excitement of the struggle to find something 'higher'; that the virtue of capitalism will also bring with it a degree of boredom to the human condition. As Fukuyama would have us see this 'end of history' condition:[1]

> The end of history will be a very sad time. The struggle for recognition, the willingness to risk one's life for a purely abstract goal, the world-wide ideological struggle that called forth daring courage, imagination and idealism, will be replaced by economic calculation, the endless solving of technical problems, environmental concerns and the satisfaction of sophisticated consumer demands.

Well, it might be argued all the better and finally so. That mankind is in the process of freeing itself from that horrific blending of an economic–political system with the fervour of a religious passion and unity that, as we have witnessed, has the result of merging the individual into a common movement with a common purpose which yields totalitarian and collectivist societies, should indeed be viewed as a movement that is spiritually uplifting and full of daring. For the struggle is thrust onto the individual and not the collective, so that it is personal enterprise that moves the society. As one observer of this development sees it: 'Capitalism, then, is the economic

ALLEGHENY COLLEGE LIBRARY

system whose central animating dynamic is invention, discovery, enterprise – in short the creative mind'.[2]

Yet if the virtue of creativity is at the core, then it is hard to accept Fukuyama's lament that when democratic capitalism becomes the prevailing system people will lead vacuous and empty lives. The very success of capitalism, say in increasing mortality or in raising the living standards of great masses of people, is largely the result of the introduction of products that may not have even existed a decade earlier. Far from agonizing over the 'end of history' we should be rejoicing over the unleashing of the creative spirit. For if democratic capitalism can bring to mankind betterment and fulfilment in an economic sense, it can also do so in the spiritual sense by sustaining an environment of free personal religious association, simply because this type of political–economic system is in no way a 'religion'. Consider the following observation:[3]

> A democratic capitalistic regime is not the kingdom of God. It is not a church or even a philosophy, and it is only in an outward sense a way of life. A domestic capitalistic regime promises three liberations by institutional means–liberation from tyranny and torture, liberation from oppression of conscience, information and ideas and liberation from poverty. The construction of a social order that achieves these is not designed to fill the soul or to teach a philosophy, or to give instruction in how to live. It is designed to create space, within which the soul may make its own choices, and within which spiritual leaders and spiritual associations may do their own necessary and creative work.

What we are saying may be obvious; but it needs to be kept at the forefront so as to appreciate what is providing the momentum away from state authority and collectivism. How ironic that not too long ago 'enlightened' or 'progressive' Western opinion had all but relegated capitalism and individualism to the archives of history (were not Western societies accused of fostering excessive individualism?), and is now sweeping away so-called 'progressive societies' with apparent ease.

Now what these remarks are leading us to is a rethinking of how one, in a fundamental way, defines what an economic system is about; that is, what is the conception of the material world that this 'reconstruction' has in mind? I think we can be reasonably certain what it does not have in mind, or at least, does not have in mind exclusively. The drawing power of democratic capitalism is not the conventional, that is, neoclassical, vision of the world where the central unifying problem is the optimum allocation of scarce resources. The attraction is certainly greater than that of a system preoccupied with the operation of a mechanism to facilitate a series of exchanges of existing goods. Certainly the animating central dynamics of capitalism are more than that of an orderly rationing system, with the obviously important result of a better allocation than that which happens to be given by an act of fortune. I do not believe we would argue that the predominant economic problem for which capitalism does provide an answer is one of providing means for rational behaviour in exchange for what is given to the system.

What must be added on, and in a very strong way, is that democratic capitalism delivers a rising real standard of life, a condition of betterment to the mass of people over time. It does so via a process of economic growth that is inextricably intertwined with the discovery and application of new techniques; this cumulative technical progress is carried on by what we can consider 'individual economic enterprise'. We are defining what economics is in terms of a system that unleashes and nourishes the creative and organizational talents of its constituents, and which uses the elements of private property and the incentive of profits to sustain a pattern of economic growth that does indeed 'lift all ships'. It is the reality that all will be better off, though unevenly so, through private economic arrangements that provides the attraction resulting in capitalism increasingly becoming the only ball game in town. This attitude is now espoused by those who at one time trumpeted the 'middle socialist road' only to see their economies stagnating, and have since been in the process of paring back the role of the state and expanding the role of the private market.

In the 1980s the governments of Margaret Thatcher and Helmut Kohl moved to privatize and stimulate growth via lowering tax rates and increasing corporate profitability. Interestingly enough, a speech by Mitterrand in 1984 conveys the extent of the change within the free societies themselves when he states: 'The French are beginning to understand that it is enterprise which creates wealth, that it is enterprise that creates jobs, and that it is enterprise that determines our standard of living and our place in the world'. And as the French Prime Minister, Fabious, observed: 'The state has encountered its outer limits; it should not move beyond them'. So much for the socialist strategy that in 1981 spoke in terms of breaking with capitalism and with 'the logic of profitability'. Perhaps we overlook the fact that along with the startling transformation of the communist world, there is the less dramatic, but nevertheless equally important change taking place in the non-communist parties of the left in the industrialized democracies, away from the doctrines of redistribution and government management. This development can be referred to as 'the death of the third way'.

If it is this dynamic mix of creativity, enterprise and growth that is the compelling force behind the 'restructuring', then we are operating within a world of economic expansiveness and almost limitless capability. The economic progress of man must be seen as being limited only by the effort and technology that he is motivated to bring to the solution of a particular production problem. We operate in a political–economic system essentially freed from the constraints of nature; it is the force of cumulative technical progress that is making man more and more dependent on himself. The gravitational centre, if you will, of the whole analysis of economics has got to reside in the learning process of the society, and thereby in constantly changing technical knowledge, and not, as tradition would have it, in the limited amount of natural resources. A realistic understanding of capitalistic societies today involves very much more than the allocating mechanism within a zero-sum environment. Indeed, the entire market apparatus so artfully applied all over the economic landscape, and so permeating the body of theory, has, in general, been shown to be a misleading analysis. Certainly it is a wrong approach to specify supply and demand curves that are separate and independent and will be automatically brought into balance through a change in the market price.

Interestingly enough, the usual tripartite division into the labour, land and capital categories should perhaps be refocused. The classicists who put forth a labour-embodied theory of value (notwithstanding its attendant theoretical difficulties) did so because they wanted to direct the central focus which would unify the whole of economic thought towards the economic problem as the struggle of man against nature in producing material wealth. What was basic was man and his role of producer as well as owner of capital. But this may not have come across very clearly due to the usual tripartition of the 'factors of production' (using the neoclassical term), which may prompt one to associate man with the factor 'labour', with the capital resource appearing as a sort of inanimate object. However, some reflection would have us realize that capital is not a separable concept from man; 'capital' embodies all the technology and knowledge that man has accumulated, it reflects all that he has learned (Kaldor recognized this straight away).

But let us consider a further step and discard the term 'property', which is generally still thought of in terms of land or structures, and replace it with intellectual property, that is with the inventions of the mind. Again, this puts 'man' at the centre. More and more our modern civilization places the mind as the core productive resource that has transformed the productive capacity of society. It is through computers, miniaturization and electronics that the emissions of the human mind are placed in more of the things that are produced. One can say that the material of the material world is more and more that of 'mind'. Now, the startling and rapid changes that result from this can only take root in a system that protects and rewards the ownership of such capital property. The idea of scarce resources in the way we normally think of this term makes little sense, it is not the 'number of hands' that we should be focusing on. The existing quantity of labour in our modern world does not (or should not) constrain or limit anything. Yet the flip-side of this thought is that creativity must essentially be unconstrained.

What then is the ethos of the political–economic system in this new world which will be put at its centre and will define for us what economics is about? It is the construction and the maintenance of an environment that promotes a growth trajectory; to be able to come to grips with the forces that result in the betterment of society in real terms over long periods of time. Economics is about the mechanics of production and the institutional arrangements of resources in the production process such as to yield an acceptable maximum economic surplus; and it is about an analysis of the interrelationship of the distribution of this surplus and growth. The core of economic analysis must deal with wealth creation and not with the designs of wealth redistribution if it is to reflect the global reconstruction. It is, I believe, fair to say that the driving force behind the social and economic changes that we see is an overwhelming acceptance of the enriching inequality of capitalism and the rejection of the poverty equalization of state authority. Will the discipline of economics become the 'vanguard' of this new 'zeitgeist', both in the core of its teaching and theoretical construction on the higher level if you will, and in its practical advising role in terms of policy?

The answer is, I would like to think, yes. The subject of economics is now clothing itself quite comfortably in a political–economic mantle that is woven around the core that we spoke of above. We find constructions drawn more and more from the world as it exists and based on some accepted principles such as private property, the existence of classes of individuals in the operation of the economy whose roles are different and whose incomes flow from different explanatory principles, profit incentives and inequality of earning outcomes (we can make this last 'principle' even stronger by saying 'necessary inequality that makes for greater absolute gains for all'). The economic analysis now emerging and exacting greater influence is not divorced from the political–economic realities of the day.

This is, of course, not new; it is a reincarnation of the classical perspective that has at the centre what can be considered as the production-surplus approach to economic reality. The great contribution of the classicists was to provide an account of the forces influencing growth and of the balances necessary to maintain the growth path. They recognized that it is the accumulation and productive investment of a portion of the social product that is the driving force behind economic growth; and under democratic capitalism this takes the form of the reinvestment of private profit.

It is the centrality of this simple notion (yet quite complex in its operation) that placed the 'capitalist' in the role of the dominant mover in the system. This class of people set commodities and labour into motion, allocated the capital stock and directed the production of the economy's output. As profit maximizers these individuals adjusted the inter-industry allocation of capital so as to equalize the rate of profit, and through this process brought about adjustments in the composition of output and in the relative quantities of industry output supplied to the market. It is interesting to note that the entire classical construction was couched in terms of 'class behaviour'; the maximization behaviour of capitalists was not explained via an elaboration of the theory of the 'firm' – an attitude that came to the forefront with the rise of neoclassical economics. In neoclassical thinking the capitalist class construct that propelled activity was removed from centre stage to be re-placed by the term 'entrepreneur', which in essence is used to designate those who control but not necessarily own the 'capital'. What this did, in one respect, was to reduce the capitalist to an owner of a resource and thereby place him on equal footing with labour, which made it easy to consider factor incomes as flowing from the same explanatory principle. What was lost was the notion of the distribution of the product being connected with the pattern of ownership of the means of production and with the performance of labour in production; what was submerged was the realistic understanding that there exists 'social relationships' in production that have a class charac-ter which, by its nature, is antagonistic, and where class income flows from the particular role played in production. How ironic that this approach to distribution that Marx wanted to emphasize and prevent from being submerged under what he considered the 'vulgar economics', and supposedly discarded for some 'co-operative relationship' in the centralized Marxist systems, is now coming back with much zeal in those very same societies as they emerge from their failed egalitarian experiment.

While it is true that in modern times the corporate entity (for example the megacorp) embodies both the ownership of capital and the control of pro-duction decisions (which for some made it easy to blur the distinction between this large impersonal entity and that of the state), we must keep in mind that the information revolution which is largely behind the recent sustained growth of Western societies is, to a great degree, the product of individuals and 'small companies'. The classical capitalist class of individu-als as an 'alive construct' is very much with us.

Another aspect of classical thinking in general was their non-compartmentalization. They recognized the interrelatedness of the activities of production, exchange of commodities, the distribution of the social prod-uct, and of the accumulation of capital. It was clear that growth depended upon the extraction of a level of surplus and the way in which the surplus was utilized; thus growth was bound up with distribution and associated class behaviour. The mechanics of production and related explanation of value became crucial, as one had to determine the rate of profit because of its connection with the accumulation of capital both as a source of investment funds and the stimulus to further investment. This has prompted modern theorists to begin to examine the relation of the firm's pricing policy to the distribution of income.

While we are recalling some thoughts about the classical approach to matters, it might be interesting to note also that while growth economics was central to their focus, they were not too sanguine about its longer-term continuance. Their pessimism contrasts with the modern day exuberance. After all, they did presume that, with a stable population and given technology, the system would be propelled to a stationary state where net investment would fall to zero and wages would stop rising. Continued growth, as they viewed the problem, required that population grow in response to capital accumulation; there must be an increase in labour and machinery. The classical population equation responded by specifying population growth to be a function of the difference between the market and the subsistence wage rates. The allocation of capital, while necessary, became an insufficient ingredient in the growth process. The population growth mechanism, though could not really save the day – due to the retarding effects of presumed diminishing productivity of a long-run accumulation which affects the demand for labour and the market wage.

It is fair to say that both Ricardo and Malthus failed to appreciate sufficiently the impact of technological change and the general learning power of human beings given the proper environment of freedom and incentives. It is not population growth which is necessary to sustain economic growth; indeed far from it. Marx, whose whole outlook was based on historical change, speaks in terms of higher profit levels resulting from degrees of exploited labour while failing to foresee the enormous possibilities of increasing productivity. It is not until much later that we have been able to forecast (and appreciate) Marx along Sraffian lines, that Marxian economics was brought out of its supposed 'fringe' and 'radical economics' position and given its rightful and firm place on the road leading from classical to current post-neoclassical thinking.

At the heart of recent developments is, as we have noted, the rejection of the neoclassical tradition, which has at its centre the analysis of an equilibrium outcome that is imposed upon the system by the existence of scarce resources. Neoclassicism turned the discussion away from the grand design of economic expansion to the myopic view of allocation of resources in relation to consumer preferences so that individuals and their wants were treated as the ultimate and independent data of the economic problem. A corollary to this is that one derives a theory of distribution as incidental to the pricing process, in that distribution is determined by the conditions of exchange. This leads to the approach that there is no need for any special analysis of the 'value' of each factor of production. One need not relate, or better yet justify, the rewards as stemming from an individual's particular role in the production process. As all factor incomes flow from the same marginal explanatory principle; it is then a short step to seeing the relationship between the designated classical constituencies of capitalist, landlord and worker as an essentially harmonious one; each makes his contribution to production and receives his appropriate (marginal) reward. In so far as there is any 'antagonism' between them, it arises merely from the competition as to who receives more of the value that has been jointly created. Of course, neoclassical analysis does not refer to these constituencies in terms of class designation, but by the anonymous 'factor of production'.

To put it more strongly, the neoclassical apparatus smothers the distributive conflict by talking in terms of 'households' that sell this service in the market-place; it maintains an analogy between the product and factor markets with the same principles operating in both. Thus the neoclassical conception of society is one of a classless society consisting of atomistic households with particular preferences and ownership of amounts of physical resources and skills. The hallmarks here are the principles of maximization and marginalism centred around individual behaviour. After all, when we think of marginal utility theory, its focus is one of subjectivity or introspection as a basis for forming hypotheses about economic behaviour – but a subjectivity that is common to all economic units in the same way. Society emerges as a property-owning democracy, based on the exchange of products in accordance with independently given preferences of classless individuals. There is, to reiterate, no basis for confrontation here, as all are governed by the same natural-mathematical laws.

Of course, as students and 'younger' professors we are normally taken up with the models and mechanics that supposedly gave credence to this harmonious world. We do not think about the hidden ideology of mainstream theory: that this neoclassical framework is in some way akin to a rationale imposed from above in centralized collectivist systems where all units are labouring under espoused uniform rules of purpose and outcome. It was not too long ago that the idea prevailed that socialism could provide the same production, order and co-ordination as that of private institutions – it was a matter of substituting one set of rules for another. But it failed to do so, fundamentally because it could not duplicate the essential disorder or 'people class mobility' inherent in democratic capitalism. Real people (not anonymous factors of production) knew well enough that society was not without classes (either in terms of property ownership or in terms of the relation of capital to labour), that the same principle does not govern all incomes, and that to acquire a greater share of the product one would have to move into a 'property relation' to production. It is this which is the underlying dynamics of economic growth in a free system; a notion which I think was well appreciated by our classical forebears. In general, people define fairness in terms of opportunity, not of outcome. It is the latter attitude, though, that is currently in vogue with 'welfare-statists' who, I think it fair but sad to say, still see the welfare state as a temporary way-station on the road to socialism.

The neoclassical model is, then far, from a representation of the real world, and its replacement can only provide a sense of reality to economics. This replacement has come to be known by different names depending, I think, on which theme is given emphasis by the particular 'school' in the link-up to classical political economy. Whether we refer to a post-Keynesian or a neo-Ricardian school, a basic approach for both is to model the operation of the economy in a real rather than an idealized world; to explain the real world as observed empirically (as much as possible) rather than to demonstrate the behaviour of economic units with regard to some optimality condition. This leads to a realistic way to model time and question the whole structure of equilibrium mechanics. Time does march on; and in the reality of historical time (as distinct from logical time) it does so in one direction: forward. To then understand economic developments as they appear over time, is to zero-in on that one overriding development that is clearly discernible from the historical data, and that is long-term uneven expansion of economic systems. For the post-Keynesian the framework is that of a 'dynamic system' where the equations incorporate time in a manner that propels the system into a state of perpetual change; thus a take-off point could very well be the 'dynamization' of the basic Keynesian apparatus.

But a take-off to which reality? Should the focus be on the secular path to come to grips with the balances required to maintain growth trajectory and thus come to consider the cyclical movements as deviations from the long term position of the economy? Or should the focus be on the shorter-term cyclical reality as basic, with the growth path emerging from the cycle? Though there is some difference of opinion among post-Keynesians, it is the 'best reality' to consider these movements as interrelated and to be analysed jointly; yet it is also fair to say that it is the underlying long-period analysis that is paramount. Now, the housing to carry on such an analysis is the steady-state mode; the aim being that we have first to come to grips with the balances that maintain the growth condition in order to appreciate what can throw the system off the track and thereby produce the cycle.

Post-Keynesians would like to make use of Keynesian tools as a means to get back to the classical time frame. The Keynesian revolutionary contribution would have to be an explanation of long-period levels of output and employment, though this was not Keynes's intent nor his design. Desired savings and desired investment are equalized through changes in income, but now they would need to be hinged to the long-period change in income. But this trend change in income requires an understanding of 'balances' more complex than the one-dimensional savings–investment relationship; that is, it requires our going beyond the Harrod–Domar models of balanced growth that are examples of the 'dynamization' of Keynes.

The standard Keynesian system does not envisage a positive rate of increase in output over time that would be necessary to accommodate the growth in capacity; it does not carry the cyclical peak (short-run) employment condition continuously forward. This limitation makes it rather straightforward to consider employment a function of income; but this is a relationship which can really only be justified over short periods of time (the cyclical framework). This approach concentrates on the demand-generating aspect of investment spending and on the non-spending aspect of saving, taking the conditions of supply as given. But this overlooks the two-sided nature of investment spending; that while it is an income-creating act it is, as well, a capacity- (supply-) creating act. Employment cannot be treated as a function of income, but must be seen as related to the ratio between national income and productive capacity. In general, the 'new classical paradigm' (post-Keynesian and neo-Ricardian) thrust puts its emphasis on the capacity-creating aspect of investment to explain an expanding economy. What is essential if we are to understand the behaviour of the system over the long term is the interplay between such matters as the determination of relative prices and income distribution; how this relates to the ability of the economy to produce a surplus; and the effect of the use of this surplus in conjunction with technological change as this affects employment and demand. Let me make the point, without getting into detail, that prices result from the mark-up behaviour of firms, which is linked directly to the need to finance planned investment by retained profits. Prices reflect the firm's requirements for planned investment, as they give rise to the appropriate surplus that is needed. Prices are, in the classical manner, production based rather than demand-determined. The role of demand is not to cause prices to adjust to cause an equilibrium condition, but in reality to shift resources among sectors through its impact on expected profits and on investment, which then spills over into price movements as firms reassess their long-term needs.

But let us go on a bit further here. The notion of equilibrium prices takes on a different meaning for neo-Ricardians than it does for the marginalists. For the former it is tied to the movement in capital and not to the pendulum analogy of market behaviour. Neo-Ricardians see capital in constant movement between producing sectors in search of maximum profitability (motivated perhaps by demand changes); and it is this movement as it alters productive capacity relative to demand that produces movements in market prices towards the 'prices of production' that reflect equalized profit rates over all sectors. It is in this sense that one speaks of 'equilibrium prices', that is prices that are related to levels of production that yield an overall rate of profit.

One does not, of course, assume that these prices and output levels will be realized; but in a state of competition the movement will be in this direction. This brings to the fore the realism of competition in the Marxian–neo-Ricardian sense; all that is really needed for competition to exist is the non-existence of barriers serving as obstacles to the free movement of capital and thereby 'new' producers and new ideas. Individual firms moving into a sector will affect supply, prices and profits. How real this is compared to the traditionalist idea of large numbers where no firm can exert any influence. The concept of competition is a meaningful element in the driving force of capitalism as societies throw off the monopoly of the state, but only if we understand the idea as it is realistically conceived and not in terms of the make-believe neoclassical mechanics.

A related point comes to mind here. In traditional thinking the position of equilibrium is one towards which the system tends as a result of particular causal changes. But how does a system get into a position that by its very nature is one that the system is already in, and has been there for some time? One can conceive a state reflective of particular characteristics, and 'equilibrium' as a condition where these features are maintained through time – say along a steady-state path with a constant rate of profit where the stock of equipment and the amount of employment are in continual adjustment to one another.

Now, one can compare two such paths with different capital to labour ratios where the outcome along each results from the interplay of the wage rate, the rate of profit and the degree of mechanization – that is, we can compare the two systems with different techniques and different distributions of the shares of output. But what one cannot do is to change the rate of profit and use this change as the causal factor explaining a move to another system embodying a different degree of mechanization. There is no corresponding one-to-one relation between existing techniques or different values of capital per man and differences in the rate of profit.

We do not want to get too far into issues dealing with how to value capital, the construction of the production function and reswitching; the point is that we should not be viewing economics essentially as the study of changing equilibrium conditions as if we could shuttle back and forth in time between them.

Let us, though, get back to the main thrust of our remarks. Neo-Ricardians give major emphasis to the role played by the rate of capital accumulation, as it determines not only the secular growth of the economy but also the resulting distribution of income. Here, we have a viewpoint that jettisons the 'microeconomic factor' explanation of income determination (Sraffa and

Robinson playing major roles here). In general, as Kalecki informs us, one has to track two related phenomena. One is the Keynesian analysis of the division of the national product between consumption and investment goods, and the other is the division of the national income between profit and wage shares. We find that savings must be shorn of their relationship to the level of income, let us say to that of the long-period level of income, and related to the long-period distribution of income. It is the 'proper' distribution that is the essential underpinning for the secular change in income and employment.

Well, in wanting to thrust Keynes into the long-term we have opened a sizeable box out of which spring many items for analysis and integration. We return to the beginning. That it is the banner of democratic capitalism which remains unfurled is the direct result of people aspiring to a better life for themselves and for future generations; that they are confident that such a political–economic system will indeed produce long-term real growth. It is all to the good that the discipline of economics has come around to making growth economics the core of what it is about. But to do this it had to override the neoclassical entrenchment, especially in the United States where the battle is, I would think, not fully over. We owe a debt to the likes of Sraffa, Joan Robinson, Kalecki and many others, not only for instruction as to what was wrong with much of heretofore accepted doctrine, but of pointing the whole of economics in the right direction. They showed the way forward, yet not without asking us to connect to what was right over 150 years ago – to see economics as the study of political economy concerned with the highest economic theme of society.

Notes

1. Francis Fukuyama (1989), 'The End of History?', *The National Interest*, Summer No. 16, p. 4.
2. Michael Novak (1989), 'Boredom, Virtue, and Democratic Capitalism', *Commentary*, September, **88** (3), p. 35.
3. Novak (1989), *Commentary*, September, p. 34.

References

Blatt, J. (1983), *Dynamic Economic Systems: A Post-Keynesian Approach*, New York: M.E. Sharpe.
Bober, S. (1988), *Modern Macroeconomics*, London: Croom Helm.
Eichner, A.S. (1985), *Towards New Economics*, New York: M.E. Sharpe.
Hamouda, O. and Harcourt, G. (1989), 'Post-Keynesianism: from Criticism to Coherence', in *New Directions in Post-Keynesian Economics*, J. Pheby (ed.), Aldershot: Edward Elgar.
Harcourt, G.C. (1985), 'Post-Keynesianism: Quite Wrong and/or Nothing New', in *Post Keynesian Economic Theory*, P. Arestis and T. Skouras (eds), New York: M.E. Sharpe.
Pasinetti, Luigi L. (1981), *Structural Change and Economic Growth*, London: Cambridge University Press.

2 The birth and death of central planning

Eva Marikova Leeds

Introduction

In economics, as in other fields, theory and practice influence one another very strongly. Some tenacious thinkers may advocate an unpopular theory until it becomes generally accepted and put into practice. The opposite causality is also encountered, as some practices persist for no apparent reason until their inner logic is illuminated by a new theory. Conversely, practices atrophy when they cannot be theoretically justified.

The historical development of the theory and practice of central planning appears to be a case in point. In this chapter I show that central planning did not develop satisfactorily because it was founded on inapplicable theory. In particular, central planning failed because it relied on static economic theory and an unrealistic understanding of human nature. (A Czech version of this paper appears in Leeds (1991).)

Marx, Lenin and von Mises

The history of central planning is a story of retreat. Karl Marx suggested planning in *Das Kapital* after analysing capitalist production. He claimed that humans conceive their plans in imagination before turning them into reality (Lavoie, 1985, p. 39). In capitalism, the lack of co-ordination may lead to the duplication of effort (Lavoie, 1985, p. 43), which in turn produces cycles in the economy. Marx envisioned direction from a central authority to improve the spontaneous, even anarchic, workings of the free market and to stabilize the economy (Lavoie, 1985, p. 40).

Marx also advocated the abolition of money to eliminate business cycles. This was a denial of Say's law, from which it is inferred that severe business cycles are not possible because supply generates its own demand. Say's law holds in a barter economy where goods are supplied for the purpose of demanding goods of equal value. Money, however, precludes perfect co-ordination because it separates the exchange of goods. In a monetary economy, the supply of goods no longer automatically generates demand for goods because goods are supplied for money, which can be easily hoarded. (See also Sowell, 1972, pp. 175–7.)

Captivated by this theory, Lenin sought between 1918 and 1921, the period of War Communism, to replace the market with central planning. He tried to appropriate goods directly from the peasants, suggested a general conscription of labour (Roberts, 1970, p. 246), and hoped to abolish money (Roberts, 1970, p. 250). Without a blueprint for socialist distribution, however, Lenin could not succeed. By 1921, 'he had come to see that the idea of the whole economy organized by a single plan was Utopian, and he was out of sympathy with those who continued to espouse the original socialist intention' (Roberts, 1970, p. 252). In the first practical retreat from central planning, he instituted the New Economic Policy which reintroduced some workings of the market into the Soviet economy.

The first major theoretical assault on central planning came from Ludwig von Mises in his famous article, 'Economic Calculation in the Socialist Commonwealth' (1920; hereafter referred to as 'EC'), later expanded into Part 11 of *Socialism* (1922; hereafter referred to as 'S'). This work was not simply a result of the experience of War Communism. Von Mises also responded to the socialist domination of thought at the time (EC, pp. 88–9), to socialist victories in Russia, Hungary, Germany and Austria (EC, p. 122) and to wartime rationing (S, p. 183). He presented three major arguments as to why central planning would fail.

First, prices are necessary for appropriate choice. To von Mises, 'economic calculation' is the process of decision-making. Men need exchange ratios to evaluate alternatives which they constantly face. Any society more complex than the household (EC, p. 102) requires a common denominator for exchange ratios (S, pp. 121–2). Prices express the value of all goods in terms of money, thus making them comparable.

Secondly, prices cannot be meaningful without private property. Von Mises claims that entrepreneurs respond to changes appropriately only when they speculate with their own property, which internalizes the consequences of their actions. Their responses are registered in the market and are reflected in prices. Thus, in modern terminology, von Mises claims that efficient markets, in which prices reflect all relevant information, cannot exist without private property. '[I]t is not possible to divorce the market and its functions in regard to the formation of prices from the working of a society which is based on private property in the means of production' (S, p. 137).

Von Mises applies the preceding arguments to the basic economic decisions of production and distribution. Because resources are limited, all societies must make choices. Even under socialism, a system of limited private property and a centrally directed economy, exchange ratios based on individual trading would emerge for consumer goods. The state must take these ratios into account when deciding what to produce and how to distribute it (EC, p. 93). With public ownership of the means of production, however, it is very difficult to make the right production decisions because the value of inputs cannot be calculated. Since prices in a market system respond to the actions of all agents, they reflect the summary valuation of all participants. Thus, using prices to evaluate alternatives provides proper social valuation.

Thirdly, individuals make the right decisions only in response to monetary incentives. Businessmen take appropriate risks when they 'subject their own wealth to risk' (Murrell, 1983, p. 98). 'The motive force disappears with the exclusion of the material interests of private individuals...' (EC, p. 118). 'Moral responsibility is but a weak substitute for financial loss' (EC, p. 122). Accountability creates the businessman. An entrepreneur behaves effectively as a result of '...his characteristic position in the production process, which allows of the identification of the firm's and his own interests' (EC, p. 121). Von Mises's observations of nationalization dampen any hopes of 'a third way', of combining the market and state sectors (S, pp. 256–7). He states that the only impetus to change in state enterprises comes from the private sector. '...[T]hey are ever driven to reforms and innovations by the business men [sic] from whom they purchase their instruments of production and raw materials' (EC, p. 118).

Von Mises claims that managers in socialist enterprises are unable to act like entrepreneurs because they are not 'vitally bound into that system' (Heilbroner, 1990, p. 1111). Administratively set prices do not perform the same function as prices set by free markets and allocate resources inefficiently. Thus, if the goal of socialists is to rationalize production, they will be disappointed. '...[H]e who expects a rational economic system from socialism will be forced to re-examine his views' (EC, p. 130).

While von Mises acknowledges that socialism is theoretically possible under static conditions (EC, p. 109; S, p. 139), he does not consider the stationary state realistic:

> The idea of a stationary state is an aid to theoretical speculation. In the world of reality there is no stationary state, for the conditions under which economic activity takes place are subject to perpetual alterations which are beyond human capacity to limit (S, p. 196).

Proper economic calculation is particularly necessary in an ever-changing economy. (See also Vaughn, 1980, p. 539.) '...[T]he problem of economic calculation is of economic dynamics: it is no problem of economic statics' (S, p. 139). Nevertheless, von Mises examines the static state of a socialist economy because '[a]ll socialist theories and Utopias have always had only the stationary condition in mind' (S, p. 163).

Von Mises argues that, even under static conditions, a socialist system would be less prosperous than a capitalist one because individuals would work with less zeal (EC, p. 120). While he acknowledges that 'purposeful labour gives satisfaction' (S, p. 165), he claims that man works fewer hours for satisfaction alone than for satisfaction combined with monetary reward (S, p. 166). Individuals are not moved by moral responsibility and do not perform efficiently under the threat of punishment (S, p. 176). Only exceptional men work for duty alone (S, p. 180). When the monetary reward does not correspond to the worker's output, as it cannot under socialism (S, pp. 173–4), the worker shirks. Thus, 'the productivity of labour must inevitably decline' (S, p. 184). Von Mises denies that human nature would change under socialism (S, p. 179). 'Thus, behind the analytics of the... dispute [between von Mises and Marx] lie two views of "human nature" ' (Heilbroner, 1990, p. 1111).

Von Mises's appraisal of socialism is grounded in his vision of capitalism. At the centre of his world is the entrepreneur (S, p. 212), who responds to two stimuli. First, he observes both the input (upstream) and output (downstream) markets. He keeps his fingers on the pulse of the market by observing prices which signal changes in market conditions. If output prices change, he may switch to a different product or develop a new one. One can call this the vertical view.

Secondly, the entrepreneur must look over his shoulder – the horizontal view – to evaluate his performance relative to competitors who are trying to solve the same problem. If input prices change, he may alter input combinations or develop new processes. For the entrepreneur to reduce costs and increase profits, that is, to succeed in both the horizontal and vertical sense, he must constantly recalculate. Von Mises's view stands in contrast with the standard neoclassical model of the economy. The simplest general equilibrium model was developed by Walras. Walras assumed that all consumers have a given amount of money and other goods, and that there is no production. Consumers bring their goods to the market, but they cannot trade until all prices are set by an auctioneer to equilibrate supply and demand.

There is an alternative partial equilibrium view of the economy with production. In perfect competition, the market is entirely impersonal:

> There is no 'rivalry' among suppliers in the market... Thus in a sense perfect competition describes a market in which there is a complete absence of direct competition among economic agents. As a theoretical concept of economics it is the diametical opposite of the businessman's concept of competition (Ferguson, 1972, p. 250).

The equilibrium model of perfect competition is based on four simplifying assumptions:

1. Producers are so small that they have no influence on price – they are price takers (p. 251).

2. Products are homogeneous so as to preclude rivalry (p. 251).
3. All resources are freely mobile (p. 252).
4. Perfect knowledge permeates the market, including the knowledge of future prices. Thus, expectations are not disappointed (p. 252).

Except for the mobility of resources, von Mises's view of the world is substantially different:

1. Producers are not small and have the power to influence prices – they are price makers (Lavoie, 1985, p. 49).
2. Products are heterogeneous to create rivalry.
3. Information is costly and dispersed. Businessmen know only a segment of the price vector. As they trade they transmit and create information, which is reflected in prices. Forecasts can be easily disappointed.

Lavoie points out that, ironically, von Mises's view of competition is very close to that of Marx, but their interpretation differs. In the long run, Marx views competition as socially destructive, while von Mises views it as an eternal engine for growth.

Lange versus Hayek
In the second stage of the development of central planning (the 1920s and 1930s), socialist economists realized they needed a theory for its justification and development. In the first theoretical retreat of central planning, Oskar Lange tried to limit central planning to input markets. In his famous article, 'On the Economic Theory of Socialism' (Lange, 1936), Lange allowed for private ownership of, and markets for, consumer but not producer goods. Prices of consumer goods would thus reflect the personal preferences of consumers. Production, however, would be ruled by a Central Planning Board according to the textbook model of perfect competition outlined above.

This system is socialistic, as it calls for public ownership of the means of production. It is market socialism because consumers would express their preferences in a free market, and the Central Planning Board would duplicate the market outcome in the production sphere. Specifically, to derive supply, Lange suggested that the Central Planning Board use 'two fundamental conditions of an explanatory model … as *operational rules*' (Temkin, 1989, p. 36) and issue them as two rules for enterprise managers (Lange, 1936, p. 62). First, managers must minimize the average cost of production by equating the marginal productivity of all factors. Secondly, they must set output so that marginal cost equals the price of the product.

In general, Lange described the Walrasian equations. Given consumers' preferences and incomes, the demand for all goods can be derived as a function of their price. Given production functions for all goods and input prices, the supply of all goods is also a function of price. Equating supply and demand for each good yields the equilibrium price for each.

Another aspect of Lange's retreat is his realization that the Walrasian equations cannot be solved analytically (Lange, 1936, p. 66) because the coefficients cannot be estimated. Thus, the Central Planning Board, like a Walrasian auctioneer, would, in effect, call out prices at random and observe whether excess supply or demand developed, in order to establish the direction in which prices should change. 'This method of trial and error is based on the parametric function of prices' (Lange, 1936, p. 66), which Lange assumed would be a suffcient motivation for managers facing budget constraints. Lange *de facto* ignored the issue of incentives (Murrell, 1983, p. 98).

Lange's proposal is based on the assumption that planning can duplicate the textbook notion of equilibrium in the economy. This assumption is seriously flawed because most economists consider the paradigm of perfect competition an abstraction from reality. The relative ease with which Lange believed the economic system could be steered suggests that, in ignoring the frictions that are inherent in all economic transactions, Lange saw the economy through Walrasian eyes. Like Marx, Lange disregarded the role of the entrepreneur in his plan for the future.

Friedrich Hayek, a student of von Mises, was an early critic of Lange's proposal. Hayek lauded the socialists for introducing competition in the consumer market, but wondered why they did not appreciate its value in the producer sector as well. Lange did not explain 'why he refuses to go whole hog and to restore the price mechanism in full' (Hayek, 1940, p. 129).

Hayek considered the role of the economist to be to explain and defend markets because '... people are not likely to let the present system work if they do not understand it' (Hayek, 1935, p. 8). Hayek recognized that the chief virtue of free markets lies in their efficient processing of decentralized information, and not in their equating prices to marginal costs. All agents can act on the information relevant to them while remaining ignorant of other influences. They need only to observe input and output prices and worry about their profits. Each agent is truly one piece in a large jigsaw puzzle. Where Marx saw anarchy, Hayek perceived spontaneous order.

Hayek responded to Lange by building upon von Mises's arguments. He presented three reasons why central planning could not function successfully. First, the economy is a dynamic system whose smooth functioning hinges on efficient responses to outside changes (Hayek, 1935, p. 212). Economists, however, have built no dynamic theory for the process of response, due to the intractability of the undertaking. Instead, they have developed static models to describe the outcome of the competitive process.

Planners thus have no guide concerning how and when to respond to constantly changing conditions. (See also Vaughn, 1980, p. 546.) Socialists greatly underestimate the number of decisions that must be constantly made for the economy to work properly, as they have been seduced by the simplicity of static theory whose equations obscure the real working of the economy (Hayek, 1935, pp. 208–10).

> ...[I]t is difficult to suppress the suspicion that this particular proposal has been born out of an excessive pre-occupation with problems of the pure theory of stationary equilibrium... With given and constant data such a state of equilibrium could indeed be approached by the method of trial and error (Hayek, 1940, p. 131).

Hayek considers finding prices by trial and error even less realistic than finding them mathematically. 'It is foolish to assume that it is easier or quicker to act out a solution than to simulate it' (Hayek, 1940, p. 131).

Moreover, as noted, models of perfect competition rest on many simplifying assumptions. Relaxing any of these renders the policy prescription of the model inapplicable to the real world. Hayek does not object to theory *per se* but to the attempt to apply it literally. For example, when goods are not homogeneous or non-standardized (see also Vaughn, 1980, pp. 546–7), price setting is much more complicated because it must be made for each version of the product after examining 'the calculations of all potential suppliers and all potential purchasers' (Hayek, 1940, p. 132).

Secondly, planning cannot function successfully because individual knowledge cannot be centralized. Hayek argues that knowledge does not exist in 'ready-made form' (Hayek, 1935, p. 210) that can easily be centralized, as assumed in static economic models. Instead, knowledge is a process, 'a technique of thought' (Hayek, 1935, p. 210) guiding individuals' responses to change, or 'a capacity to discover any improvement' (Hayek, 1935, p. 211). Dynamic knowledge is intangible and cannot be collected by a central planning board. Thus, the Walrasian equations that the socialists seek to solve, which are based on a particular technology, do not really exist.

Thirdly, central planning ignores the incentives needed for economic progress consisting of the development of new products and practices. Since invention and innovation are risky, they must be properly rewarded. In free markets, private property and profits motivate businessmen to be creative and inventive by rewarding them for their efforts. The rivalry of competition in the market engenders new products and processes that would not exist otherwise. Competition gives rise to new ideas by ensuring that individuals bear the consequences of their own actions.

Central planning offers no credible substitutes for private property and profits to motivate individuals, nor is it able to assign responsibility clearly. If the central plan decrees the expansion of a facility, for example, it is unclear whether the manager should be responsible for its success. The socialists trust that managers would follow instructions and duplicate the actions of entrepreneurs. Hayek is less hopeful. 'To assume that it is possible to create conditions of full competition without making those who are responsible for the decisions pay for their mistakes seems to be pure illusion' (Hayek, 1935, p. 237; 1940, p. 145). With no clear reward system, Hayek hypothesizes that the fear of failure would lead individuals to avoid risk entirely, the logical consequence of which is stagnation (Hayek, 1935, p. 235). Moreover, managerial talent would be misallocated. 'Where profit or loss no longer serves as an objective test of managerial success, as it likely would not under socialism, it becomes exceedingly difficult to weed out inefficient managers' (Vaughn, 1980, p. 548). Hayek is not happy that planning lacked a theoretical foundation because he saw socialism as the main driving force of the time. 'In a world bent on planning, nothing could be more tragic than that the conclusion should prove inevitable that persistence on this course must lead to economic decay' (Hayek, 1935, p. 242). Hayek wishes that he could conclude otherwise:

> To relieve the unmitigated gloom with which the economist today must look at the future of the world... Even for those who are not in sympathy with all the ultimate aims of socialism there is strong reason to wish that now the world is moving in that direction it should prove practicable and a catastrophe be averted (Hayek, 1935, pp. 242–3).

Hayek is naturally pessimistic, however, about any possibility of overcoming the inherent weaknesses of planning.

The death of central planning
The socialists never responded to the criticism of von Mises and Hayek except to dismiss it. Undeterred, they pressed on. In the third stage of central planning, the practice was introduced to varying degrees in Eastern Europe after World War II. No expansion of Marx's or Lange's theory was attempted. A new literature about planning developed (planometrics), but it was more applied mathematics with emphasis on computational technique than a theory of central planning (Lavoie, 1985, p. 94).

Given the lack of planning theory, one would not expect centrally planned economies to be successful. A set of criteria is necessary for a systematic evaluation, however. Von Mises and Hayek suggest three.

First, Hayek considers opportunity costs by comparing the outcome of central planning with what would have happened under free markets. Hayek, referring to the 'Russian Experiment,' notes that one would expect lower output under central planning due to 'excessive development of some lines of production at the expense of others' (Hayek, 1935, p. 204). Thus, Hayek does not view the technological accomplishments of the former Soviet Union as proof of success because they were achieved at the cost of diverting resources from more highly valued uses.

Secondly, both von Mises and Hayek judge central planning on its provision of consumer goods. To von Mises, industrialization alone is not a sign of success. Large plants are not necessarily evidence of useful capital accumulation (von Mises, 1922, p. 203). Hayek states that empirical evidence suggests that the masses are not better off than under the Tsar (Hayek, 1935, p. 205).

Thirdly, Hayek judges central planning on the rationality of the decisions of the central authority (Hayek, 1935, p. 205). '...[T]he rulers of Russia had to learn by experience all the obstacles which a systematic analysis of the problem reveals' (Hayek, 1935, p. 206). Hayek's evaluation of the pre-World War II experiment can now be directly applied to the post-World War II experience.

What was obvious to Hayek became generally accepted 30 years later. Many attempts at reform were undertaken in the 1960s in response to the inefficiency of planning. Within the socialist framework, only a partial reintroduction of the market was possible – and the verdict on this experiment is in. Hayek clearly foresaw that the combination of a free market of consumer goods with a planned producer sector would be inferior to free markets in all spheres (Hayek, 1935, p. 241).

Centrally planned economies entered a crisis in the 1970s. The timing is not coincidental. The 1970s were rocked by many technological and institutional changes stemming from the development of microcomputer technology. Even the free market economies had difficulty in coping with these large changes. Central planning, however, was particularly poorly suited to respond to such pressures. While free markets were eventually able to respond to changing relative prices and to harness the wealth of technological innovation, centrally planned economies were considerably less successful and thus fell relatively further behind. The practice of central planning, bereft of both empirical appeal and of theoretical backing, has quickly withered. This historical outcome fully vindicates von Mises's and Hayek's view of central planning, which is conceivable under static conditions, but highly impractical under dynamic conditions.

References
Ferguson, C. E. (1972), *Microeconomic Theory*, Homewood, Illinois: Richard D. Irwin.

Hayek, Friedrich A. (ed.) (1935), *Collectivist Economic Planning*, London: George Routledge & Sons.

Hayek, Friedrich A., 'The Nature and History of the Problem', in Hayek, 1935, 1–40.

Hayek, Friedrich A., 'The Present State of the Debate', in Hayek, 1935, 201–43.

Hayek, Friedrich A. (1940), 'Socialist Calculation: The Competitive "Solution"', *Economica*, VII, (27), May, 125–49.

Heilbroner, Robert (1990), 'Analysis and Vision in the History of Modern Economic Thought', *Journal of Economic Literature*, XXVIII, (3), September, 1097–1114.

Lange, Oskar (1936), 'On the Economic Theory of Socialism', *Review of Economic Studies*, IV, (1), October, 60–71.

Lavoie, Don (1985), *Rivalry and Central Planning*, New York: Cambridge University Press.

Leeds, Eva Marikova (1991), 'Zrod a skon centralniho planovani', *Promeny*, 28, (2), 81–9.

Mises, Ludwig von (1920), 'Die Wirtschaftsrechnung im sozialistischen Gemeinwesen', *Archiv fuer Sozialwissenschaft und Sozialpolitik*, 47, 86–121, reprinted (1935) as 'Economic Calculation in the Socialist Commonwealth', in F. Hayek (ed.), 1935, Collectivist Economic Planning, London: George Routledge & Sons, 87–130 (EC).

Mises, Ludwig von (1922), *Socialism*, New Haven: Yale University Press, 1951 (*Die Gemeinwirtschaft*, 1922).(S)

Murrell, Peter (1983), 'Did the Theory of Market Socialism Answer the Challenge of Ludwig von Mises? A Reinterpretation of the Socialist Controversy', *History of Political Economy*, 15, (1), 92–105.

Roberts, Paul Craig (1970), 'War Communism: A Re-examination,' *Slavic Review*, 29, 238–61.

Sowell, Thomas (1972), *Say's Law: An Historical Analysis*, Princeton: Princeton University Press.

Temkin, Gabriel (1989), 'On Economic Reforms in Socialist Countries: The Debate on Economic Calculation under Socialism Revisited', *Communist Economies*, 1, (1), 31–59.

Vaughn, Karen I. (1980), 'Economic Calculation under Socialism: the Austrian Contribution', *Economic Inquiry*, 18, 535–54.

3 The advantage of relative backwardness: an input–output approach

William Milberg and Bruce Elmslie

Introduction

The recently rekindled debate over the degree to which productivity levels have converged among industrialized countries since the late 19th century is not without relevance for the newly privatized economies of Eastern and Central Europe.[1] Their relative backwardness *vis-à-vis* other European countries suggests that the issues inherent in Gershenkron's 'advantages of relative backwardness' hypothesis are equally relevant for countries which have recently opted to move in the direction of the free market.

An understanding of their experiences will require, at a minimum, an acceptable methodology for measuring productivity growth. We will make a case for using a vertically integrated measure that will enable us to compare the productivity experiences of different sectors within particular economies, as well as among the economies of Germany, Japan, Italy, Norway and Portugal, for the period 1959–1975. The availability of consistent input–output data dictated this choice of countries for inclusion. The results of our study have enabled us to evaluate whether, and to what extent, there has been an experience of productivity convergence.

Besides laying a further foundation for empirical testing of input–output data, our study also provides a rationale for examining alternative hypotheses about productivity growth. Our findings not only contradict the sectoral productivity convergence findings of Dollar and Wolff (1988), but also Baumol's findings of productivity convergence at the aggregate level (Baumol, 1986).

The experience of Portugal, which is the most 'backward' of the countries studied, and which grew at a much slower rate than the other countries in our sample, is of particular interest because it suggests that the growth 'catch-up' anticipated by the countries of Central and Eastern Europe may not be as reliably attainable for these relatively backward economies as the Gershenkron hypothesis suggests.

Our sectoral productivity data reveal another interesting pattern: that the degree of productivity convergence at the sectoral level may be cyclical and, with a lag, directly correlated with long-term growth trends. Accordingly, we argue for a more general framework which is able to account for alternating periods or cycles of divergence and convergence. Two hypotheses are proposed; one based on spurts of technological innovation and diffusion, and the other based on hysteresis resulting from long periods of growth or decline. We argue that while growth slowdowns have an impact on both high productivity and low productivity countries, the impact on the low productivity countries is more severe.

This dynamic describes a cycle of convergence in high growth periods when diffusion makes foreign technologies accessible to low productivity countries, and divergence when these technological avenues are cut off. By drawing on the extensive literature on uneven development, we propose a more general approach than Gershenkron's 'advantages of relative backwardness' hypothesis.

This paper contains five sections. In Section 1 we describe the nature and extent of backwardness in Portugal, the low income country in our sample. In Section 2 we briefly discuss uneven development models as an alternative to the Gershenkron hypothesis, and in Section 3 we consider the evidence using input–output data for five countries over the 1959–1975 period. In Section 4 we propose some alternative explanations of the divergence trend, and in Section 5 we try to summarize the productivity convergence debate and speculate on its future direction.

Portugal's 'backwardness'

Following Veblen (1915), Gershenkron (1952) argued that countries which, for whatever reason, lag behind others in terms of productivity, are able to catch up quickly by imitating the superior technology of the leaders. Such catch-up is facilitated by investment (through capital-embodied technological change) and demand growth, and premised on the existence of an adequate institutional base.[2] According to Gershenkron (1952, p. 6):

> Assuming an adequate endowment of usable resources as given, and assuming that the great blocks to industrialization had been removed, the opportunities inherent in industrialization may be said to vary directly with the backwardness of the country.

Even 40 years after Gershenkron, there are a number of reasons why observed divergence of sectoral productivity levels across OECD countries run counter to our expectations. Trends toward the globalization of production, the apparently large role of multinational corporations in international technology diffusion, and increased international competition which drives out inefficient technology, all lead to the expectation of productivity convergence.

Portugal fits rather well Gershenkron's description of a country whose 'great blocks to industrialization had been removed'. From the late 1920s when the fascist government of Oliveira Salazar came to power, through the period of our study, Portugal's government emphasized economic development. Salazar maintained close structural ties to business, regulating economic co-ordination, improving export quality and regulating imports. The government also made the development of Portugal's infrastructure a symbol of the 'new state'. Road building was a top priority, as was the development of port facilities (which would allow longer ships and more traffic), and expanded telephone and telegraph services. According to the historian Marques (1976, pp. 198–9):

> [T]he public works policy bore fruit, making possible – along with the general expansion of Europe – the rapid economic development of Portugal in the 1950s and the 1960s... [E]xports rose ten times between 1926 and 1951 (mostly after World War II), then doubled to 1964... The development of exports was a result of industrialization... Imports hardly changed in character. Portugal continued [throughout the period] to order all kinds of manufactured items, like machinery and transportation equipment.

Finally, we note that 70 per cent of Portugal's imports came from developed countries, suggesting that Portugal had access to technology through imports. Portugal was clearly in a position to take advantage of its relative backwardness.

Table 3.1 reports gross domestic products per capita in dollars at 1970 purchasing power parity (PPP) exchange rates for the years 1958, 1965 and 1970, and at 1975 PPP exchange rates for 1976, for the five countries in our study: Germany, Italy, Japan, Norway and Portugal. Clearly, based on per

Table 3.1: Gross domestic product per capita*

Country	1958	1965	1970	1976
Germany	1 483	2 914	3 979	6 001
Italy	955	1 912	2 856	4 124
Japan	507	1 403	2 866	4 668
Norway	1 457	2 566	3 809	6 804
Portugal	476	824	1 426	2 422**

* The population data are taken from 1963, 1970 and 1976. Purchasing power parity exchange rates are used for the years 1958, 1965, 1970 and 1975.
** Based on 1970 population figure.

Sources: United Nations (1970) *Statistical Yearbook 1969* (New York: United Nations) Tables 16 and 177; United Nations (1978) *Statistical Yearbook 1977* (New York: United Nations) Tables 18 and 186; Ward (1985).

capita GDP, Portugal is the least developed country in the sample.[3] Therefore, given that Portugal's social network of education, infrastructure and
technical training for workers is adequate, the Gershenkron hypothesis suggests that Portugal will show signs of productivity convergence with the
productivity leader country over the sample period.

Productivity convergence or uneven development?
Much of the recent research on productivity convergence is a reinvention of
the Gershenkron wheel. But the extensive literature on uneven development,
which predicts productivity divergence, not convergence, has received short
shrift in the recent debate.

Theories of technological divergence between advanced and underdeveloped countries pre-date Adam Smith. The mercantilist link between interest
rates and the balance of trade provided an explanation of divergence. The
mercantilists understood that 'the quantity of the domestic circulation and
the domestic rate of interest are primarily determined by the balance of
payment' (Keynes, 1964, p. 348). Thus, a surplus in the balance of trade
leads to lower rates of interest, increased investment and increased wealth
and power.

Smith's underlying dynamic theory of exchange led him to the theory that,
when trade is based on 'artificial' differences between countries, exchange
through international trade leads to divergence in development and technology.[4] To understand this, we must realize that Smith's theory of exchange is
not the modern static, endowment-based theory. For Smith, exchange breeds
differences where few existed before because it leads to the division of
labour.[5] Applying his theory of exchange to trade between nations, Smith
found that historical accidents, such as access to waterways large enough to
allow seagoing vessels, form the basis of trade and result in large differences
between rich and poor countries. Nations with access to waterways are the
first to become open to international markets, which allows them to be first
in extending the division of labour; this leads to increased labour productivity, more extensive use of machinery in production, and faster rates of
technical progress (Smith, 1937). The cycle of exchange, market extension,
greater division of labour, increased opulence and a still greater volume of
exchange, creates a divergence between rich and poor nations. This virtuous/
vicious cycle creates the advantage in goods which are capable of an extensive division of labour (that is manufactures) for the most open trading
countries, and relative advantages in non-extensive division of labour goods
(that is agriculture) for the less open countries. The eventual result is specialization in dynamic-returns goods for the most open economies and specialization in non-dynamic-returns goods for those less open. In comparing
the 'opulent nations' of Britain and France with a 'poor country' such as

Poland, Smith states: 'In Poland there are... scarce any manufactures... [because] it can pretend to no... competition in its manufactures' (ibid., p. 6). Trade leads to underdevelopment because historical accident causes some countries to specialize in non-dynamic-returns goods. This pattern, once begun, is self-perpetuating.

The Smithian description of economic and technological divergence has its direct modern counterpart in the modern theories of uneven development. Kaldor (1985) is most closely associated with emphasis on the cumulative causation of an initial productivity lead, based on the existence of dynamic scale economies. Krugman (1981) put this into an international trade framework. Given the existence of external economies, the country with a small head start in an industry will continually increase its productivity advantage over lagging countries. In a trade context the model posits that the opening of trade causes the 'head start' advanced countries to specialize in external economies to scale industries, while the lagging countries are forced out of these industries. We do not expect advantages to relative backwardness because continual productivity gains are caused by external economies which are not transferable as are technologies. Trade and time cause initial productivity differences to be magnified so that the advantages of relative backwardness are negative.

The Marxian tradition also has a number of well-developed models of productivity divergence or uneven development.[6] These are mainly built on Lenin's (1917) theory of imperialism and monopoly capitalism. Baran and Sweezy (1966) and more recently Dutt (1984) have rooted uneven development in the monopoly power of firms in the initially more advanced country. Such power results in a persistent edge in capital accumulation and effective demand growth.

Another strain of Marxian thought on unequal development stresses the role of capitalist competition, not monopoly power. For Amin (1977), unequal development is the outcome of a unified world capitalist system. Uneven development within this single system results from the 'unequal specialization' pattern imposed on the 'periphery nations' by international trade relations with the 'centre'. The direction of trade is determined by absolute (not comparative) advantage, which is a function of productivity and wages. Centrally located countries have an absolute cost advantage in industry because of their relatively early development of capitalist sectors. The result, which Amin calls 'peripheral capitalism', is blocked development in the periphery. This implies that countries that are located in the periphery are likely to specialize in natural resource and agricultural products. The infusion of foreign capital helps these sectors to develop most rapidly. Accumulation in the periphery is thus 'extroverted', that is, geared towards exports. Pre-capitalist sectors continue to function since such a large part of the population is excluded from the capitalist sector.

Shaikh's (1980) model also finds the roots of uneven development in capitalist competition, especially free trade. Competition leads to imbalanced trade which, in turn, leads to interest rate changes which encourage investment in the surplus country and squelch it in the deficit country. This sequence of unequal rates of accumulation (and thus technological development) is matched by a similar sequence of trade imbalances. Countries which have chronic deficits must ultimately rely on capital inflows to balance international payments. International debt accumulation is the result.

Empirical results
The recent revival of interest in productivity convergence has been spurred by concern about the declining US position in the global economy, and the provision of a consistent data set on productivity for over 20 nations over the period of 1870–1979 (Maddison, 1982). Abromowitz (1986) used these data to show the considerable convergence in productivity levels that occurred during this period. He attributed any lack of convergence to the different 'social capabilities' (for example, education and financial institutions) in different countries. In particular he showed that the convergence was characterized by a continuous, if unsteady, 'catching up' by backward countries with respect to the leading productivity country (the US or the UK during the period he considered). This evidence supports Gershenkron's 'advantages of relative backwardness' hypothesis. Baumol (1986) offered a more detailed analysis of Maddison's data, and found strong support for the Gershenkron phenomenon for a group of 16 countries over the 110 year period. De Long (1988) criticized the Baumol results on the grounds of sample selection bias. That is, De Long showed that Baumol's results were a function of the countries he selected to include in the sample. A larger sample, based on *ex ante*, not *ex post*, considerations of country characteristics showed much less evidence of convergence, and for significant periods actual divergence. Baumol and Wolff (1988) accepted De Long's critique and went on to observe that any sample of countries larger than and including their original 16 shows signs of considerable divergence, especially after 1961.

Only one major study of productivity convergence at the sector or industry level emerged out of this debate. Dollar and Wolff (1988) found that convergence occured in 27 of the 28 industries studied in 12 industrial countries during the 1963–1982 period. They found convergence to the US level of productivity to be strongest among light industry sectors and less, on average, for all manufacturing. Changes in the composition of employment do not account for the convergence at all manufacturing levels. Dollar and Wolff further located the sources of productivity convergence in the conver-

gence in industry capital–labour ratios and 'technology levels' across countries.

Our analysis adopts the vertically integrated measure of productivity, that
is we look at direct and indirect labour productivity in a sector. This approach captures the interdependence of sectors, providing a more comprehensive measurement of labour productivity than simple direct measures.[7]
The vector of vertically integrated labour coefficients (vilcs) is calculated as
follows:

$$v = l(I–A)^{-1}$$

where v = the 1xn vector of vilcs
   l = the 1xn vector of direct labour coefficients
   I = the nxn identity matrix
   A = the nxn transactions matrix.

Not only is v a more comprehensive measure than the direct measure, it also
captures dynamic scale economies, since productivity in a given vertically
integrated sector is a function of productivity in all its intermediate sectors.[8]
Because of the wide variance in input composition among final goods sectors, we would not expect each sector to share equally the advantage of
dynamic scale economies. Vertically integrated analysis thus captures the
importance of Kaldor–Young dynamic returns at a disaggregated level. The
simple direct measure fails to capture the dynamic returns, since each final
goods sector's performance is considered in isolation.

In input–output analysis, changes in production over time take the form of
changes in the matrix of technical coefficients – a vector for each sector.
However, the direction and magnitude of this change is ambiguous. Vertically integrated analysis reduces the input–output current flows matrix to a
vector, that is a scalar for each sector. Productivity change can be measured
as changes in this single coefficient. Such a measure of technical change is
unambiguous, yet retains the information provided by input–output tables.[9]

We have used the vertically integrated measure of productivity to test for
productivity convergence at the sectoral level among five OECD countries
over the period 1959–1975. The countries used in the study were Germany,
Italy, Japan, Norway and Portugal. These countries were selected because
they are the only ones in the Economic Commission for Europe (ECE)
sample with consistent data over the entire period. Aggregation of the input–
output tables to 14 sectors is summarized in Table 3.2. This was the greatest
degree of disaggregation possible while still maintaining cross-country compatibility. The Appendix gives details on data sources, aggregation procedures and variable construction.

Table 3.2:   Final aggregated industrial sectors

Sector industry group	Corresponding original sectors in the input–output database	
	1959–1965	1970–1975
1 Agriculture, hunting, fishing and forestry	1	1
2 Coal mining, crude petroleum and natural gas	2	2, 3
3 Metal ore and other mining	3	4, 5
4 Food, beverages and tobacco	4	6
5 Textiles and clothing	5, 6	7
6 Wood, wood products, paper and printing	7	8, 9
7 Chemicals and rubber	8, 9	10
8 Petroleum and coal products	10	11
9 Non-metallic mineral products	11	12
10 Ferrous and non-ferrous metals (basic metals)	12	13
11 Machinery, transport and other manufactured goods	13, 14	14, 15
12 Electricity, gas and water	15	16, 17
13 Construction	16	18
14 Trade, distribution, transportation, storage and communication	17, 18	19, 21, 22

We measure convergence in two ways: first, we take the ratio of highest to lowest vilc per sector across countries. An increase in this ratio implies divergence, and a decrease implies convergence. Second, we calculate the coefficient of variation[10] (cv) in each vertically integrated sector across countries over time. Declines in the cv imply convergence and increases imply divergence in a given sector. The results of these two measures are presented in Tables 3.3 and 3.4.

The bottom line of Table 3.3 shows the median of the sectoral ratios of highest to lowest productivity by year. This ratio declined to 3.62 in 1975 from 4.86 in 1959, implying that on average the country with the lowest productivity in each sector partly 'caught up' to the leading country in that

Table 3.3:   *Ratio of highest v to lowest v, by sector (five country sample) 1959–1975**

Sector	1959 High/low	Countries	1965 High/low	Countries
1	3.76	[J/G]	3.36	[J/G]
2	10.93	[J/N]	11.70	[J/N]
3	6.96	[P/I]	4.05	[P/I]
4	2.41	[I/G]	2.23	[J/G]
5	5.92	[I/N]	3.15	[I/N]
6	4.38	[I/G]	3.66	[J/G]
7	4.20	[I/N]	2.86	[J/N]
8	4.12	[J/N]	6.56	[J/N]
9	4.02	[P/N]	2.71	[P/N]
10	6.29	[J/N]	3.50	[J/N]
11	5.19	[J/N]	3.87	[J/P]
12	8.95	[J/N]	10.68	[J/N]
13	6.74	[P/N]	4.37	[P/N]
14	4.52	[J/N]	4.10	[J/N]
MEDIAN	4.86		3.77	

Sector	1970 High/low	Countries	1975 High/low	Countries
1	2.97	[P/G]	4.11	[P/G]
2	5.97	[G/P]	9.86	[I/P]
3	13.75	[I/J]	2.31	[P/J]
4	3.60	[P/G]	4.67	[P/G]
5	3.28	[J/N]	6.46	[P/N]
6	2.37	[J/I]	4.85	[P/I]
7	2.41	[P/N]	3.54	[P/N]
8	3.44	[G/I]	5.43	[P/I]
9	2.44	[P/N]	3.53	[P/N]
10	2.87	[G/P]	1.90	[G/N]
11	2.28	[J/N]	2.43	[J/N]
12	1.86	[P/N]	3.20	[P/I]
13	3.65	[P/N]	3.70	[P/N]
14	2.69	[P/N]	3.54	[P/N]
MEDIAN	2.92		3.62	

* The countries included in this table are Germany, Italy, Japan, Norway and Portugal. Note that the ratio of highest v to lowest v is equivalent to the ratio of lowest to highest total productivity.

Table 3.4:   Coefficients of variation of vertically integrated labour coefficients (five country sample) 1959–1975*

Sector	1959	1965	1970	1975
1	0.4599	0.5035	0.4413	0.6567
2	0.8438	0.7266	0.6061	0.9444
3	0.8454	0.5754	0.9839	0.3826
4	0.3069	0.2960	0.5408	0.7370
5	0.6414	0.4640	0.4267	0.7390
6	0.4730	0.4511	0.3943	0.7250
7	0.5854	0.3887	0.2960	0.4866
8	0.5946	0.7187	0.5156	0.7259
9	0.5465	0.4003	0.4011	0.6207
10	0.7297	0.4382	0.3742	0.2423
11	0.6746	0.6014	0.3460	0.2965
12	1.1706	1.2936	0.2754	0.5936
13	0.7536	0.6223	0.6222	0.6069
14	0.5722	0.5060	0.3739	0.5290
Median	0.6180	0.5047	0.4139	0.6138

*The countries included in this table are Germany, Italy, Japan, Norway and Portugal.

sector. This provides support for the Gershenkron hypothesis, and is consistent with a number of the recent studies discussed above.

Looking at the coefficient of variation of specific sectors in Table 3.4, we find no clear-cut tendency for divergence or convergence over the entire period. The number of sectors in which there was convergence was exactly equal to the number of sectors in which divergence was observed over the 1959–1975 period.

Not surprisingly, the comparison of end points (1959 and 1975) hides some interesting fluctuations over the sample period. Specifically, there was considerable convergence between 1959 and 1970, and then equally large divergence between 1970 and 1975. In Table 3.4 we see that between 1959 and 1965 11 of 14 sectors showed convergence. Again, between 1965 and 1970, convergence occurred in 11 sectors. But from 1970 to 1975, convergence occured in only four sectors: metal ore and other mining; basic metals; machinery, transport and other manufactured goods, and construction. Moreover, the median coefficient of variation rose from 0.4139 to 0.6138 from 1970 to 1975. The median for 1975 increases almost to the original 1959 level of 0.6180.

This break in the convergence tendency observed in the 1975 data is confirmed by the ratios in Table 3.3, comparing the lowest to highest productivity in each sector over time. The median of the ratios of highest to lowest sectoral vilc levels declines steadily from 1959 (4.86) to 1970 (2.92) and then jumps back up in 1975, practically to its 1965 level. The picture from our sample is thus considerably less definite than the Dollar and Wolff results indicate. Certainly, it requires an explanation which goes beyond the simple Gershenkron hypothesis.

The evidence from our input–output study demonstrates, however, that convergence did not occur. The third and fifth columns of Table 3.3 show the country with the lowest total sectoral productivity relative to the country with the highest total sectoral productivity. The country listed in the numerator is the low productivity country in that sector. In 1959 and 1965, Portugal was the low productivity country in three sectors: metal ore and other mining; non-metallic mineral products, and construction. Japan was the low productivity country in six sectors in 1959 and ten sectors in 1965. In 1970 and 1975, Portugal was still the low productivity country in the same three sectors, but in 1970 it ranked as the low productivity country in seven sectors.[11] In 1975 it was the low productivity country in 11 of the 14 sectors. Over the sample period, Portugal experienced a general productivity divergence between itself and the other, more advanced, countries in the sample. The data do not support the Gershenkron hypothesis.

To further develop this point, we re-evaluate our data, this time excluding Portugal. Table 3.5 reports total productivity ratios for the low and high productivity country in each sector. By excluding Portugal we note that overall convergence occurs between sample countries in each period. The median total productivity ratio falls from 4.29 in 1959 to 1.91 in 1975. Moreover, the median ratio falls in the 1970 to 1975 sample period. The strong divergence observed in this period in Table 3.3 can be attributed to Portugal's divergence from the other sample countries.

The convergence trend does show signs of slowing down during the 1970 to 1975 period for Germany, Italy, Japan and Norway. This is shown by the fact that even though the median ratio falls, seven of the 14 sectors diverged over this period. This is compared to five sectors diverging from 1959 to 1965, and four sectors diverging from 1965 to 1970. However, the fact remains that Portugal is responsible for the median divergence reported in Table 3.3.

Portugal's role is again confirmed using the coefficients of variation for Germany, Italy, Japan and Norway reported in Table 3.6. From 1959 to 1975 only sector 8, petroleum and coal products, diverges. From 1959 to 1965, six sectors diverge, and from 1970 to 1975, seven sectors diverge. However, over the sample period the median coefficient of variation falls to 0.2818 in

Table 3.5:   Ratio of highest v to lowest v by sector (excluding Portugal) 1959–1975*

Sector	1959 High/low	Countries	1965 High/low	Countries
1	3.76	[J/G]	3.36	[J/G]
2	10.93	[J/N]	11.70	[J/N]
3	2.36	[J/I]	1.88	[J/I]
4	2.41	[I/G]	2.23	[J/G]
5	5.92	[I/N]	3.15	[I/N]
6	4.38	[I/G]	3.66	[J/G]
7	4.20	[I/N]	2.86	[J/N]
8	4.12	[J/N]	6.56	[J/N]
9	2.13	[I/N]	2.25	[I/N]
10	6.29	[J/N]	3.50	[J/N]
11	5.19	[J/N]	3.87	[J/P]
12	8.95	[J/N]	10.68	[J/N]
13	2.54	[J/N]	2.13	[I/N]
14	4.52	[J/N]	4.10	[J/N]
MEDIAN	4.29		3.43	

Sector	1970 High/low	Countries	1975 High/low	Countries
1	2.24	[J/G]	1.87	[J/G]
2	3.61	[G/J]	6.32	[I/J]
3	13.75	[I/J]	1.57	[N/J]
4	2.41	[J/G]	2.04	[J/G]
5	3.28	[J/N]	3.46	[J/N]
6	2.37	[J/I]	2.34	[J/I]
7	1.98	[J/N]	1.92	[J/N]
8	3.44	[G/I]	4.59	[G/I]
9	1.56	[J/N]	1.73	[J/N]
10	1.86	[G/N]	1.90	[G/N]
11	2.28	[J/N]	2.43	[J/N]
12	1.19	[G/N]	1.26	[G/I]
13	1.55	[I/N]	1.53	[J/N]
14	2.32	[J/N]	1.86	[J/N]
MEDIAN	2.30		1.91	

* The countries included in this table are Germany, Italy, Japan and Norway. Note that the ratio of highest v to lowest v is equivalent to the ratio of lowest to highest total productivity.

Table 3.6:   *Coefficients of variation of vertically integrated labour coefficients* excluding Portugal*

Sector	1959	1965	1970	1975
1	0.5267	0.5586	0.3577	0.2936
2	0.9193	0.8374	0.4424	0.8063
3	0.3311	0.2501	1.1092	0.2160
4	0.3256	0.3258	0.3924	0.3230
5	0.7662	0.5133	0.4655	0.5013
6	0.5481	0.4895	0.4183	0.3836
7	0.6462	0.4489	0.2707	0.2699
8	0.6413	0.7725	0.6028	0.7704
9	0.3393	0.3808	0.2045	0.2624
10	0.7022	0.4754	0.2547	0.2596
11	0.6540	0.5448	0.3316	0.3454
12	1.2319	1.3279	0.0783	0.0944
13	0.3434	0.3533	0.2146	0.1949
14	0.6337	0.5638	0.3434	0.2465
Median	0.6375	0.5291	0.3506	0.2818

* The countries included in this table are Germany, Italy, Japan and Norway.

1975 from 0.6375 in 1959. Moreover, from 1970 to 1975 the median falls from 0.3506. The divergence observed in Tables 3.3 and 3.4 for the 1970 to 1975 period is due to the divergence of the least developed country, Portugal.

Clearly, one possible explanation of Portugal's failure to keep pace with the more advanced countries in the sample is Portugal's political instability. From 1968, when Oliveira Salazar died, to 1974 when the military took over the country, political instability increased. Along with this internal instability (from 1968–1975) came increasing resistance in Portugal's colonies. However, Portugal held on to its major colonies, Mozambique and Angola, until well after the 1974 revolution (June 1975 and November 1975, respectively).

Despite the political turmoil (both internal and external), Portugal's economy remained relatively stable until 1975, a year after our sample period. With respect to the colonial wars, most economic analyses suggest that the captive markets and cheap supplies of raw materials more than offset Portugal's military and administrative expenses in keeping the colonies. In general, Portugal was only slightly less stable than the EEC in 1974. Portugal's growth rate remained positive in 1974 at 1.1 per cent. This compares to the EEC growth rate of 1.6 per cent. But in 1975 Portugal's growth rate fell to –4.3 per cent, while the EEC fell to –1.5 per cent. Unemployment and output gap data also indicate that Portugal's economy remained relatively stable until 1975. The unemployment rate grew slightly from 3.1 per cent to 5.6 per cent between 1973 and 1974, but exploded to 11.7 per cent in 1975. The output gap stood at 0.5 per cent in 1973 and 1.88 per cent in 1974, and rose to 4.93 per cent in 1975. Thus, while political instability came to a head in 1974, major economic instability came in 1975 and continued through the rest of the 1970s.[12]

Cycles of relative productivity change

An issue often ignored in the recent productivity convergence debate is the contingency of the Gershenkron hypothesis,[13] that is the ability to capture the advantage of relative backwardness depends on a certain level of institutional development; a capacity to absorb the new technology in order to catch up or to leapfrog to leader status (Soete, 1985). We have argued that Portugal was beyond the threshold of institutional development; that is of absorptive capacity. And yet even in this case convergence did not occur between 1959 and 1975. But what the Gershenkron hypothesis and the neo-Schumpeterian emphasis on absorptive capacity are perhaps missing are two features of the the post-1973 global economy – the product life-cycle and the hysteretic effects of growth and decline. We deal with each in turn.

While the explanations of cumulative causation and productivity divergence are accurate in describing cases of underdevelopment, they lack an explanation of cases of productivity convergence. A complete model of the process of productivity dynamics must be general enough to explain both divergence and convergence, as exhibited in our study of five OECD countries. The reversal of the convergence trend after 1965 depends on the unequal impact of the forces for productivity change on different countries. Models of productivity growth are inadequate since they generally lack the asymmetry which is at the core of our divergence results. We look instead to the theory of technical change and the theory of growth.

The technology diffusion literature provides one explanation of the phenomenon of alternating periods of convergence and divergence. If the product life-cycle allows for catching up through technological diffusion (leading to the mature product phase), it also leaves open the possibility of forging ahead, in the sense of creating a new variant (for example, generation) of the mature product, and shifting the industry to a new wave in the product life-cycle. This is depicted in Figure 3.1(a), which shows recurrent product life-cycles in a given industry.[14] The recurring product life-cycles translate into cycles of productivity convergence and divergence. Such cycles, corresponding to successive product life cycles, are depicted in Figure 3.1(b). Of

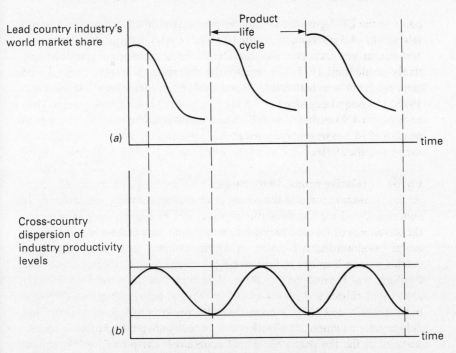

Figure 3.1:   The product life cycle and productivity convergence

course, there is a microeconomic explanation, which would require significant inter-industry linkage to be operative at the aggregate level. Among
developed countries (such as those in our sample) such linkage is quite
evident (see Milberg and Elmslie (1992) for evidence of this).

The product life-cycle is appealing in its simplicity, but it fails to account
for the growth–productivity dispersion link observed in our sample. For the
whole sample, the sectoral productivity divergence was observed in times of
slower productivity growth on average in the five countries. The period of
most rapid productivity growth was the period of most significant convergence. The weighted average annual productivity growth rate for the entire
sample began to fall in the 1965–1970 period and then remained low in the
post-1970 period. It is possible, then, that productivity divergence occurs
during periods of overall productivity slowdown, but with a lag. Productivity growth slowdowns may affect low productivity countries relatively more
than high productivity ones, in the same way that, implied by the Gershenkron
hypothesis, periods of productivity growth affect low productivity countries
relatively more than high productivity countries. In this case, long-run convergence would depend on the existence of longer periods of productivity
growth than of productivity slowdown.

One possible explanation, then, is the asymmetric effect of growth and slowdown on high and low productivity countries. Low productivity countries may tend to specialize in sectors with relatively high income elasticity of demand. Periods of rising world economic activity would result in some catch-up by low productivity countries. But in periods of falling world demand, low productivity countries see a drastic fall in profits and investment potential, and thus a worsening of their relative productivity position *vis-à-vis* the high productivity countries.

The argument parallels that of the Prebisch and Singer hypothesis on the terms of trade in developing countries. The result is that cycles of relative productivity change would be unstable, tending towards increased divergence. Such 'hysteresis' assumes an inequality in technological diffusion in high and low growth periods. One explanation for this might be the link between diffusion and the use of foreign capital either through direct trade in capital goods or through foreign direct investment, and the correlation of foreign capital use and productivity growth (Elmslie, 1990; Onida, this volume).

The hysteresis hypothesis emphasizes that technology gaps may converge or diverge depending on the endogenous rate of technical progress in leading and lagging countries. While demand factors are important (as described above), supply considerations will also play a role. Rosenberg (1963) argued that low productivity countries lack the strong domestic capital goods industry necessary for the endogenous development of new technologies. In part, this is due to their small domestic markets, which prevent capital goods firms from taking advantage of the economies of specialization associated with the production of heterogeneous capital goods.

The lack of a domestic capital goods industry makes low productivity countries largely dependent on the diffusion of technology from abroad. Technology is transferred either through the purchase of advanced foreign capital goods, the purchase of technology through licensing or through direct foreign investment. In periods of economic slowdown, all of these avenues dry up. The foreign exchange required to purchase technology becomes scarce because of decreased exports and tighter credit, while multinational enterprises cut back on direct foreign investment. These factors became increasingly important with the breakdown of the Bretton Woods agreement in 1973. Flexible exchange rates imposed a greater burden on high inflation countries than on low inflation ones. This factor might have contributed to the severe divergence observed in the 1970–1975 period.

Two other important factors, not pursued in detail in this paper, are likely to have worked along with the generalized cycle of divergence and convergence described above. One is the unequal impact of the burden of a flexible exchange regime. That is, low income and high inflation countries are more heavily burdened by the required discipline of flexible exchange rates than are low inflation countries. This may have led to the relative decline of Portugal in the 1970–1975 period. Secondly, the role of the state is of crucial significance. A government concerned with 'catching up' will impose policies that encourage technological imports, export expansion and thus productivity convergence.[15] Among the countries in our sample, the Portuguese government did not vigorously pursue such a course, whereas the Japanese government clearly did.

Our conclusions are not only relevant for Portugal, of course. The non-inevitability of 'catching up' is an important lesson for Eastern European countries seeking to attain a Western European standard of living. Such catch-up cannot be assumed inevitable, but is created by government policy and the development of social institutions.

Conclusion
In this paper we have provided evidence based on a small sample of OECD countries which contradicts Dollar and Wolff's results on sectoral productivity convergence, and supports De Long's scepticism of Baumol's assertion of convergence at the aggregate level. We argue that not only is selection bias a problem in this debate, but so is the measurement of productivity. We use a vertically integrated measure of productivity and show that the case for convergence at the sectoral level is not strong, even for a group of advanced market economies in the OECD.

Portugal, relatively 'backward' in our sample, saw its productivity grow at a much slower rate than the other countries. This amounts to a clear-cut counter-example to the Gershenkron hypothesis, since Portugal exceeded the threshold level of development of infrastructure, education and trade openness required to be in a position to 'catch up'. In this case, models of divergence, not convergence, would be most appropriate.

Technology diffusion is clearly not the linear and monotonic process implied in the simple convergence model; unequal, rather than convergent, development may be the more likely global dynamic.

To the extent that our preliminary results hold up in further testing, it would seem that the simple Gershenkron hypothesis is in need of amendment. A few extensions have been proposed, including the recurrent product life-cycle and asymmetric effects of growth and slowdown on high and low income countries. We have, hopefully, laid the groundwork for future empirical testing of these alternative explanations.

Notes
1. In this paper we deal only with the 'backwardness advantages' school. For a discussion of the trade theory implications, see Elmslie and Milberg (1992).

2. For a critical review of 'catching up' theories, see Ames and Rosenberg (1963), Gregory (1974) and Fagerberg (1988) .
3. Japan rivals Portugal in 1959.
4. For a more complete analysis of Smith's theory of trade and development see Elmslie and James (1992).
5. Smith emphasized this point by arguing that the apparent natural intellectual differences between the philosopher and the 'common street porter' are the result of the societal division of labour, rather than inherent differences in intellect (Smith 1776; pp. 15–16).
6. For a review of these theories, see Brewer (1980) and Barone (1985).
7. Momigliano and Siniscalco (1984) argue that the direct approach may be misleading if indirect effects are significant. On this point, see also Milberg and Elmslie (1992).
8   This notion can be expanded to include fixed capital goods:

$$v* = 1\,(I–A–D)^{-1}$$

where D = the nxn matrix of fixed capital depreciation coefficients.
9. See Pasinetti (1973).
10. The coefficient of variation is the standard deviation divided by the mean.
11. The exception is that Italy appears as the low productivity country in sector 3 in 1970. This is obviously a data error. Italy was the high productivity country in sector 3 for 1959 and 1965. Moreover, the ratio jumps from 4.05 in 1965 to 13.75 in 1970 and back down to 2.30 in 1975.
12. For full references see Elmslie (1988).
13. Abramowitz (1986) and Nelson (1990) are exceptions.
14. The possibility of recurrent technology gaps has been raised by Abernathy *et al.* (1974), Magee (1977), Branscomb (1989) and Fagerberg (1988) .
15. Amsden (1990) has shown this clearly for the case of South Korea.

References

Abernathy, W., Kantrow and Clark (1974), *Industrial Renaissance*, New York: Basic Books.

Abromowitz, M. (1986), 'Catching Up, Forging Ahead, and Falling Behind', *Journal of Economic History*, **XLVI**, (2), 385–406.

Ames, E. and Rosenberg, N. (1963), 'Changing Technological Leadership and Industrial Growth', *Economic Journal*, **73**, March 13–31.

Amin, S. (1977), *Imperialism and Unequal Development*, New York: Monthly Review Press.

Amsden, A. (1990), *Asia's Next Giant*, Oxford: Oxford University Press.

Baran, P. and Sweezy, P. (1966), *Monopoly Capital*, New York: Monthly Review Press.

Barone, C. (1985), *Marxist Thought on Imperialism: Survey and Critique*, Armonk: ME Sharpe.

Baumol, W. (1986), 'Productivity Growth, Convergence, and Welfare: What the Long-Run Data Show', *American Economic Review*, **76**, December, 1072–85.

Baumol, W. and Wolff, E. (1988), 'Productivity Growth, Convergence and Welfare: Reply', *American Economic Review*, **78**, (5), 1155–9.

Branscomb, L. (1989), 'Technological Change and Its International Diffusion', in J. Cassing and M. Husted (eds), *Capital Technology and Labour in the New Global Economy*, Washington, DC: American Enterprise Institute.

Brewer, A. (1980), *Marxian Theories of Imperialism*, London: Routledge and Kegan Paul.

De Long, B. (1988), 'Productivity Growth, Convergence, and Welfare: Comment', *American Economic Review*, **78**, (5), 1138–54.

Dollar, D. and Wolff, E. (1988), 'Convergence of Industry Labour Productivity Among Advanced Economies, 1963–1982', *Review of Economics and Statistics*, **LXX**, (4), 549–58.

Dutt, A. (1984), 'Monopoly Capital and Uneven Development: Baran Revisited', *Journal of Development Economics*, **12**, 161–76.

Elmslie, B. (1988), 'Capital Mobility and International Trade: A Cambridge Contribution', unpublished PhD Dissertation, University of Utah.

Elmslie, B. (1990), 'Capital Good Imports and Total Productivity', mimeo: Department of Economics, University of New Hampshire.

Elmslie, B. and James, A. (1993), 'The Renaissance of Adam Smith in Modern Theories of International Trade', in R. Hebert (ed.), *Perspectives on the History of Economic Thought*, vol. IX, Aldershot: Edward Elgar.

Elmslie, B. and Milberg, W. (1993), 'International Trade and Factor Intensity Uniformity: An Empirical Assessment', *Weltwirtschaftliches Archiv*, forthcoming.

Fagerberg, J. (1988), 'Why Growth Rates Differ', in G. Dosi *et al.* (eds), *Technical Change and Economic Theory*, London: Pinter.

Gershenkron, A. (1952), 'Economic Backwardness in Historical Perspective', in B. Hoselitz (ed.), *The Progress of Underdeveloped Areas*, Chicago: University of Chicago Press.

Gregory, P. (1974), 'Some Empirical Comments on the Theory of Relative Backwardness: The Russian Case', *Economic Development and Cultural Change*, 21, 654–65.

Kaldor, N. (1985), *Economics Without Equilibrium*, Armonk: ME Sharpe.

Keynes, J. M. (1964), *The General Theory of Employment, Interest and Money*, New York: Harcourt Brace Jovanovich, first published 1936.

Krugman, P. (1981), 'Trade, Accumulation and Uneven Development', *Journal of Development Economics*, 8, 149–61.

Lenin, N. (1975), *Imperialism: the Highest Stage of Capitalism*, Moscow: Progress Publishers, originally published in 1917.

Maddison, A. (1982), *Phases of Capitalist Development*, Oxford: Oxford University Press.

Magee, S. (1977), 'Information and the Multinational Corporation: An Appropriability Theory of Direct Foreign Investment', in J. Bhagwati (ed.), *The New International Economic Order: The North-South Debate*, Cambridge: MIT Press.

Marques, A.H. de Oliveira (1976), *History of Portugal*, New York: Columbia University Press.

Milberg, W. and Elmslie, B. (1992), 'Technical Change in the Corporate Economy: A Vertically Integrated Approach', in W. Milberg (ed.), *The Megacorp and Macrodynamics: Essays in Memory of Alfred Eichner*, Armonk: ME Sharpe.

Momigliano, F. and Siniscalco, D. (1984), 'Technology and International Specialization', *Banco Nazionale del Lavoro Quarterly Review*, No. 150, 257–84.

Nelson, R. (1990), 'US Technological Leadership: Where Did It Come From and Where Did It Go?', *Research Policy*, 19, 117–32.

Onida, F. 'Economic and Monetary Integration, Real Exchange Rates and Patterns of Industrial Specialization', this volume.

Pasinetti, L. (1973), 'On the Notion of Vertically Integrated Analysis', *Metroeconomica*, 17, 1–12.

Rosenberg, N. (1963), 'Capital Goods, Technology and Economic Growth', *Oxford Economic Papers*, 15, 217–27.

Shaikh, A. (1980), 'The Laws of International Exchange', in E. Nell (ed.), *Growth, Profits, and Property*, Cambridge: Cambridge University Press.

Smith, A. (1937), *An Inquiry into the Nature and Causes of the Wealth of Nations*, New York: Modern Library Edition, first published 1776.

Soete, L. (1985), 'International Diffusion of Technology, Industrial Development and Technological Leapfrogging', *World Development*, 13, (3), 409–22.

Veblen, C. (1915), *Imperial Germany and the Industrial Revolution*, New York: Macmillan.

Ward, M. (1985), *Purchasing Power Parities and Real Expenditures in the OECD*, Paris: The Organization for Cooperation and Development.

Appendix: data sources and manipulation

Input–output tables
The A matrices of each country were constructed from the *Standardized Input–Output Tables of ECE Countries for Years around 1959, 1965, 1970 and 1975* published through the United Nations by the Economic Commission for Europe.

Each transaction matrix for years around 1970 and 1975 is aggregated to 24 sectors by the ECE, utilizing the post-1965 International Standard Industrial Classification (ISIC). Most sectors are aggregated to the two-digit level. Each matrix for years around 1959 and 1965 is aggregated to 20 sectors by the ECE using the pre-1965 ISIC.

In order to make the tables compatible with each other and the available labour data, certain manipulations of the data were performed. First, the tables were made compatible. Italy had one sector that was not reported in 1970 and 1975; this sector had to be filled in order for the results to be comparable between countries. The missing sector is 'other mining' (ISIC 29). The methodology to develop the Italy sector was to take the data from France and assume $x_{ijy}/l_{iy} = x_{ijz}/l_{iz}$ where i and j are standard input–output sectors, and y and z are each country. The x_{ij} for Italy was then divided by its purchasing power parity exchange rate (z/y) to make it conform with the rest of the table. The sectorial output data are derived by assuming that $x_{iy}/l_{iy} = x_{iz}/l_{iz}$. Again, this is divided by the purchasing power parity exchange rate.

The vertically integrated labour coefficients were made compatible between countries by converting the country currency denominated output to a dollar denominated output, and multiplying by the United States purchasing power parity exchange rate from Ward (1985). Also, the output was deflated by dividing by a wholesale price index (1970 = 100) for general goods published in the *Statistical Yearbook* (1977).

Secondly, in order to make the tables consistent with the labour data, we aggregated the 24 sectors for 1970 and 1975 and the 20 sectors for 1959 and 1965 into the 14 sectors shown in Table 3.1.

Labour data

The labour data used to develop the direct labour coefficients are taken from the *Yearbook of Industrial Statistics*, Vol. 1, 1976, edition published by the United Nations, and from *Labour Force Statistics*, OECD, 1986. To obtain the missing sector for Italy the following methodology was employed: $l_{iy}/X_{iy} = l_{iz}/X_{iz}$ for countries y and z.

4 Defining property rights after the 'Velvet Revolution'

Nicholas W. Balabkins

Introduction

In the early 1970s, the property rights debate echoed throughout the academic halls of American universities. The existing property relations were taken out of the *ceteris paribus* cage, and the institutional and legal environment was added to the analysis of the maximizing behaviour of firms and households. In particular, the different property relations, enforcement costs of contractual activities, and exchange and policing activities were brought into maximizing models of economic theory. The seminal essay on the entire property rights analysis was written by Erik G. Furubotn and Svetozar Pejovich in 1972 (pp. 1137–62). Their main point was that:

> Property rights do not refer to relations between men and things but, rather, to the sanctioned behaviour relations among men that arise from the existence of things and pertain to their use. Property rights assignments specify the norms of behaviour with respect to things that each and every person must observe in his interactions with other persons, or bear the cost for nonobservance...the crucial task for the new property rights approach is to show that the content of property rights affects the allocation and use of resources in specific and predictable ways... (p. 1139).

It is clear, then, that existing property rights influence incentives and behaviour. Every economy, no matter how organized, must be able to co-ordinate demand and supply in order to avoid surplus and prevent shortages, enforce efficiency, and to create and preserve incentives. Because the traditional model of perfect competition has abstracted the occurrence of externalities, it cannot address the problem they pose for the attainment of Pareto optimum and the achievement of maximum economic efficiency. Externalities arise as side effects in the course of producing and consuming some commodities. They may be either harmful or beneficial and fall upon firms and people not directly involved in the production or consumption of the commodities; so that they incur external costs when they are harmful and external benefits when they are beneficial (Pigou, 1932, pp. 129–30). Air pollution is a familiar example of an external cost, while persons inoculated against typhus generate an external benefit because they reduce the potential spread of the disease.[1]

Why, we might ask, do externalities arise? The answer is that they arise when property rights are not adequately specified (Knight, 1924). The best contemporary statement is the so-called Coase theorem, which clearly established that when property rights are clearly defined and transferable, externalities are avoided (Coase, 1960). But apart from externalities, restrictions on the property rights of ownership are usually imposed by government. The insights of Knight and Coase take on new relevance as economies in which the means of production were state-owned make the transition towards markets.

State ownership of the means of production

It seems relevant to recall that, since 1917, the Soviet Union has banned all privately owned means of production. Its institutional framework was characterized by the complete absence of private and/or corporate ownership of the means of production. Because privately owned means of production were considered instruments of exploitation, the Bolsheviks proceeded to expropriate the former owners soon after they came to power in 1917. It was expropriation without any compensation. Such expropriation was followed by an imposition of the expropriation tax, designed to soak up the liquid funds of the former owners. Thereafter, the former owners were forever called 'former exploiters' and were typically deported to some Siberian camp for 're-education'.

The satellite countries of Central and Eastern Europe, as they were known for more than four decades, were created with the assistance of the Red Army after the end of World War II. The ideological foundation on which they were built was supposedly Marxism with a Leninist twist, which called for the elimination of privately owned means of production, the substitution of quantitative-output planning (popularly known as central planning) for a market economy, and a shift of political power to the communists. These changes were supposed to produce a material nirvana, a worker's paradise. Yet, they failed to do so, as the people in Central Europe and the Soviet Union well know. Instead, by Western standards, communist bosses left behind an economic wasteland. The capitalist welfare states of Western Europe, Australia, New Zealand and even North America provide a level of material well-being that is the envy of all former Soviet-type societies. The civil rights and freedoms assured by contemporary capitalist welfare states have made material progress possible. Furthermore, the Soviet Union and the former satellite countries missed the high-tech revolution of the 1960s.

For these reasons, the socialist states were swept away in 1989, as though by a tidal wave. This wave was actually the beginning of the 'Velvet Revolution' or what in the 1950s and 1960s used to be called the 'convergence theory' of different social orders as they cope with upheaval, disorganization and different degrees of crisis.

Since the focus of this paper is on the emerging property rights after the demise of Soviet-type social order, it is necessary to sketch briefly the salient features of state ownership of the means of production. As interpreted by Janos Kornai in his recent volume (Kornai, 1990), which basically deals with the remaking of two dimensions of the Hungarian social order, specifically, how to revamp the institution of property ownership to create favourable conditions for the emergence of privately owned means of production, and, secondly, how to move the economy from a highly centralized and bureaucratic system of control to a market economy. The two tasks are intertwined.

Kornai writes that in Hungary, 'the private sector, private initiative and private property, had almost fallen victim to a series of nationalization, collectivization, and confiscation campaigns' (Kornai, 1990, p. 36). Furthermore, he notes: 'the critical deficiency of socialist state property consists in the impersonalization of ownership. Since state property belongs to everybody, i.e., nobody, nobody really cares for it' (Kornai, 1990, p. 51). State ownership creates a permanent government bureaucracy. In consequence the threat remains that direct bureaucratic regulation will be replaced by *indirect* bureaucratic regulation, even if reforms dismantle the quantitative-output plan economy (Kornai, 1990, p. 59). To prevent this, he recommends setting up an office to manage the privatization of state property (Kornai, 1990, p. 72).

As the 'Velvet Revolution', with its difficult corollary process of the privatization of the means of production, unfolds in the Central European countries, a clearer understanding and perspective of the true condition of the vast state sector is emerging. It is becoming apparent that state ownership of the means of production contributed little to balanced economic growth and continuous improvement of material welfare. State ownership is so invariably inefficient that one might even equate it with what was once called the 'inefficient property rights doctrine' (Furubotn and Pejovich, 1972, p. 1140). Von Mises anticipated such a state of affairs in the 1920s in his work *Die Gemeinwirtschaft*, recently elaborated by D. Lavoie (1985) in his *Rivalry and Central Planning: The Socialist Calculation Debate Reconsidered*. From the perspective of American property rights theory, the deficiencies of the state-owned means of production are numerous. In 1917, under Lenin, the Soviet Union embarked (in the name of Marx) on the course of nationalizing all privately owned means of production without compensation, for private property was viewed as the fruit of exploitation. It was to prevent exploitation in the Soviet Union that all lands and factories were to be owned by the government. To avoid the misuse and abuse of the state-owned property, the Soviet government set up the 'Department to Combat the Misappropriation of Social Property'.[2]

On occasion, property theft was subject to punishment by death. Actually, it was red managers who stole large quantities of state-owned machinery, equipment and raw materials and sold it to the vast 'underground business world' of the Soviet Union (Simis, 1982, pp. 144–79). Since 90 per cent of Soviet laws have never been published, illegal activity by the party bosses was the order of the day, and they exacted tribute from those who were producers in the not so legal sector of the economy.

Since socialist state ownership of the means of production means total impersonalization of property, it really belongs to nobody and nobody cares very much what happens to it. One consequence widely observed in the Soviet Union is that more and more arable land has been left uncultivated. This was not supposed to happen, but it did; factory premises were supposed to be kept clean and in good repair, yet that was often not the case. State-owned factories were also supposed to be among the most modern in the world, yet we now know of their sorry condition. Idle capacity is another characteristic which emerged, as an unintended consequence of the quantitative-output planning. To be assigned lower output quotas, Soviet managers developed the habit of hiding their true productive capacity from government inspectors. It was not unusual to hide 10–15 per cent of the available productive capacity successfully. In other words, state ownership of the means of production and quantitative-output planning led to the emergence of the permanent existence of excess capacity in the Soviet Union. Since bankruptcy did not exist and interest charges were not used for decades, the concept of economic efficiency as it is used in market economies did not exist.

Technological backwardness has also accompanied state ownership. State-owned firms have substantially missed out on the high tech revolution, and they face immense productivity problems if and when they try to compete in the world market. Elsewhere in the world, assembly-line production methods with their 'large volume-standard commodity – low unit costs' have given way to the 'flexible production methods' of the computer age. The property rights framework of state-owned enterprises has not had the capacity for either gathering information or absorbing technological advances into its production methods to increase efficiency. Privatization of these firms will clearly not enable them to confront their immense productivity problems to enable them to compete in the world market.

The task ahead: updating the 'socialist' property rights doctrine
The on-going 'Velvet Revolution' is, in fact, a valiant process of convergence, meaning the eventual transformation of the socialist 'inefficient

property rights' doctrine into the conventional, Western 'property rights doctrine' of Coase and Furubotn and Pejovich.

In the aftermath of the 'Velvet Revolution', three dimensions of the former social orders are becoming redefined. The first is their totalitarian political structures, which have been abandoned, giving way to multi-party democracies. In the economic sphere, they have moved away from quantitative-output planning towards a price-driven market economy, or, more precisely, towards a capitalist welfare state. The herculean task of reducing the vast state sector, with its 100 per cent state ownership of the means of production, is probably the most difficult – as the current privatization experiences in Poland, Czechoslovakia and the former DDR indicate.

In Germany, an agency called *Treuhandanstalt*, located in Berlin, is in charge of the privatization process of the former state-owned enterprises.[3] Since the two Germanies were united economically in the summer of 1990, the *Treuhandanstalt* has been able to privatize more than 5 000 enterprises.[4] It still has roughly 2000 firms to sell; because of the technological obsolescence of these enterprises there are few takers. The *Treuhandanstalt* has been regularly advertising properties for sale in the *London Economist*, but many of the firms are probably not economically viable in the short run.[5]

Apart from privatizing entire 'going concerns', the unification treaty of 1989 (which fused West Germany and the Deutsche Demokratische Republik into one economic entity), insisted that communist-expropriated property must be returned to its former owners or their heirs. In other words, West Germans insisted on the 'return first principle' of expropriated property. Even though East German officials urged the 'compensation first principle' because many different and difficult property relations emerged during the 40 year rule of the communists, West German ideas prevailed. At present (three years later), in consequence of the return first principle, numerous large East German cities are virtually paralysed waiting for lawyers to untangle the incredible legal problems of establishing ownership. In Leipzig, for instance, the inner city is virtually paralysed because nobody knows who owns what.[6]

As private ownership of the means of production emerges, private contracts will become enforceable and violations of contracts will, as in Western societies, entitle the injured party to a court hearing. Enforcement of contracts in the former satellite countries remains quite haphazard for the simple reason that nobody quite knows what the sanctioned behaviour will be. Though there are laws on the books, political expedience rules supreme and the costs, if any, of non-observance remain unclear. Nor is the bankruptcy concept extensively known in satellite countries. As the former socialist property rights give way to Western property rights, it will be necessary to create a judicial apparatus, with properly trained lawyers and a suitably detailed body of civil law (Kornai, 1990, p. 45). This legal or judicial infrastructure is not yet in place. The situation is something of a 'legal limbo'; the old laws are not enforced and the new ones are in the process of being written. With the passage of time, as privately owned means of production take root, the new property rights will specify 'sanctioned behaviour' and identify the costs 'for non-observance' of the norms of behaviour. In the meantime, property rights in the newly privatized economies remain poorly defined and the price in terms of economic inefficiencies remains correspondingly high.

Notes

1. Five types of externalities are generally identified. First, *external diseconomies of production* refer to uncompensated costs imposed on others by the expansion of output by some firms. For instance, increased discharges of industrial wastes into rivers may lead to tougher anti-pollution legislation, which is likely to increase the waste disposal costs for all industrial firms in the area. Secondly, *external diseconomies of consumption* are the uncompensated costs imposed, for example, by the noisy and reckless riders of snowmobiles on cross-country skiers or the hardy folks doing the ice fishing. Third are the *external economies of production* which are uncompensated benefits conferred on others by the expansion of output by some firms. For instance, some high-tech firms may train workers, and these, after the completion of the training, go to work for other firms which don't have to pay for their training costs. Fourth are the *external economies of consumption* which refer to uncompensated benefits bestowed on others by the increased consumption of a given commodity. For instance, extra expenditures to maintain the lawn, or the property, increase the value of the neighbour's home. Such costs or benefits are also called 'neighbourhood' effects. Under the implicit assumptions of perfect competition, private costs are assumed to equal social costs and private benefits to equal social benefits, which simply omits the externalities catagorized above. The type of externality that arises under monopoly is a technical externality beyond the power of even government regulation to control by means of setting design to achieve competitive marginal cost price.
2. Alas, for decades, quite a few American academic economists tended to disregard the above-mentioned 'inefficient property rights' doctrine for a number of reasons. For instance, at the end of 1949, Joseph A. Schumpeter, in his much celebrated presidential address to the American Economic Association (known as 'The March into Socialism'), claimed that the capitalist system tends to destroy itself over time, and that centralist socialism is its heir apparent. For Schumpeter, capitalism, with its innovations and the process of 'creative destruction', was likely to destroy itself, almost willy-nilly (J.A. Schumpeter (1950), *Capitalism, Socialism, and Democracy*, third edn, New York: Harper, p. 416). Secondly, the Soviet launching of the Sputnik in 1956 shook America virtually to the core. This technological feat was a tangible manifestation of the technological creativity and sophistication of the Soviet centralist socialism. Many American academics expected more and greater technological wonders in the future. Finally, the older academic economists forever recalled with horror the sufferings of the American people during the Great Depression, and in the American academic halls 'socialism' was popular. At a safe distance from the Soviet Union, many academics felt that socialism was more 'just' than 'capitalism.'
3. See, for instance, the German report on this matter by P. Christ, 'So rar wie ein weisser Rabe. An der Spitze der Treuhand-anstalt folgt die Politikerin Birgit Breuel auf den Unternehmer Detlev Rohwedder', in *Die Zeit*, No. 17, April 26, 1991, p. 7.
4. 'The Visible Treuhand,' in *The Economist*, March 21, 1992, p. 20.

5. For an illustrative ad. see *The Economist*, March 28, 1992, p. 106.
6. T. Kleine-Brockhoff, M. Menge, R. Neubauer, 'Der Häuserkampf', in *Die Zeit*, March 27, 1992, p. 7.

References
Coase, Ronald (1960), 'The Problem of Social Costs', *The Journal of Law and Economics*, **3**, October, 1–44.
Furubotn, Erik G. and Pejovich, S. (1972), 'Property Rights and Economic Theory: A Survey of Recent Literature', *Journal of Economic Literature*, **10**, (4), December, 1137–62.
Knight, Frank (1924), 'Fallacies in the Interpretation of Social Cost', *Quarterly Journal of Economics*, **38**, May, 582–606.
Kornai, Janos (1990), *The Road to a Free Economy*, New York: Norton.
Lavoie, Donald (1985), *Rivalry and Central Planning; The Socialist Calculation Debate Reconsidered*, Cambridge University Press.
Mises, Ludwig von (1922), Socialism, New Haven: Yale University Press, 1951 (Die Gemeinwirtschaft, 1922). (S)
Pigou, A.C. (1932), *The Economics of Welfare*, 4th edn, London: MacMillan.
Schumpeter, J.A. (1950), *Capitalism, Socialism and Democracy*, 3rd edn, New York: Harper.
Simis, K. (1982), *USSR: The Corrupt Society*, New York: Simon and Shuster.

5   A critical analysis of the change to a market economy

Linwood T. Geiger

Tracing the world-wide trend to market economies[1]

The transformation of the countries in Eastern Europe and the newly established nations in what was formerly the Soviet Union from centrally planned socialist economies to primarily private market economies is without historical precedent. No one foresaw or predicted these amazing changes involving many new and complex governmental, institutional and economic reforms. Yugoslavia began to experiment with economic reform in the 1950s; in the German Democratic Republic (East Germany) there was price reform (along with greater flexibility in decision-making at the enterprise level) in the mid-1960s, and Czechoslovakia and Hungary initiated reform programmes in the late 1960s; but the first really successful economic reform programmes in a communist country began in China in 1978. With the death of the three major leaders, Mao Zedong, Zhou Enlai and Zhu De, in 1976, the end of the cataclysmic 'cultural revolution', and a reduction in the economic rate of growth, the reforms initiated by Deng Xiaoping in 1978 were readily accepted by Chinese society. These reforms accelerated in the 1980s, with the result that China has experienced one of the highest real growth rates in the world during the past decade.

In the 1980s, there was an increased use of prices and the market mechanism to allocate production and consumption of goods throughout the world. During the decade, there was a gradual shift from autocratic and, primarily, command economies to market economies in a number of Third World countries. This was prompted in part by concern regarding stagnant economies, and in part by stipulations on loans (structural adjustment loans) imposed by the World Bank and the International Monetary Fund (IMF). The movement to market economies and the use of the market mechanism gathered momentum during the latter part of the 1980s because of the 1985 introduction of *perestroika* and *glasnost* in the Soviet Union, accelerating at the end of the decade because of the rapid political changes in Eastern Europe. Between the summer of 1989 and the winter of 1989–1990 the Cold War between the East and the West ended as seven Eastern European countries declared their independence from the Soviet Union. Following is a brief summary of these changes in Eastern Europe:

Summer 1989   A peaceful transition to an elected coalition government in Poland occurred when the Solidarity labour union was legalized in April, and Solidarity and its allies won the elections in June.

Autumn 1989   In Hungary, border guards permitted 30,000 Eastern Europeans to cross the border into Austria in September; on 7 October the Hungarian Communist Party formally abolished itself. A democratic government was established in elections in the spring of 1990.

Autumn 1989   In Czechoslovakia, after a number of public protests, Communist Party leaders resigned on 24 November. Early in December a new government was formed with a non-communist majority. Elections in June 1990 confirmed the non-communist government.

Autumn 1989–spring 1990   East Germany opened its borders by demolishing the Berlin Wall on 8 November, and early in December the Communist Party leadership resigned. Free elections were held in the spring, and the official unification of East and West Germany occurred on 3 October, 1990.

Winter–spring 1990   Romania's transition to non-communist rule was violent in contrast with the predominantly peaceful revolutions in other countries. After a brief civil war, the former communist leader, Nicolae Ceausescu, was arrested and executed on 25 December 1989. A new government was formed in the spring under the leadership of Ion Iliescu, who has been criticized for being autocratic, pro-communist and only 'lukewarm' about market reforms.

Spring 1990   In February a new government was formed in Bulgaria after pro-democracy demonstrations forced the communist cabinet to resign, and Zhivkov, the communist dictator, was jailed. The Communist Party (which was renamed the Socialist Party) continues to be a strong political force. Yugoslavia's reaction to the political revolution in the area is confused. Although the Yugoslavian Communist Party agreed to yield its monopoly power in January 1990, an effective democratic federation was not formed, primarily because of the desire for independence on the part of a number of the republics within the country.

The changes in the Soviet Union were equally dramatic. In the Spring of 1990 the Baltic republics (Estonia, Latvia and Lithuania), which had been annexed by the Soviet Union in 1940, announced their independence. During the following year a number of the other republics expressed an interest in independence, and in December 1991, with the creation of the New

Commonwealth of Independent States, all 15 republics became sovereign states. Some critical information about the five largest countries created when the Soviet Union was dissolved is summarized in Table 5.1.

Table 5.1:   *Population and relative size of industry and agricultural sectors of the five largest countries created by dissolution of the USSR*

	Population in 1989 (thousands)	Industry (% of total)	Agriculture (% of total)
Russia	145,743	63.7	50.3
Ukraine	44,186	17.2	17.9
Uzbekistan	16,689	2.4	5.5
Byelorussia	10,036	4.2	5.1
Kazakhstan	8,136	2.5	6.4

Source: Vol. 1, *A Study of the Soviet Economy*, pp. 204, 214.

Table 5.2:   *Eastern Europe and the Soviet Union – population and per capita GNP (1988)*

Country	Population (millions)	GNP/capita (dollars)
Bulgaria	9.0	5630
Czechoslovakia	15.6	7600
East Germany	16.6	9360
Hungary	10.6	6490
Poland	38.0	5450
Romania	23.0	4120
Soviet Union	286.4	5550
Yugoslavia	23.6	4900

Sources: Population, CIA *Handbook of Economic Statistics, Per Capita GNP, PlanEcon* reports.

The other new nations created with the end of the Soviet Union were the Baltic countries (Estonia, Latvia, Lithuania) and Moldavia; the Muslim countries (Kirghizia, Tajikistan and Turkmenistan); and the Caucasus (Armenia, Azerbaijan and Georgia). As illustrated in Table 5.2, the Eastern European countries and the former Soviet Union represent a significant portion of the world population and world GNP. These nations accounted for between 13 per cent and 18 per cent of world GNP in 1988, depending on whether the estimates come from CIA data or from PlanEcon (a private consulting firm specializing in Eastern Europe and the Soviet Union).

An important reason for the widespread interest in economic reform among the former socialist nations was concern about inefficiency, bottlenecks, poor quality and low productivity, all of which became obvious in the 1970s. It was very difficult for the central government to make efficient allocative decisions, particularly with consumer goods. There were increasing shortages of desired products and there were surpluses, and ultimately wastage, of products that nobody wanted. In many of the former socialist countries, economic growth started to decline. Even when there was satisfactory growth, it was primarily because of the increased use of resources rather than because of an increase in the productivity of the resources. The decline in real output in the Eastern European countries in the 1980s is illustrated in Table 5.3.[2]

Table 5.3:   Eastern Europe – comparison of real growth rates in the 1970s and the 1980s

Country	% Annual change in real output	
	1970s	1980s
Bulgaria	7.1	3.7
Czechoslovakia	5.0	2.1
East Germany	4.9	4.0
Hungary	5.4	1.6
Poland	6.6	–0.1
Romania	9.7	4.5
Yugoslavia	6.1	0.7

Source: The Institute of Int. Finance, Inc, Table 2.2, p. 13.

In basic terms, economic growth is determined only by the following two factors:

1.   An increase in resources (land, labour or capital).
2.   An increase in the productivity of these resources.

Well over 90 per cent of the growth in the socialist countries was due to a growth of resources. After World War II, these countries were very effective in mobilizing labour and capital. In China there were many underemployed (particularly in the rural areas) who were put to work. While there were fewer underemployed in Eastern and Central Europe because of the large loss of life during World War II, most of the younger men were transferred from rural areas to heavy industry. The non-agricultural sectors concentrated on manufacturing producers' goods and capital goods, that is, machines, trucks, tools and factories. During the 1950s and 1960s, people in the social-ist countries essentially sacrificed consumer goods in order to build a sub-stantial industrial base.

On the other hand, Taiwan, Korea, Hong Kong, Singapore, Japan and most of the Western world not only mobilized labour and capital resources effectively, but also increased the output of their workers with innovations and incentives. They provided an environment in which people were moti-vated to develop new and more effective ways of producing goods. In other words, there was technological growth. For example, in South Korea, im-provement in the productivity of resources was responsible for 60 per cent of the nation's total growth. In the United States, during the first part of the 20th century, 43 per cent of the economic growth was due to an increase in productivity.[3] In the late 1970s, when growth gave way to stagnation, the socialist countries realized that they had to improve the productivity of their resources so that they would not continue to fall behind the Western nations.

Will the trend to market economies in Eastern Europe and the former Soviet Union continue?

In the first half of the 19th century, Charles MacKay wrote a book entitled *Popular Delusions and the Madness of Crowds*, which effectively illustrated how, throughout history, people made wrong decisions time and again based on trends occurring in their lifetime. Trends never continue indefinitely; there will always be changes.

The assumption that life will always continue as it has been helps to explain the shock which reverberated throughout the world when the Eastern European countries declared their independence from the Soviet Union in 1989, and again in December 1991 when the Soviet Union broke up into 15 separate, independent nations.

As the Eastern European countries and the newly established nations which were formerly republics in the old Soviet Union are finding out, the task of transition to a market economy has been, and will continue to be, very difficult. The problems are more complex than with the Latin American countries, for example, where some market economy institutions were al-ready in place and the number of firms to be privatized was in the hundreds rather than in the thousands. The initial excitement and euphoria have changed to pessimism, disappointment, anger, confusion and a greater appreciation of the challenges of reform. The task of building a market economy after decades of central planning will be long and arduous. Now that the rejoicing over their new-found freedom has subsided, the people are struggling with the new problems of unemployment, inflation, corruption and general economic confusion. Most of the Eastern European countries are expecting GDP in 1992 to be 20 to 40 per cent less than in 1987, and unemployment is expected to range from 15 to 18 per cent. The attractiveness of a market economy could prove to be short-lived, and the people could decide that they prefer a system with many sectors of the economy controlled by the state.

In addition to the difficulties of the transition, the express train to a market economic system may become derailed; first, because of political instability and secondly because the people in Central and Eastern Europe do not understand the way the market mechanism works; they may prefer the security of a system with central controls.

Political instability

Important sources of political instability derive from the self-interests and entrenched positions of the former bureaucrats and communists. Various self-interest groups such as the army, workers' organizations, managers of the state-owned firms and the newly formed political parties are manoeuvring to obtain the best possible outcome for their own groups as changes occur during the transition. Many people in the large central government bureaucracies have been resisting reform, since these changes will reduce their power and wealth.

Some of the newly created political parties in the Eastern European countries include communists who are resisting liberalization efforts, changes and loss of control. For example, in Bulgaria, 33 per cent of the members of parliament were ex-communists, and in Czechoslovakia 14 per cent were communists. Reform efforts have been slow in Romania because of a split between the former communists and the people who want to see rapid change; and in Albania, the ex-communist Albanian Party was in control with 68 per cent of the vote.

While many of the new political parties favour capitalism, there are also a number that prefer welfare and Civil liberties programmes. In the Ukraine, the former communist bureaucrats now in charge are not committed to the same level of reforms going on in Russia; and in the Crimea, to the South of Ukraine, the local communist party is in control. Byelorussia remains basically a command economy, although the price liberalization in Russia in 1992 is forcing some reforms in this country. The small, recently established, Muslim-dominated countries in the far south of the former USSR are still under the control of the former communist leadership.

In addition, ethnic and regional problems contribute to political instability. With the dismantling of communist regimes and the resulting political liberalization, ethnic tensions (some of which have existed for decades and even centuries) have created substantial instability within the countries. The war begun in 1991 between Serbia and Croatia in Yugoslavia has resulted in deaths which are estimated to be between five and ten thousand people, including the massacre of hundreds.

Ethnic tensions in the former Soviet Union have even more potential for explosion. Within the former 15 republics, there are 20 autonomous republics, eight autonomous regions and ten smaller autonomous areas, all of which include 25 million people from 200 ethnic groups. There has been fighting between people within Azerbaijan, Armenia and Georgia, with deaths estimated to be well over a thousand, and there is potential for conflict in many other areas. In Czechoslovakia, there is tension between Slovakia and the Czech lands. In addition to these ethnic problems, there is the possibility of political instability between the central government and regional governments in a number of the countries.

Preference for more central control

While people in transitional economies recognize that market economies have been highly successful in creating wealth and producing large quantities of goods and services, they have little appreciation of how the system works. It is difficult for many citizens of former communist societies to understand how the market allocates resources, because the government has made these allocative decisions during all of their lives. Even prior to the establishment of communism in 1945, very few of the countries in Eastern Europe had ever really been democratic; the same is true of Russia – throughout its history, almost all change, including Christianity, has been imposed from above. For centuries in Poland the vast majority of the people have had little experience with the market, as they let the Jews do all the buying and selling.

Large inequalities of income and massive lay-offs of workers during recessions or when an industry is in decline because of technological change, are anathema to many people in Eastern Europe and Russia. There is a predisposition towards interventionist policy, that is, if there are problems, the government should resolve them. Personal accountability for failure is a concept that many of the citizens neither understand nor appreciate.

These attitudes have been evident in opinion surveys. A *Times Mirror* survey conducted in May 1991, which included 2210 people in Russia, the Ukraine and Lithuania, revealed that the vast majority (76 per cent) favoured state control of heavy industry, banks, the telephone system, trains, radio, television and electrical utilities. There was a clear preference for the private sector in farming only. When asked to choose among alternative economic systems, more of the citizens chose socialism than capitalism. However, younger and better educated people supported the market system.

Naturally, these attitudes vary from country to country. They are probably less evident in Hungary and Yugoslavia, which have been experimenting with markets and private property reforms for some time. If the reform trends continue, it will probably be because a majority of people within the transitional economies are willing to sacrifice in order to enjoy, eventually, the assumed higher standards of living of the market economy.

Possible characteristics of the evolving market economies

It would be unrealistic to assume that the market economies which evolve from the transition of the former communist countries will be the *laissez-faire*, Adam Smith-type market systems with very little government intervention, and with prices determined and goods and factors of production allocated almost entirely by the interaction of supply and demand forces. This pure kind of market system is unlikely (particularly when considering the former Soviet bloc area from a historical perspective), the government sector may continue to be significant.

All governments interfere with their economies to some degree. The governments of many successful East Asian countries such as Japan, Taiwan, South Korea and Singapore have intervened aggressively to influence industrial output and patterns of trade in ways they thought desirable. For a number of decades, the Scandinavian countries (Denmark, Finland, Iceland, Norway and Sweden) have combined market economies and private ownership with substantial regulations and government intervention to achieve an egalitarian income distribution, low unemployment, reasonable growth and protection for all members of their society. A number of European nations also have large government sectors and intervene in their economies in many ways. As Table 5.4 indicates, these market economies possess many state-owned enterprises which compete with the private sector.

Table 5.4: Value added by state-owned sector by country

Country	Mid-1980s State-owned sector as share of value added (per cent)
France	17
Italy	14
West Germany	11
Britain	11

Standard of living

During recent decades the communist countries have been experiencing increasing economic problems. Subsidies have continued to rise; losses have grown at state-owned firms; there have been increasing inventories of poor quality products and goods that no one wants to consume; and economic growth, such as there has been, has been due almost entirely to an increase in labour and/or capital – that is, there has been very little improvement in productivity.

There are good reasons to believe that the standard of living will improve in the former communist countries if the people have the patience to establish macroeconomic stability (small fiscal deficits and price stability) and also to create the laws and institutions, and to develop the educated workers, necessary for an efficient market economy.

In general, the market system allocates resources efficiently with relatively little effort. Incentives are provided for the development of new, more efficient production techniques. The threat of losing business to competition keeps managers and owners alert and looking for ways to improve their operations. If the system is working effectively, it is sensitive to consumers' needs, and the tremendous surpluses of unwanted goods common in command economies are avoided.

The other major plus for this system is the great emphasis on personal freedom. With competition, the consumer is protected from coercion by the seller because of the opportunity to purchase from other sellers. The employee is also protected from coercion, because he can work for another employer if he is not satisfied with the arrangement with his current boss

The superiority of an outward trade orientation

In the past, international trade of the nations of the former Soviet bloc was constrained by decisions of the CMEA (Council for Mutual Economic Assistance), which established a complex bilateral system of trade relations between the Soviet Union and the East European Countries. The quantity and prices of the export products were determined by central authority for all the CMEA countries. These countries have, or are now in the process of liberalizing their trade; quotas are being eliminated, tariffs are being lowered, realistic exchange rates are being established and currency convertibility is being adopted. There seems to be little doubt that the trade liberalization will lead to a substantial expansion in trade for these transitional economies.

Research spanning almost two decades and indicating the superiority of an outward orientation, or export promotion policy, over a policy of import substitution, confirms the probability that the change to market economies will significantly improve the standard of living of the transitional economies.[4] Empirical investigations support a positive relationship between export expansion and economic growth for developing countries in total, as well as for various groupings of countries for different periods of time. (See Balassa, 1978, 1980, 1984, 1985; Feder, 1982; Kavoussi, 1984, 1985; Krueger, 1978, 1980, 1983; Michaely, 1977; Nishimizu and Robinson, 1984; Ram, 1985.[5])

The analysis has also been expanded to include the industrial nations. The results were similar – there was a strong statistical significance between export growth and GDP growth.[6] The results of all of the empirical studies consistently confirm that export expansion is an effective strategy for improving economic development. There is a positive and significant correlation between export growth and economic growth for nations at all levels of development. The effectiveness of this strategy is enhanced as the share of manufactured goods in exports increases.

The reason for the effectiveness of an outward orientation is straightforward. Exports and trade enable a country to exploit its comparative advantage, resulting in more efficient allocation of resources, an increase in capital formation and an improvement in factor productivity.

One of the reasons for the productivity improvement is 'economies of scale'. The domestic markets in many countries are often too small to support plants of efficient size. The international market enables export firms to expand and to realize economies of scale, with the result that there will be a reduction in unit production costs. As the process continues, non-exported products may also be produced more efficiently. The increased activity often promotes the growth of supporting firms and other industries within the country. Scale effects resulting from the increased demand are transmitted to other sectors of the economy.

The presence of a reasonably well developed or developing capital goods sector provides an even larger multiplying effect because of the strong backward linkages. The greater competition also creates greater efficiencies– innovation, more incentive for technological improvements, a better use of resources and a quicker response when opportunities are perceived. All of this activity encourages investment, increases capital formation and attracts entrepreneurs. The increased exports provide additional foreign exchange, permitting the purchase of more competitively priced intermediate goods, raw materials and machinery and equipment, which become available at world prices.

World Bank examples of the advantages of macroeconomic stability, openness and competition
World Bank studies also lend support to the likelihood that the market economies will improve per capita GNP. In addition to the strong correlation between an outward orientation (export expansion) and economic growth discussed in the previous section, the empirical work of the World Bank

confirms the advantages of macroeconomic stability and competition in terms of improving economic performance and a nation's standard of living. An evaluation of 1200 World Bank and IFC public and private projects illustrated that the economic rate of return was high when trade restrictions were low, when the currency was not significantly overvalued, when real interest rates were positive, and when the fiscal deficit was low. The data, which covered a period from 1968 to 1989, also showed a positive relationship between non-distorted exchange rates (that is, where the currency is not overvalued) and the economic rate of return for industrial projects, agricultural projects and transportation and energy projects.

Other studies showed a positive association between productivity growth and various measures of openness such as liberal trade and exchange rate policies. They also suggested that the long-run gains from increased competition and technology transfer are probably greater than the short-run gains. Table 5.5 illustrates the relationship between policy distortions for the 1200 World Bank projects for the period 1968–89 and the economic rates of return.[7]

Table 5.5:   Evaluation of World Bank projects 1968–1989

Policy distortions	Percentage return
Trade restrictions	
High	13.2
Moderate	15.0
Low	19.0
Real interest rate	
Negative	15.0
Positive	17.3
Fiscal deficit	
High (>8%)	13.4
Moderate (4–8%)	14.8
Low (<4%)	17.8

Source: World Bank data from Table 4.2, 1991 WDR (p. 52).

Basic needs of all members of society
There is a possibility that the lower income members of society will be worse off in the market economy. Communism was designed to be a benevo-

lent economic system. The Marxist vision included responsibility for the
hungry, the poor and the oppressed.

A nation's budget decisions provide a good picture of its priorities, and
the allocation of resources by the communist countries during the past three
decades clearly confirms their concern for their people. Table 5.6 uses 1986
food prices in the former Soviet Union to illustrate the government's heavy
subsidization of basic foods.

Table 5.6: Per cent subsidization of basic food prices in 1986

	Bread	Beef	Mutton	Pork	Poultry	Milk	Butter
Retail price (R)	0.18	1.77	1.50	1.85	2.63	0.25	3.38
Cost to state	0.25	6.44	5.74	4.10	3.62	0.54	10.09
Cost excess over price (%)	38.6	265.1	282.6	121.6	37.6	116.0	198.5

Housing was also priced considerably below cost. At the beginning of
1991, rents had been basically unchanged since 1928, and householders
spent less than 3 per cent of their income on rent and utilities. In addition,
urban and rail transportation, as well as entertainment and many cultural
activities, were subsidized so that they were available at affordable prices to
all members of society. For example, prior to 1991 one could ride the
Moscow Metro system (possibly the best in the world) anywhere in the
greater metropolitan area for just five kopecks, and the highly regarded
Leningrad Circus performance was available to the public for just 25 kopecks (a few US cents). The subsidies, of course, were costly; in 1988 in the
USSR they totalled 131.5 billion rubles, almost 30 per cent of total state
expenditure and 15 per cent of GNP.[8]

Health care and education were made available to all. While the quality of
health care reflected the modest standard of living of the country, the universal education system resulted in substantial improvement in the education of
the population in both the Eastern European countries and the former Soviet
republics. It produced a relatively larger percentage of competent engineers
than in the Western industrialized countries.

Income equality is also a good indicator of a country's concern for all
members of its society. Generally, income inequality was the lowest in the
world in the communist countries (the exception being the Scandinavian
countries), with Gini coefficients for Eastern European countries averaging
25.4. (The highest level of income inequality is found in the developing

nations, particularly in the Latin American countries, where a small group of people have a high percentage of the income.)

When development progresses and the middle income sector grows, the Gini ratios start to fall. Table 5.7 records Gini coefficients for selected countries and areas of the world. It is likely that the Gini coefficients for the transitional economies will increase as the countries shift to an economic system where the market allocates goods, services and income, and where there is a greater opportunity to concentrate wealth.

Table 5.7:   Gini coefficients for select countries

Country or area	Gini
Eastern Europe	25.4
Czechoslovakia	20.7
Hungary	24.4
Poland	24.3
Yugoslavia	32.1
USSR	25.6
Western Europe	31.4
United States	32.6
Sweden	20.5
Asian NICs and Japan	38.3
Latin America	49.5

Source: Milanovic (1989).

Crime, exploitation and oppression

Oppression in a closed society
While all countries with market economies are not necessarily democracies, increased freedom and openness naturally accompany liberalized economies that are active in the world market. Because of the greater interaction required with all kinds of people in order to compete effectively in a market economy, it is not surprising that there is pressure on the political system to be less autocratic and more democratic. However, with a large private sector, whether or not a democratic political system is in place, there is considerably more freedom of action and openness than there would be under communism.

This increased openness and greater freedom should bring about a reduction of the mass murder, exploitation and corruption that occurred in the former communist countries. There is little question that the atrocities resulting from Stalin's purges would not have occurred if there had been freedom of the press in the USSR, and if the world had been made aware of these activities.

During the past five years, Soviet citizens have been shocked by revelations of the mass exterminations by Stalin in the 1930s and the early 1940s, with numbers estimated to range from 5 to 40 million people. The world was also shocked when information was made public about Nicolae Ceausescu's oppression of the Romanian people.

An open economic and political system not only serves to prevent these mass tragedies, but also frequently exposes any kind of exploitation and criminality to the 'light of day', and, in the process, tends to reduce intimidation, oppression and conditions which are not compatible with human dignity and not acceptable to society.

With *glasnost*, the world has become aware of the high level of corruption which existed in the former Soviet Union. Illegal private activities took place in almost every major city in the union. The theft and resale of food, precious stones and other products occurred frequently, but the more sophisticated operations involved factories within factories, where workers and managers would work slowly in existing state factories during the day, then work illegally, but often more efficiently, at night for their own gain.

Involved in such schemes were a plant in Bashkiria producing women's shoes and plastic goods, a fur factory in Odessa and many different factories in Georgia. A major cotton scam existed in Uzbekistan for decades and involved thousands of people (Telmud Gdlyan, the investigator of the case, estimated hundreds of thousands of people involved) and millions of rubles. Obviously, this level of endemic corruption required collusion at all levels of government, including Moscow, so it would have been most prevalent with corrupt leaders like Stalin and Brezhnev. (Much of the corruption in Georgia was exposed by Eduard Shevardnadze, who was appointed by Gorbachev to fight and eliminate political corruption.)

It is also obvious that there is no lack of corruption in societies with market systems. However, it is likely that economic crime and oppression would probably be less widespread and would not continue for as long in a more open society.[9]

Crime in market economies
The concern shared by most people in Central and Eastern Europe, that an increase in crime will accompany the increase in private business activity, is not just the result of many years of communist propaganda. In the transitional economies, as the central planning systems broke down and the legal infrastructure and competition, both of which are essential for the market

system to work efficiently, were not yet in place, there was a vacuum in which unprincipled entrepreneurs could exploit society.

The high level of economic crime during the past few years in the former Soviet bloc is evidence of this exploitation, and confirms the legitimacy of peoples' concern. However, there is also an apprehension that the high level of economic crime will continue even after legal and judicial systems and other appropriate market institutions are in place, because of the individual greed that is unleashed with the new economic system.

Most surveys and polls indicate that Eastern European and Russian people associate crime with the market economy. The rising crime rates within these countries in recent years reinforce their views. An opinion poll in Poland indicated that the majority consider corruption the biggest problem facing their country; the many corporate and banking scandals have disillusioned ordinary Poles.

Economic crime in mature market economies   Unfortunately, economic crime and economic exploitation resulting from the greed and selfishness of business people, and often involving the complicity of government policy-makers, are, and have been, widespread in mature market economies. This is amply illustrated by recent revelations in newspapers and periodicals; for example, the Robert Maxwell fraud, where apparently well over $1 billion was stolen, much of it from pension funds; the $9 billion BCCI international banking fraud which involved a number of supposedly reputable banks in America, England and dozens of other countries, and whose illegal activities included money laundering, tax conspiracy violations, assisting criminal clients and collusion in fictitious loans; or Sagawa Kyubin, a parcel delivery firm in Japan, which made approximately $4 billion worth of bribes and illegal loans, many of them to gangster-linked companies, and which reportedly involved over one hundred Japanese politicians in the fraud.

Crime and ethical standards   It is obvious that the level of crime would be less if high moral and ethical standards were ingrained in the hearts and minds of businessmen and all members of society. The financial scandals mentioned above would not have occurred if the commercial and investment banks, auditing firms, directors of pension funds, directors of the companies directly involved in the scandals, government policy-makers, and others were alert and maintained high ethical standards in their business relationships. Apparently they were concerned only if there was an obvious violation of the letter of the law and often (sadly) only if this illegality implicated their institutions.

Too often, governments' actions (or inactions) imply that they accept economic fraud, exploitation, criminality and occasional government complicity as a cost of doing business in a market economy; they will initially decry the incident for public edification but, with the passage of time, little effective action will be taken to prevent a recurrence.

Unfortunately, unethical practices are not limited to top executives but permeate all levels of work and all segments of society. At a small liberal arts college in the United States, round-table discussions with business leaders and the business faculty are required for MBA students in the ethics class. It has been discouraging to note the frequency with which both the executives and the students will rationalize almost any activity that will improve the profits of a firm as long as it is not clearly illegal. This attitude was evident over a ten year period during which these business ethics meetings occurred two or three times each semester.

Japan is an extreme example of pervasive criminal activity which seems to be accepted as a cost of doing business in a market economy. The country is periodically 'rocked' by scandals involving top government officials and businesses. The most recent is the Sagawa affair, which emerged in 1992 and promises to eclipse the other scandals.

The second largest parcel delivery firm in Japan, with 25,000 employees and 1991 sales of ¥909 billion ($7.3 billion), Sagawa is accused of bribing over 100 politicians (one estimate was 130 members of the Diet, the Japanese parliament), with bribes and illegal loans amounting to about $4 billion over a number of years. Much of Sagawa's money has been traced to Inagawa-kai, one of Japan's largest crime syndicates, which helped the company expand into rival companies' territories, using strong-arm tactics when the competition resisted the intrusion. Before his arrest, Mr Saotome, a director of the firm, said that politicians were coming over to Sagawa's Tokyo offices 'almost every day' to collect money.

Increased freedom and openness in market economies: (other positive results)

More reliable information

One of the pluses resulting from the higher level of openness in market economies, which is important to an educator and researcher, is the improvement in the quality of data which will be coming out of the former communist countries in Eastern Europe and the former Soviet Union. Statistics from a closed society are frequently inaccurate and misleading. Even if there had been a high level of technical competence in the gathering and manipulation of statistical data (which is often not the case), there was good reason to be sceptical about information emanating from communist countries during the past four decades.

Private consultants (such as PlanEcon) and international statistical teams from the International Monetary Fund, the World Bank, OECD and the European Bank for Reconstruction and Development, working with statisticians from Eastern Europe and the former Soviet Union during the past three years, confirm problems with old data. There were strong incentives to distort data because bonuses were generally paid upon proof of fulfilment of the goals of the state plan. Even as late as the last half of the 1980s, output, on average, is estimated to have been inflated by 3 per cent, with output in some of the raw material sectors exaggerated by as much as 25 per cent.

Technical problems also created distortions in the economic data – comparisons of data with those of other countries were very subjective because of vast differences in the relative prices (since the prices in the USSR were set administratively) and also because of the absence of a market-clearing exchange rate to convert the Soviet accounts into dollars or yen or marks. Analysts now estimate that the growth rates between 1966 and 1985 ranged from 2.2 to 2.9 per cent rather than the official growth rate of 5.3 per cent. Statisticians at the USSR Institute of World Economy and International Relations estimate real growth between 1913 and 1987 to have been about one-third of the official rate. Similar confusion exists with regard to estimating per capita income for the Eastern and Central European countries. For example, estimates of per capita GNP in the Soviet Union in the latter half of the 1980s vary from $9230 (CIA) to $5550 (PlanEcon) to $1735 by World Bank/IMF/OECD researchers.[10]

False bookkeeping was naturally required to support the widespread corruption. A good example of this is the cotton fraud in Uzbekistan. Here the government kept raising the cotton quota for the republic until it reached an unrealistic 5.5 million tons in the mid-1980s, 65 per cent of the entire Soviet cotton crop. False reports were created indicating that the plan was met, and money was paid for cotton which was not grown. The pay-off was divided among everyone involved in the scam – all the way up to Moscow. False bookkeeping and phony records were also needed to support the illegal underground factories mentioned in the previous section.

Development of Potential

The freedom of the market economy probably provides the best opportunity for people to utilize and develop their talents. In my years in China, I have been impressed with many people who seem to find dignity in their work, no matter how menial. They do not shirk unpleasant work, but do accept responsibility for accomplishing the task as effectively as possible.

The communist countries have also established significant budgets in the arts and sport, and have invested in people who demonstrate talent in these areas. However, in the arts the government frequently provided incentives and disincentives to motivate the focus of paintings, writing and other forms of art so that Marxist ideology was lionized. Expressions expanding the spiritual dimension, for example, were not encouraged and at times were not even permitted.

The greatest restrictions, however, have been in the general work area, where citizens in communist societies were normally assigned to work units by the government. While full employment was the norm (although disguised unemployment was substantial as many organizations hoarded labour), and some workers were involved in the decision-making process at the plant level, very little job mobility was permitted. Most people were stuck with work in a particular field no matter how unsuitable it may have been, and there were few opportunities to expand their horizons and enjoy the creativity of work. One of the challenges that workers in the transitional economies are now facing is how to live with the new-found freedom of job mobility, and how to maximize the opportunities for self-expression that are provided.

Freedom of worship

The freedom of people to develop spiritually becomes very important because of the vacuum which may be created as society moves from the Marxist ideology, which espouses justice, to a market economy where the emphasis is on the individual and the accumulation of assets. The members of the Supreme Soviet, when they met with 19 American evangelical leaders in the autumn of 1991, repeatedly talked about the 'paramount significance of the acquisition of spiritual and moral values'. With the rise in crime, the editor-in-chief of *Pravda* emphasized that 'morality is the worst crisis, worse than the economic and political problems'.[11]

Conclusion

The world will probably be a better place in which to live if the transition continues and market economies are established in most of the countries of the world – where resources are allocated primarily by demand and supply forces, reflecting the desires of consumers and costs of producers, and where the possibility of exploitation is reduced by a competitive environment. The 'if' should not be overlooked because of the very real possibility that Eastern and Central Europe will remain in a muddle. Indeed, authoritative economic systems may continue in some of these countries indefinitely.

The freedom and openness which normally accompany market economies are the major reason for optimism about the current trend. The freedom for people to select dignified employment which makes the best use of their talents, plus the openness which will reduce the likelihood that cruel and sick people will be able to harm large segments of society for extended periods of time, are ample reasons to be pleased with the changes. The higher rate of economic growth, and the improvement in the standard of living which should follow, will be even more welcome if the increased wealth filters down to the nation's lower income groups.

However, it is necessary for citizens in the transitional economies to recognize the weaknesses in the market system. If they are going to control crime and establish a caring society that assumes responsibility for marginalized individuals, they must understand that some of the characteristics of the market economy – like materialism, selfishness, greed and an obsession with the accumulation of assets – which contribute to the dynamic nature of the economic system, also cause the problems which are inherent in the system. The self-interest which is the driving force of the system creates the difficulty; the most effective way to accumulate and protect wealth is to eliminate competition, but if this occurs, freedom and openness will decline and the market system will eventually self-destruct. Thus there is a very pragmatic reason for ethical behaviour and a recognition of the obligations people have as citizens and entrepreneurs.

Notes

1. Information concerning the trends in economic reform comes from many sources. Committee reports, IMF and World Bank Working Papers, and articles from periodicals and journals are particularly important since the shift to market economies is on-going and current. We are in the midst of a historic period.

    The following is just a partial list of the sources of information concerning economic reforms in Eastern Europe and the former Soviet Union.

    Dozens of articles have been written and are continuing to be drafted by various departments of the World Bank. In addition, the Socialist Economic Reform Unit of the Country Economics Department in the World Bank publishes a monthly newsletter entitled *'Transition'* which provides excellent current information about economic reform in the transitional economies, particularly the countries in Eastern Europe. The most comprehensive source of information concerning economic reform in Russia and the former Soviet Republics is the three-volume report entitled *A Study of the Soviet Economy* which was published in 1991; it is still very useful, even with the dissolution of the USSR. Hedrick Smith's *The New Russians* provides an interesting historical perspective concerning the changes in Eastern Europe and Russia. Three *Economist* sources are listed below because each is a detailed survey. However, almost every edition of this publication contains some information concerning current reforms in the former communist countries.

    Susan Collins and Dani Rodik (1991), *'Eastern Europe and the Soviet Union in the World Economy'*, Washington, DC: Institute for International Economics.

    Stanley Fischer and Alan Gleb (1990), *'Issues in Socialist Economy Reform,'* Washington, DC: Policy, Research and External Affairs, Country Economics Department, World Bank, December, WPS 565.

    E. Iasin (1991), 'Problems of Making the Transition to a Regulated Market Economy', *Problems of Economics*, **33**, (12), April, 6–32.

    IMF, World Bank, OECD & European Bank for Reconstruction and Development (1991), *A Study of the Soviet Economy*, Volumes 1, 2 & 3, Paris: OECD Publication Service.

    IMF, World Bank, OECD & European Bank for Reconstruction and Development (1990), *The Economy of the USSR*, Washington, DC: Government Printing Office.

Institute of International Finance (1990), 'Building Free Market Economies in Central and Eastern Europe: Challenges and Realities', Washington, DC: Institute of International Finance Inc., April.

Hedrick Smith (1990), *The New Russians*, New York: Random House, Inc.

'A Survey of Perestroika', *The Economist*, April 28, 1990.

'A Survey of the Soviet Union', *The Economist*, October 20, 1990.

'A Survey of Eastern Europe', *The Economist*, September 21, 1991.

World Bank Socialist Economies Unit, Country Economics Department (1991), 'The Transformation of Economies in Central and Eastern Europe: Issues, Progress, and Prospects,' April 3.

John Williamson (1991), *The Economic Opening of Eastern Europe*, 1 Washington, DC: Institute for International Economics.

2. More recent calculations show the annual percentage change in real income for the Eastern European countries to be much lower. Data calculated by the IMF, ECE and PlanEcon (a private consulting firm specializing in Eastern Europe), estimate that Bulgaria, Poland and Hungary experienced negative growth in the 1980s and that Czechoslovakia's growth rate for the decade was well below 2 per cent.

3. A number of items, including technological change, education and training, and allocative efficiency, influence factor productivity. Edward F. Denison's *Trends in American Economic Growth, 1929–1982* (Washington: The Brookings Institution, 1985) details the sources of growth of real income in the United States for the period from 1929 to 1982.

Much of the increase in productivity in the United States during the first half of the 20th century was due to the improvement in the quality of labour, caused in part by a higher level of education. For more information concerning factor productivity in economic growth in the United States during this period, see *World Development Report 1991* (New York: Oxford University Press, 1991).

Increases in factor productivity stem from many sources, for example innovations (like the steam engine, computers, calculators and fax machines), education, incentives and improved working conditions (which motivate people to work harder and smarter), improved discipline in the work-force and changes in an assembly line. About 20 years ago when I was working in industry, our division decided to purchase metallic piston rings from a Japanese producer because of the lower cost. When we visited the supplier's plant in Japan, we were surprised to observe that their competitive advantage was not lower labour costs or more sophisticated equipment, but was derived from many, many small changes in their production line. They did a better job of paying attention to the details of production.

4. *Import substitution* is the substitution of domestic production for foreign imports of manufactured goods and requires policies which include high tariffs, quotas, production subsidies and overvalued exchange rates. While the terms 'outward orientation' and 'export promotion' are occasionally used interchangeably, they have different meanings. *Export promotion* implies the use of policies to create an export bias, like export subsidies or an undervalued exchange rate. On the other hand, an *outward trade orientation* places the emphasis on the elimination of both trade barriers and trade incentives, that is, the establishment of what is popularly called a 'level playing field'.

5. Extensive work has been done in the area of import substitution/export expansion. Following is just a partial list of some of the best-known articles about the topic. A more complete list is included in the bibliography. During the past five years, the World Bank has strongly supported export expansion strategy for developing nations and has included interesting results of many studies in recent World Development Reports.

Balassa, Bela (1978), 'Exports and Economic Growth: Further Evidence', *Journal of Development Economics*, 5, (2), June, 181–9.

Kavoussi, Rostam M. (1984), 'Export Expansion and Economic Growth', *Journal of Development Economics*, 14, (1 & 2), Jan/Feb, 241–50.

Kruegar, Anne O. (1983), 'The Effects of Trade Strategy on Growth', *Finance and Development*, June, 20–2.

Michaely, Michael (1977), 'Exports and Economic Growth: An Empirical Investiga-tion', *Journal of Development Economics*, **4**, March, 49–53.

Nishimizu, M. and Robinson, S. (1984), 'Trade Policies and Productivity Change in Semi-industrialized Countries', *Journal of Development Economics*, **16**, 177–206.

Ram, Rati (1985), 'Exports and Economic Growth: Some Additional Evidence', *Economic Development and Cultural Change*, **33**, (2), January, 415–25.

6. The paper I presented at the International Trade Theory Session (#410–1) at The Twenty-fifth International Atlantic Economic Conference in London on 19 April 1988 established a positive correlation between export growth and GDP growth for a sample of 93 developing and industrial nations. The correlation was statistically significant at the 99 per cent level (t-statistic 4.35).

7. Anyone interested in information about the World Bank's research concerning the association between economic health (rates of return, productivity and so on) and various measures of the openness of the economy should refer to the World Develop-ment Reports published during the past five years and, in particular, to the *World Development Report 1991*. Additional detail concerning the studies can be obtained by contacting the World Bank directly in Washington DC.

8. The source of the subsidy data is from Volumes 1 and 2 of *A Study of the Soviet Economy* (Paris, IMF, World Bank, OECD, EBRD, 1991).

9. In Chapter 8 of *The New Russians*, Hedrick Smith chronicles the Stalin purge in Byelorussia. In what is considered to be the most authoritative study of the Stalin exterminations, Roy Medvedev's *Let History Judge* (New York: Knopf, 1989) estimates the Stalin death toll to be 40 million. Hedrick Smith's detailed book also contains many examples of economic corruption in Russia. Konstantin Simis's *USSR: The Corrupt Society* (New York: Simon and Schuster, 1982) probably provides the most extensive information about the networks of illegal entrepreneurs in the Soviet Union in the 1970s.

10. Collins and Rodrik's *Eastern Europe and the Soviet Union in the World Economy* and Hedrick Smith's *The New Russians* discuss problems involving the accuracy of infor-mation in the former communist countries. However, the most extensive coverage of the topic is in Appendix 'II-2–Statistical Issues', pp. 133–69, in Volume 1 of *A Study of the Soviet Economy*.

11. See the article by Philip Yancey 'Praying with the KGB' in the 13 January 1992 issue of *Christianity Today*. This covers the emotional experience of the 19 evangelical leaders from the United States meeting with the Soviet leaders in the Kremlin in the autumn of 1991. Dr John Bernbaum, one of the 19 guests of the Supreme Soviet and a member of our team (which is working with the Russian State Committee on Higher Education to develop a graduate business programme), said that the communists mentioned time and again during the four day meeting the importance of increased morality and a higher level of ethical behaviour.

References

Balassa, Bela (1978), 'Exports and Economic Growth: Further Evidence', *Journal of Devel-opment Economics*, **5**, (2), June, 181–9.

Balassa, Bela (1980), 'Structural Change in Trade in Manufactured Goods Between Industrial and Developing Countries', *World Bank Staff Working Paper No. 396*.

Balassa, Bela (1984), 'Trends in International Trade in Manufactured Goods and Structural Change in the Industrial Countries', *World Bank Staff Working Paper No. 611*.

Balassa, Bela (1985), 'Exports, Policy Choices and Economic Growth in Developing Coun-tries after the 1973 Oil Shock', *Journal of Development Economics*, **18**, (1), May/June, 23–35.

Collins, Susan and Rodik, Dani (1991), *Eastern Europe and the Soviet Union in the World Economy*, Washington, DC: Institute for International Economics.

Denison, Edward F. (1985), *Trends in American Economic Growth, 1929–1982*, Washington: The Brookings Institution.

Feder, Gershon (1982), 'On Exports and Economic Growth', *World Bank Staff Working Paper No. 505*, World Bank, February.

Fisher, Stanley and Gleb, Alan (1990), '*Issues in Socialist Economy Reform*', Washington, DC: Policy, Research and External Affairs, Country Economics Department, World Bank, December, WPS 565.

Iasin, E. (1991), 'Problems of Making the Transition to a Regulated Market Economy', *Problems of Economics*, **33**, (12), April, 6–32.

Institute of International Finance (1990), 'Building Free Market Economies in Central and Eastern Europe: Challenges and Realities', Washington, DC: Institute of International Finance Inc., April.

Kavoussi, Rostam M. (1984), 'Export Expansion and Economic Growth', *Journal of Development Economics*, **14**, (1, 2), Jan/Feb, 241–50.

Kavoussi, Rostam M. (1985), 'International Trade and Economic Development: The Recent Experience of Developing Countries', *Journal of Developing Areas*, **19**, (3), April, 379–92.

Krueger, Anne O. (1978), *Foreign Trade Regimes and Economic Development: Liberalization Attempts and Consequences*, Cambridge, Massachusetts: Ballinger Publishing Co.

Krueger, Anne O. (1980), 'Trade Policy as an Input to Development', *American Economic Review*, **70**, (2), May, 288–92.

Krueger, Ann O. (1983), 'The Effects of Trade Strategy on Growth', *Finance and Development*, **20**, (2), Washington, DC: World Bank Publications, June, 6–8.

Lourie, Richard (1991), *Predicting Russia's Future*, Knoxville, TE: Whittle Direct Books.

Mackay, Charles (1841), 'Popular Delusions and the Madness of Crowds', New York: Noonday Press (reprinted 1974).

Medvedev, Roy (1989), *Let History Judge*, New York: Knopf.

Michaely, Michael (1977), 'Exports and Economic Growth: An Empirical Investigation', *Journal of Development Economics*, **4**, March, 49–53.

Nishimizu, M. and Robinson, S. (1984), 'Trade Policies and Productivity Change in Semi-industrialized Countries', *Journal of Development Economics*, **16**, 177–206.

Ram, Rati (1985), 'Exports and Economic Growth: Some Additional Evidence', *Economic Development and Cultural Change*, **33**, (2), January, 415–25.

Simis, Konstantin (1982), *USSR: The Corrupt Society*, New York: Simon and Schuster.

Smith, Hedrick (1990), *The New Russians*, New York: Random House.

Tyler, William G. (1981), 'Growth and Export Expansion in Developing Countries', *Journal of Development Economics*, **9**, August, 121–30.

Williamson, John (1991), *The Economic Opening of Eastern Europe*, Washington, DC: Institute for International Economics.

World Bank (1991), *World Development Report 1991*, New York: Oxford University Press.

World Bank, IMF, OECD & European Bank for Reconstruction and Development (1990), *The Economy of the USSR*, Washington, DC: Government Printing Office.

World Bank, IMF, OECD & European Bank for Reconstruction and Development (1991), *A Study of the Soviet Economy*, Vols 1, 2 & 3, Paris: OECD Publication Service.

World Bank, Socialist Economies Unit, Country Economics Department (1991), 'The Transformation of Economies in Central and Eastern Europe: Issues, Progress, and Prospects', April, 3.

Wright, John W. (1991), (General Editor), *The Universal Almanac 1991*, New York: Andrews and McMeel.

6 The pricing problems of Eastern Europe

Christine Rider*

Introduction

In no other part of the world is the challenge of global restructuring so pressing as in Eastern and Central Europe. To use United Nations terminology, these economies are no longer 'socialist centrally planned economies', rather they are 'economies in transition'. But in transition to what? While there is an increased role for markets to accomplish the reforms these post-planning, post-communist societies hope to achieve, it is important that they do not fall into the error of adopting a reform simply because it is 'not planning'. That there are serious flaws in the private free market system is all too evident when the focus is directed to the many roles which prices are required to fulfil in a free market system.

Given the opportunity to rethink and remake the key elements of their economic system, reformers must take care not to miss the chance to restructure the economy to incorporate features that are appropriate. In particular, this might involve reliance on markets for the allocation of consumer goods, while demand management policies and institutional controls over investment might be put into place to support growth and stability at the macroeconomic level.

The problems of the Eastern European and Soviet economies derive from two failures: lack of flexibility (or adaptability) and lack of accountability. An accountability approach, which establishes a mechanism for assigning responsibility for economic activity along the lines suggested by Bowles and Gintis (1986) and Gintis (1991), offers an advantage over the narrow price theoretic approach whose very limited focus is on equilibrium conditions. Its advantage lies chiefly in its policy applications; but it also has theoretical implications which relate to the feasibility and maintainability of competitive markets in a given real-life situation. Although market-determined prices *may* help with the flexibility problem, the privatization envisaged by reformers is unlikely to solve the problem of responsibility.

This paper begins with an examination of the problems resulting from the highly centralized planning model that the reforms are intended to remedy. The next section describes restructuring itself; in particular, the abolition of the central planning bureaucracy, enterprise independence, the introduction of the 'market mechanism' and privatization. Section 3 evaluates the results of restructuring, and the concluding section summarizes both theoretical arguments and pragmatic realities to suggest that if these economies are to achieve their aims, then it is insufficient to make a 180 degree turn from 'planning' to 'the market'. The creation of new institutions and new behavioural patterns must be carefully thought through to achieve the ends desired. As difficult as it is for those eager to see results from restructuring, what is required will involve a long, slow process of adaptation and change.

While this paper is general and does not focus on the specifics of any one country, these generalizations focus on the key elements common to all the restructuring proposals.

The failure of centralised planning

Planning was first adopted in the Soviet Union in the 1920s to speed up the process of industrialization and modernization – at a time when the USSR was still predominantly rural and agricultural (Ofer, 1987; Zaleski, 1971). With the accession to power of Josef Stalin in the late 1920s, planning became highly centralized, and it was this version that was adopted by the Eastern European socialist economies in the 1940s, again to speed up economic modernization. There were differences in the level of economic development and industrialization, ranging from the relatively sophisticated, industrial economies of the Democratic Republic of Germany and Czechoslovakia, to Albania, which had hardly been touched by modern technologies. Because these countries were socialist, the means of production had become state-owned, although there were exceptions (such as farmland in Poland, which remained privately owned).

The process of socializing agricultural land ownership, usually through the creation of large collective or co-operative farms, was not a smooth process, and peasant resistance was not uncommon. Socialization of industrial enterprises was accomplished by expropriating the private owners; state ownership of industrial property was effected most easily in the less industrialized economies through the process of establishing new enterprises which were state-owned from the start.

Production decisions were made 'at the centre'; the chain of command was vertical, running from the central planning board through financial and industrial ministries to enterprises which were operating and not decision making units. Ideally, there would be a flow of information back to central planners so that adjustments could be made. But in practice, and in the absence of horizontal competition between enterprises, a type of vertical competition took place: ministries and the enterprises under their control competed for scarce resources with other ministries.

Once the central plan had been determined, the allocation of resources and inputs to enterprises was made in physical terms, with output goals and targets also established in physical terms. This practice of physical planning was originally intended to set enterprises free from the burden of showing short-run financial profits to permit them to concentrate on the long-run task of improving technical efficiency. But again, a sensible ideal became warped in practice: ministries and enterprises defended their turf, and those with the best political connections, usually the more powerful enterprises, were the most successful in gaining privileged access to scarce resources.

As a consequence of the desire to speed up the industrialization process – seen at the time as being necessary for the creation of a strong modern state – several characteristics of planning appeared. Over time, these characteristics led to the emergence of the problems now being grappled with by the socialist economies in transition.

First, planning was taut: the plans set over-optimistic targets in terms of the resources available for two reasons. Planners wanted to speed up industrialization as much as possible, and they also wanted to motivate the working population to work harder. Such non-material incentives were also thought desirable because there was less emphasis on material (money) rewards as a motivator – possibly to avoid the money fetish associated with capitalism.

The second characteristic was that priority was given to heavy industry, the symbol of modern industrialization, at the expense of consumer goods, agriculture and a supportive infrastructure. Thirdly, closely associated with this characteristic, was the desire to encourage the development of energy-providing industries. This was done by underpricing energy inputs so as to encourage greater use of energy by users, thus permitting the exploitation of economies of scale by energy producers and justifying the original decision. Finally, there was a significant amount of political input into the planning process. Originally this was intended to add a democratic element by adding the workers' input to industrial decision-making – to avoid the lack of economic democracy associated with capitalist industrialization – but this political input became monopolized by the Communist Party *nomenklatura*.

In fact, the early results of planning, as measured by growth rates and industrialization, were impressive. The centrally planned economies 'outscored' the Western mixed market economies.[1] However, from the late 1960s onwards, it became harder to maintain this momentum, and various problems associated with declining labour productivity and slowing growth momentum began to be identified. Some of these are associated with the difficulties of the economic development process itself, but others are the outcome of the actual practice of planning.

There were many early attempts to remedy these problems in some of the countries of the area. In the 1950s and 1960s, efforts to introduce some elements of decentralization (in effect liberalizing the plan) were tried, but were succeeded by a period of recentralization in response to the new problems created by decentralization (Asselain, 1984; Hewett, 1988; Kornai, 1986, 1990; Zimbalist *et al.*, 1989). By the late 1980s (earlier in Hungary) simply tampering with the planning process was rejected in favour of a complete switch towards adopting private ownership and relying on the profit motive and the price mechanism to direct resources (Bergson, 1987; *Financial Times*, 1990; Kornai, 1990; Lipton and Sachs, 1990; Nuti, 1988).

Again, with variations in the different countries, it was hoped that this switch would solve the seven most easily identifiable problems. If one were to choose a single word to summarize these problems, it would be 'inefficiency'. This done, it becomes easier to appreciate the appeal of the move to free market pricing: in the idealized model of a free market, *laissez-faire* private enterprise economy, the outcome of all economic agents' decentralized decisions is efficient, producing maximum output at lowest cost.

The seven problems are therefore apparent examples of inefficiency. First, production itself is inefficient and wasteful in terms of resource use when compared with Western economies. Because priority in the use of resources was given to the build-up of heavy industry, enterprises were encouraged to use more intermediate goods and energy inputs through a system of deliberate underpricing and subsidies. This inefficiency showed in higher intermediate goods, labour and energy input coefficients per unit of output.

While possibly excusable in the early years given the aim of planning, this problem in fact got worse over time. The planning process did not encourage innovation or changes in production techniques in response to changing resource supplies. Enterprise managers had little incentive to economize on these inputs if it meant that future supplies would be cut, or if increased output implied an upward revision of output targets in the plan.

So long as the Eastern bloc remained closed to world competition, this inefficiency remained localized. But once these trading barriers came down, then with the opening up of the Eastern European economies, their non-competitiveness became a serious problem. The case of the fall in East Germany's industrial production following union with West Germany due to unsold, uncompetitive products is instructive here.

There is a second related problem: specifically, inflexible prices. Prices in a planned economy play a different role from those in a market economy, and thus were not changed very often. Originally intended to reflect production costs and to provide an approximate balance between supplies and demands, they ceased to perform even that function because they were rarely changed.

In addition, as production of some items was subsidized, the resulting price structure became arbitrary. Prices neither balanced supplies with demand nor reflected changing information, nor did they serve to finance enterprise expansion: the financial results of enterprise activity cannot be compared with those of Western enterprises, and it is often difficult to tell whether an operation is even viable. This inflexibility underscored the lack of incentive to economize on resources or to innovate, and as the economy grew over time, it intensified the pattern of imbalances.

The pattern of imbalances, the third problem, is the most visible among the planning failures of socialism. It is marked by shortages coexisting with bottlenecks, by a shortage of consumer goods, an incomplete supportive infrastructure and, in many cases, an inefficient agricultural sector. The early emphasis on heavy industry failed to stimulate the general expansion of all sectors that was supposed to be the reward for the early years of sacrifice. The way the system worked encouraged extensive growth using more resources to increase output rather than, as was more common in the West, intensive growth based on new technologies and the knowledge-based industries to get more output from the same inputs.

Unfortunately, this path of growth can continue only as long as resources are available. Once resource limits appear it is no longer possible to continue along these lines, but the overall inflexibility of the economy prevented a search for new solutions; hence the imbalance of shortages plus bottlenecks plus wastage – characteristics of resource-constrained economies.

This situation gives rise to a fourth problem – chronic shortages. The behavioural response to the third problem does not solve but rather worsens it; that is, the usual response to a shortage in this type of economy is to expand investment. Because the power and prestige of an enterprise is not measured by profitability but by its size and its access to the central corridors of power, both enterprises and centre have every incentive to try to expand. When resource constraints exist, the result is half-finished projects and a lengthening of the construction period – examples of further inefficiency that do not solve the problem of pervasive shortages. In addition, because enterprises are not responsible for financing their own investment, there are no financial constraints on expansion plans. The centre gives in to requests for finance not only because investment is perceived as the key to growth, but also because of the commitment to the full utilization of resources.

Ironically, commitment to full employment and full resource utilization was intended to demonstrate the economic superiority of the planned socialist economy over the cyclical instability of the market capitalist economy. By planning the rational use of all resources at all times, socialism could avoid the waste of recessions. The cost, as it turned out, came in the form of underutilized labour resources (disguised unemployment), incomplete projects and a shortage of high quality consumer goods: in this environment, whatever can be produced can be sold. In contrast, in Western capitalist economies, demand is the constraint – from the point of view of producers, buyers are in short supply. Hence the competitive struggle for market share results in attention to quality, style, service and so on. These do not have to be attended to in a sellers' market environment.

Shortages lead to a fifth problem – repressed or actual inflation. On the one hand, a commitment to full employment implies relatively high incomes and earning power. On the other hand, shortages of consumer goods, low and subsidized prices for consumer goods, free or heavily subsidized provision of social goods and services, and lack of alternative uses for financial funds has resulted in the accumulation of liquid assets in the hands of the public.

The final problems are not the outcome of planning *per se*, but either the result of deliberate policy or of an unfortunate combination of circumstances. Relative isolationism is the result of a deliberate policy move. Initially, the creation of the Comecon trading group was meant to encourage the rapid development of the Eastern bloc countries by creating a customs union. Within its protected borders, comparative advantage was to determine what should be produced and in which country. As customs union theory indicated, this provided a large potential market, enabling economies of scale to be tapped by producers located in countries with only small domestic markets. However, after 1989, the opening up of the Eastern European economies further served to underscore precisely how inefficient their economies had become. The former East Germany is perhaps the clearest example. The German Democratic Republic was the pre-eminent producer of capital goods within Comecon, but lost both its own domestic market to West German competition and its export markets in the other Eastern countries (which are now able to import from whichever supplier they choose). Protection plus rigidity did not encourage improved industrial production but only inefficiency, low quality and uncompetitiveness (Kurz, 1992).

The final problem of concern, the full extent of which is still being uncovered, is the environmental damage widespread in the area. This is neither the result of planning – good environmental practices are not incompatible with planning – nor of a commitment to socialist principles. Environmental damage also occurs in private enterprise market economies. The reason that it is somewhat less in the advanced Western economies (but not in the developing ones where there is mounting evidence of extensive damage occurring) has nothing to do with ownership rights or economic coordinating mechanisms. It has more to do with attribution of responsibility and the ability of concerned people in mature democracies to bring political and social pressure to bear, effectively, on polluters.

Restructuring the centrally planned economies
Although attempts at reform of the centrally planned economies date back to the 1950s, it is those of the late 1980s that are of particular interest. In

general, today's reformers seem to view earlier attempts to improve the functioning of the planning mechanism as misguided, hence a wholesale 'conversion' to a market system dominated by the profit motive and set in a framework of private ownership of productive resources seems to be the common element. It is hoped that giving enterprises decision-making authority (the decentralization aspect), introducing market institutions and permitting profit incentives to guide behaviour will produce better results and remedy the problems identified above (especially the first six).

Possibly the most widely publicized reform is Poland's Balcerowicz plan, which is better known in the US as the Lipton/Sachs plan, after the Polish government's advisers. However, certain common elements inform all the actual practices (Hungary is furthest along the restructuring process) or the proposals.

The key reform is the replacement of the bureaucratic planning mechanism by enterprise independence, permitting decentralized markets and market-determined prices. Enterprises are to be financially self-sufficient; they will be subject to the discipline of a hard budget constraint (to use Kornai's phrase), and will only be able to finance new expenditures out of profits or by borrowing on market-determined terms. This reform is intended to introduce market discipline to control activity: only those enterprises that are efficient and make profits will survive; those that cannot adapt and that cannot cover their costs will be permitted to fail and will not be bailed out by the state.

Second is the replacement of administered prices with market-determined prices, the price liberalization aspect. Replacing vertical competition with horizontal competition between enterprises is intended both to improve efficiency and to result in prices that are better reflections of production costs and relative scarcities. Being subject to market competition will force firms to innovate and become more efficient just to survive.

Replacement of the economic mechanism is to be accompanied by a change in ownership of productive resources, from state to private hands. There are many proposals for accomplishing this; the reality of introducing private property rights is extremely complex. The simplest change has been to permit the establishment of new privately or co-operatively owned enterprises; this has particularly affected small service and retail enterprises. More difficult is the privatization of state-owned enterprises, especially the large ones that dominate the economic landscape of Eastern Europe.

Various schemes have been advanced to accomplish privatization. These include turning enterprises over to their workers and managers; selling them in whole or in part to their workers, managers, general public or to specially created mutual funds or foreign buyers; and simply giving away shares in them to the first four of the above groups. Any of these schemes may or may not be preceded by a liquidation of the firm or by breaking up a large enterprise into smaller, presumably more manageable, subunits.

That this has been problematic is no surprise, because these economies lack two essential ingredients for the introduction of private property. The first is an accurate valuation of what the enterprise is worth: given the arbitrary nature of the pricing system, it is impossible to use existing prices to value enterprises, and presumably accurate prices will not emerge until economically viable enterprises are competing to produce market prices.

The second difficulty is a lack of all the supportive institutions that make private property workable elsewhere. For example, the legal system must be changed to permit it, new accounting techniques need to be introduced so that accurate valuations may be established, and the necessary institutions for the transferrability of shares must be created – this last requirement has led to a flurry of activity as Western central banks, stock markets and stock brokers have been called on for advice on the movement to a monetised free enterprise system.

In some economies – Poland is the best example – restructuring has been preceded by stabilization. In practice, this has meant the deliberate creation of recession conditions and control of inflation with the aim of reducing the amount of liquid assets held by the public. It is hoped that this will reduce the excessive demand characteristic of resource-constrained economies. This is thought to be a necessary prerequisite for price liberalization and enterprise restructuring.

In addition, various political changes have been effected – the economic impact is intended to remove the influence of the Communist Party over economic decisions, hence it parallels enterprise decentralization. In practice, however, even without official party labels or affiliation, many of the decisions are still likely to be made by the same individuals.

Underlying all these reforms seems to be the implicit belief that the market mechanism is an inherently superior one for co-ordinating the actions of individuals, and that private property and the profit motive will generate the right incentives. That is, that the results of atomistic decision-makers in freely working competitive markets will produce the right prices. These prices are the right prices because they reflect opportunity costs, thus the resulting output mix is both technologically and socially efficient, and is the one that maximizes social welfare.

In addition, because prices reflect consumer preferences, any change in preferences will be followed by an output adjustment (in the right direction) as profit-maximizing producers rush to meet consumers' wishes. This can only be done in a demand-constrained economy where there are penalties – for example, pecuniary losses – for not meeting consumer needs, or slack resources that can be put to work to meet increased demands for output.

Evaluation

The question of whether restructuring will be successful can be addressed on several different levels. While the above was oversimplified – real-life prices of course do not maximize welfare or minimize costs – it can be useful to use an ideal-type exposition to clarify the issues. If the ultimate justification for introducing the price mechanism depends on maximizing consumer well-being via the efficient allocation of resources, it is easy enough to demonstrate theoretically that success is unlikely (Rider, 1992). In brief, the requirements for the price mechanism to produce this result are so restrictive that they have never, and will never, be met in any real economy. These are the familiar constraints from neoclassical price theory: perfect competition; atomistic units with no market power; no economies of scale or externalities to lower costs as output expands; substitutability of factors of production in response to marginal price changes, and so on. If these are met, then prices do reflect the true opportunity costs of using resources, and the appearance of pure profits or losses results in the reallocation of resources in accordance with consumer wishes. Thus the appearance of economic profit or loss, and the consequent adjustment of behaviour, gives validity to the role of the profit motive in real life.

This theoretical exercise, however, is sterile because it does not address real-life concerns (Kaldor, 1972, 1975, 1979; Sawyer, 1993). A more useful exercise is to attempt to show whether or not restructuring can remedy the problems identified above and help make improvements in these economies, that is improvement rather than maximization takes centre stage. These seven problems in one way or another can be reduced to two basic shortcomings: lack of flexibility and lack of accountability.

Will there be more flexibility and a sense of responsibility after the restructuring? The answer has to be a qualified 'yes'; qualified because the conditions required for the complete effects expected by the pure pricing model are not present. For example, taking input use, output and pricing decisions out of the hands of a politicized bureaucracy and putting them into the hands of independent profit motivated enterprises will result in different decisions being made, but there may well be a new source of inflexibility arising from the monopoly elements in the economy.

The characteristic industrial enterprise of the centrally planned economy was large because of economies of scale and because dealing with a few vertically integrated enterprises was easier than dealing with many smaller units. In the economies in transition, what will happen to these large units? How they can be restructured without losing the advantages of size is still being worked out. It is likely that, as in the Western market economies, monopolization (or oligopolization to be more precise) will remain a very real problem: if these entities are left intact, they have a tremendous advantage in perpetuating their power in the new market situation. Sheer size and dominance will enable them to make profits due solely to their market power, and these profits can then be used to consolidate that power by financing further expansion.

There are further incentives towards monopolization if international competition is to be dealt with. The larger the company, the easier it is to attract resources and employees with the right skills and to get finance capital on favourable terms; hence they are likely to be at a further advantage. Alternatively, if co-operation (perhaps via joint ventures) with foreign companies is sought, in spite of all the problems, a link with an already established operation is likely to be preferred by the foreign partner than a link with an inexperienced start-up – especially if considerations of national control and sovereignty are added.

In fact, the existence of monopolization is the main reason why any flexibility resulting from restructuring is likely to be limited, and for the same reasons that neoclassical price theory tells us that monopolization is bad. From the theoretical point of view, the greater the degree of imperfection in the market mechanism, the greater the divergence between price and costs, the smaller the output, and the less likely it is that lowest cost production and maximum consumer welfare will be achieved. These are reasons why most Western governments have attempted some form of anti-monopoly measures, especially to curb the abusive practices associated with market dominance.

Unfortunately, this is precisely an area where the post-communist governments are most inexperienced: there is no similar tradition of anti-monopoly policy. Unless there is a critical approach rather than the unfortunate presumption that 'the market mechanism always makes the right decisions', there may well be a lengthy period of pain before effective industrial policy and a legal environment that includes such provision is put into place. It must also be remembered that large size is a prerequisite in many areas for economies of scale, and so on, so the issue becomes how to encourage the 'good' attributes of size so that the large enterprises will be a force for improvement.

In summary, plan inflexibility may be replaced by a new type of inflexibility associated with monopoly elements. In any event, the characteristic operation of industrial enterprises is not like that of neoclassical theory: if firms adopt mark-up pricing and favour quantity rather than price adjustments to demand changes, then prices will not operate as signalling devices. Prices, in fact, have more than just an allocative role (Sawyer, 1993). If production does become more efficient, and if the inherited imbalances of the economy are worked out, the explanation does not depend on the elements of pure price theory becoming operational. In addition, there is no way that market forces alone can solve the environmental problem; this requires a restructuring of the political sphere and the acceptance of an ethic that truly does empower the people.

The lack of accountability is also the cause of many of the problems of these economies. It can be traced to many contributing elements: the dominance of the Party in economic affairs; the role of the *nomenklatura* in decision-making; the anonymity of the plan; the lack of any accounting mechanism that is able to reward or penalize good or bad decisions and encourage good work efforts. It seemed as though decisions or behaviour were good if they suited the Party's purposes. Hence the end result was that no one felt responsible for their decisions; if they did, pervasive shortages of resources would prevent effective action, so demoralization was widespread.

To remedy this, the reformers hope that privatization and the threat of unemployment will be the answer. Apologists for private property rights maintain that ownership does give feelings of responsibility. Hence by selling or giving ownership shares to citizens, it is hoped that the pride of ownership will induce people to work harder and improve the economy.

However, the flaw in this argument is that private ownership *per se* does not automatically lead to the best decisions or accountability, and that public ownership *per se* does not automatically produce bad ones. One can point, without difficulty, to many privately owned companies in the West that are glaring examples of inefficiency and poor decision-making (some American savings banks, for example), and to many publicly owned enterprises that outperform equivalent private ones (European rail systems, for example). The separation of ownership from control in large organizations further reduces individual accountability. What matters is not private property rights as such, and introducing them into societies which have learned to look with suspicion on private property will not be easy. The important lesson to be learned is that if people have a sense of responsibility for what they do, then the outcomes are likely to be preferable – and this makes the question of property ownership a *non sequitur.*

Thus, if there are incentives and rewards (which can be either material or non material) for doing the right thing, and disincentives and penalties for not doing it, the outcome is likely to be preferable.

Summary
To summarize, lack of flexibility manifests itself in inefficient production, rigid prices, economic imbalance and the failure to come to terms with sound environmental practices. Lack of a sense of responsibility derives from the rigidity and overpoliticization of the planning process as actually practised. It reinforces the other problems and makes it difficult to derive a

practical solution in keeping with the best of the inherited socio-cultural traditions of these societies while eliminating the destructive elements.

Some restructuring *is* necessary; any economy that shows obvious signs of inefficiency and stress must attempt improvement. The scale of the restructuring at the present time, however, is unprecedented. How often does a society have the chance to remake itself without undergoing a bloody revolution?

The problem with the current proposals is that they seem focused on marketization and privatization to the exclusion of other requirements. They have not considered all the other institutions and behaviour patterns and general psychology that makes markets work well elsewhere. Modern market economies are mixed economies, and function well not because they are closer to the *laissez-faire* end of the market planning spectrum, but because they have developed those institutions that curb the destructive potential of unbridled market activity. It is culturally arrogant to suppose that a Western economist's vision of an ideal-type market economy can be simply superimposed on the socialist economies in transition; how much input has come from the region's own economists who are most familiar with them?

Market-oriented activity is not totally foreign to these economies – witness the fairly extensive black market or moonlighting activities that coexisted with the plan, or the upsurge in new entrepreneurial activity that followed the demise of the Communist Party's hold on power. What do not fit in easily with their prevailing social ethic are some of the other accompaniments of market capitalism, such as lack of concern for the disadvantaged and an acceptance of significant inequality.

Several general conclusions and recommendations can therefore be derived. First, restructuring to produce a price system that is intended to allocate resources efficiently and to maximize social well-being will not succeed unless careful attention to supportive institutions is also undertaken. The conditions required to produce the 'right' set of prices are too restrictive. Rather than trying to meet them, a clearly impossible task, it is necessary to look at everything else that is needed for a well-functioning economy, an opportunity that rarely comes twice. That is, it is necessary to determine what it is that markets *do* do best, and incorporate this into the restructuring, finding other tools and other mechanisms to accomplish other improvements that are needed.

What is most important here, given cultural traditions, is to structure non-market institutions to provide greater stability. For example, ideally control over investment at the macro level should be retained to even out cyclical movements of investment. If investment expenditures remain solely the responsibility of the enterprises, then the already strong will get stronger and new imbalances will appear in the economy.

Other types of policy or forms of government intervention should also be implemented. In areas where markets fail – in the provision of public goods or infrastructure, or where externalities exist, for example – it is necessary to intervene in or complement the market so as to accomplish the social ends desired. Control of the macroeconomy with industrial, fiscal and monetary policies is another area where these governments are inexperienced, but which needs to be addressed. The two particular areas covered in the body of this paper, monopoly trends and environmental damage, should be dealt with as rapidly as possible.

Thirdly, altering behaviour patterns to generate better decisions cannot be left to chance, but this is an area where many changes will take a long time. In the short run, training managers and supervisors to manage their new work-place tasks and deal with their personnel is the easiest to accomplish. Over the longer run, developing a sense of responsibility for personal actions will require different types of education and reinforcing mechanisms. The issue of incentives and disincentives has to be worked through; when do material rewards/penalties work best? When are non-material ones more appropriate?

Closely associated are the political changes that are already proceeding. Greater democratization of a society is not accomplished with just an election; it is a process that goes deeper and affects many other areas of the society. This will be difficult and time-consuming in many countries which moved rapidly from semi-feudalism through communism to post-communism. Perhaps the length of time required will be frustrating, but it is a process that needs to be finished.

Democratization in these societies should not mean just political change. It should also mean economic democratization, thus realizing one of the aims of socialism: true involvement of people in every aspect of life.

Notes

*   The author would like to express appreciation for the helpful input of Philip Arestis, Gary Mongiovi and Ingrid Rima.
1.   Not until the late 1970s did the growth rate of the USSR (as officially reported) fall below that of the US. For example, in the five year period 1961–65, the average annual growth rate of real GNP of the USSR was 5 per cent, compared with 4.7 per cent for the US; in 1966–70, it was 5.3 per cent and 3 per cent respectively; 1971–75, 3.4 per cent and 2.5 per cent respectively; 1976–80, 2.3 per cent and 3.4 per cent respectively; 1981–85, 1.9 per cent and 2.4 per cent respectively (data from Table 5.4, p. 156, Zimbalist *et al.*, 1989). Zimbalist *et al.* (1989) present a useful comparison of the growth of these two countries, pp. 145–64; see also Hewett (1988).

Bibliography

Asselain, Jean-Charles (1984), *Planning and Profits in Socialist Countries*, London: Routledge & Kegan Paul.
Bergson, Abram (1987), 'The Gorbachev Revolution', *Challenge*, **30**, (4), September/October.

Bowles, Samuel and Gintis, Herbert (1986), *Democracy and Capitalism,* New York: Basic Books.
Financial Times (1990), 'The Soviet Economy', FT Survey, 12 March.
Gintis, Herbert (1991), 'Where did Schumpeter Go Wrong?', *Challenge,* **34**, (1), January/February, 27–33.
Hewett, Edward (1988), *Reforming the Soviet Economy,* Washington, DC: Brookings.
Kaldor, Nicholas (1972), 'The Irrelevance of Equilibrium Economics', *Economic Journal,* **82**, (328), December.
Kaldor, Nicholas (1975), 'What's Wrong with Economic Theory?', *Quarterly Journal of Economics,* **LXXXIX**, (3), August.
Kaldor, Nicholas (1979), 'Equilibrium Theory and Growth Theory', in Michael J. Boskin (ed.), *Economics and Human Welfare: Essays in Honor of Tibor Scitovsky,* New York: Academic Press.
Kornai, Janos (1986), *Contradictions and Dilemmas: Studies on the Socialist Economy and Society,* Cambridge, Mass.: MIT Press.
Kornai, Janos (1990), 'The Affinity Between Ownership Forms and Coordination Mechanisms: The Common Experience of Reform in Socialist Countries', *Journal of Economic Perspectives,* **4**, (3), Summer, 131–48.
Kurz, Heinz (1992), 'Whatever Happened to the East German Economy?', in Mark Knell and Christine Rider (eds), *Socialist Economies in Transition: Appraisals of the Market Mechanism,* Cheltenham: Edward Elgar Publishing.
Lange, Oscar (1936), 'On the Economic Theory of Socialism', Review of Economic Studies, **IV**, 53–71, 123–44.
Lipton, David and Jeffrey Sachs (1990), 'The Case of Poland', *Brookings Papers on Economic Activity,* Washington, DC.: Brookings Institution, 293–333.
Nuti, Mario (1988), 'Perestroika: Transition from Central Planning to Market Socialism', *Economic Policy,* **8**.
Ofer, Gur (1987), 'Soviet Economic Growth, 1928–1985', *Journal of Economic Literature,* **XXV**, December, 1767–1832.
Rider, Christine (1992), 'Justifying the Need for Reform: The Price-Theoretic Approach', in Mark Knell and Christine Rider (eds), *Socialist Economies in Transition: Appraisals of the Market Mechanism,* Cheltenham: Edward Elgar.
Sawyer, Malcolm (1993), 'The Nature and Role of the Market', *Social Concepts,* **6**, (1).
Zaleski, Eugene (1971), *Planning for Economic Growth in the Union, 1918–1932,* Chapel Hill: University of North Carolina Press.
Zimbalist, Andrew, Sherman, H.J. and Brown, Stuart (1989), *Comparing Economic Systems: A Political-Economic Approach,* 2nd edn, San Diego: Harcourt Brace Jovanovich.

7 The transition to a free market: the case of the Polish economy

Walter W. Jermakowicz

Introduction

Germany's 1948 currency reform and Poland's 1990 'shock' reform substantially transformed their respective economies into free market systems by adopting heroic macroeconomic measures.[1] A comparison of their respective experiences, although they are separated by more than 40 years is, nevertheless, revealing. Though sceptics will question whether the German experience during the period between 1 July 1948 and 30 June 1949 had much in common with that of Poland between 1 January and 31 December 1990, their similarities reveal many of the requisites for successful transition to a market economy. German specialists claim that the German situation was more complicated; Polish experts claim that, on the contrary, they are introducing reforms under more tangled conditions. Who is right?

There is agreement that the two countries were similarly depressed at the time their reforms were initiated. In early 1948 the German economy was in dire straits. As a result of extensive war damage, manufacturing production was at little more than 40 per cent of its 1936 level, and real per capita consumption was about two-thirds what it had been in 1936. The severity of the scarcity of basic goods is evident in daily food rations that provided only 1 200 calories. War financing had also left a public debt that almost amounted to 300 per cent of the GNP, which created vast excess liquidity. Internationally, Germany was confronted with the requirement to pay large war reparations. Her difficulties were compounded by the dismantling of productive equipment; in 1948 alone more than 600 plants were stripped in the American and British occupation zones.

The Poland of 1989 was in equally difficult straits following the so called 'consolidation of the national economy', put in place by the government of Mieczyslaw Rakowski. Indexation of wages forced through by Solidarnosc and the National Council of Trade Unions (OPZZ) produced an inflation that was close to 900 per cent; consumption goods prices rose by 739 per cent and food prices rose by 977 per cent. National income was 15 per cent lower in 1989 than in 1979, and real wages were 17 per cent lower than they were ten years earlier.

Money had virtually lost its function as a means of exchange in Poland, as it had earlier for Germany where American cigarettes became the medium of exchange. The medium of exchange in Poland was the US dollar. Black markets undermined the system of price and wage controls as well as the production and distribution of goods. The amount of money in circulation exceeded the value of available goods in the market by approximately 15 times. The international debts of both the Polish state in 1989 and Germany in 1948 were so large that normal interest and debt repayment was an impossibility in both countries.

The administrative systems which prevailed in Germany and in Poland before their reforms were also similar. A hierarchical command system characterized both countries. Both economies were operated according to their respective central plans: four year plans in Germany and five year plans in Poland. Their measures to control inflation included price controls, wage and rent controls, central allocation of labour and natural resources, agricultural quotas and procurement, housing controls and a rationing system. Both countries established managers at the plant level (*Betriebsleiter* or Director), and political party representatives (NSDAP in Germany called *Parteifuehrer*; PZPR in Poland called *I Sekretarz POP*) who supervised business operations and to whom plant managers were subordinate.

The end of the war and allied occupation brought little change to the West German situation. Although central plans were removed, and the *Wirtschaftsministerium* was replaced by the *Wirtschaftsrat* (Economic Council), and NSDAP *Parteileiters* by the officers of Allied armies occupying Germany, the system remained essentially the same. The 1946 *Plan for Reparation and After War State of Germany's Economy* provided for the reduction of her industrial capacity to 50–55 per cent of its 1938 level. This was to be achieved by disassembling factories and lowering the German standard of living (Hamel, 1989, p. 27) within the structure of a centralized command system.

Poland's administrative system in 1982 was not substantially different from that of post-war Germany in 1946. Planning discipline ceased, the system became directed by individually given preferences, yet it remained bureaucratic. It has been said that the command-distribution economic system was replaced by the 'persuasion-distribution system'. What emerged in both Germany and Poland was a situation without either a plan or a market.

The year preceding reform was also characterized by similar political climates in both countries. Social-democratic ideas dominated, and there was strong support for central planning, the nationalization of coal mining and the steel industries, and co-determination by employees. Both countries had also accumulated large monetary overhangs which created severe deterioration of public sector finances. Both countries thus needed action to stabilize their economies.

Both Ludwig Erhard and Leszek Balcerowicz – architects of their country's new programmes – were faced with problems of stabilizing prices and obtaining international help in order to stabilize their currencies and ease debts. Both undertook actions and policies that led to the marketization of the economy. The differences in the starting conditions of the two countries generally relate to their international situation and the institutional characteristics that prevailed in each. The international situation seemed to favour Polish reforms. The Germany of 1948 was occupied by Allied powers with differing attitudes towards a market economy. At one extreme were the Soviets, who practised a pure command economy model, and the French, who were experimenting with the Plannifique Commission (Hamel, 1989, pp. 25–34). Then came the British, whose Labour Party tried to make Germany a 'laboratory' for new central planning methods. At the other extreme, the Americans favoured a free uncontrolled economy.

These differences, unfortunately, excluded the possibility of co-operation among the Allies in the transformation of the German economy. Quite the opposite occurred: the introduction of monetary reform in June 1948 gave the Soviets a reason to blockade Berlin, and the ensuing division of Germany lasted for more than 40 years.

Polish '1990 shock therapy' started in quite a different international situation, and was regarded by the Soviets and other Central European countries as an experiment, which, if successful, could be introduced into their own economies. Illusions about the superiority of central planning methods over market forces and about the benefits of state ownership of production means had substantially disappeared by 1990. The polls in Poland indicated that some 64 per cent of the population supported the economy's privatization; only eight per cent of those polled opposed ownership transformation ('Privatization', 1990, p. 3).

In spite of the differences between the Germany of 1948 and the Poland of 1990, the similarities of their starting conditions make it clear that the transformation of any centrally planned economy into a market mechanism requires the fulfilment of three tasks:

1. Macroeconomic stabilization of the economy.
2. Liberalization of economic activity.
3. Privatization of state-owned enterprise and the concurrent creation of financial institutions necessary to a market system.

The timetables for undertaking these tasks were substantially different in the two countries.

West Germany circa 1948

Macroeconomic stabilization

The necessity for reforming German monetary conditions was apparent by 1945 (Moeller, 1961). The impetus was a deteriorating economic situation marked by hunger strikes and a changing international climate. The American point of view, which was expressed in the 'Colm–Dodge–Goldsmith Plan' of 1946 (Moeller, 1961, p. 429), was to concentrate on financial recovery for German banks and foreign exchange roles.

On 20 June 1948, military authorities enacted three laws: the currency law, the conversion law, and the issue law. The currency law of 1948, (*Waehrungsgesetz*, 1948) established the Deutschemark as the only legal tender. It provided an initial advance of 40 DM in June and 20 DM one month later to each inhabitant of the western sector of occupied Germany.

The new currency was issued to individuals upon presentation of their rationing and personal identity cards. It also established a supply of new currency to public authorities and businesses against payment of an equal amount of Reichsmark (RM). Interestingly, the law did not disclose the eventual conversion rate of RM into DM; this imposed a one week moratorium on all RM obligations and required that cash denominated in RM be deposited in bank accounts for later conversion into DM.

The law for monetary reform, otherwise known as the conversion law (*Gesetz zur Neuordnung*), contained detailed regulations for the conversion of RM assets and for the liabilities of the banking and non-banking sectors. Part one stipulated that the RM accounts of private non-banks were to be converted into DM accounts at a rate of 10:1 (a few months later at about 15:1). One-half of the DM assets were credited to demand deposits and could be accessed freely after conversion; the other half were credited to escrow accounts until a decision on their treatment was made in the following 90 day period.

Part two of the conversion law regulated the liabilities of the non-banking sector. Current payment obligations such as wages, salaries, rents and pensions were converted, as prices were, at the rate of 1:1. An equalization of burdens was foreseen in principle, but detailed provisions were left to German legislation to be enacted by 31 December 1948.[2]

Liberalization measures

Extensive efforts towards reform were launched after the appointment of Erhard as the chairman of *Verwaltung fuer Wirtschaft* in March 1948. While Allied military authorities concentrated on developing and mastering the technical side of monetary exchange, Erhard focused his efforts on preparing a set of legal acts to create the environment for reforms. The law called the

Guiding Principles of Rationing and Price Policy after Monetary Reform came into force on 20 June 1948. This law liberalized by 50 per cent the prices for food, agricultural products and most raw materials; housing and public transportation, however, remained controlled, and their supply was rationed. Textile and shoe prices were also liberated, but their supply was rationed. Law No. 64 was enacted on the same date and became effective on 22 June 1948. This lowered tax rates on personal and corporate incomes, wealth, inheritance and tobacco. The 'guiding principles' and other laws were accepted by the *Wirtschaftsrat* during an all-night session from 17–18 June 1948, and the decision to free prices was made the following day.

Changes in prices required a prior exact approval by the occupation forces. The threat of renewed inflation led Erhard courageously to announce the liberation of prices by radio without the Allied powers' permission because he had insufficient time to arrange compliance. When General Clay, the American Governor, accused him two days later of ignoring the Allied powers' directives forbidding any change in price and rationing regulations, he replied that he did not *change* them, he merely *removed* them, an act for which, according to the quoted directives, permission was not required. General Clay was impressed by Erhard's courage and the 'guiding principles' were undersigned by the military government, becoming effective on 7 July 1948 (Wuensche, 1986, p. 182).

Institutional changes
The changes made in the institutional machinery needed for effective functioning of financial markets had been suspended but not dismantled from the years before 1936, so that the changes needed in the institutional sphere were minimal. Property rights were generally in private hands. Stock exchanges (in Frankfurt, Hamburg and Munich) reopened just four weeks after reform on 17 July.

The interruption in the market economy's regular functioning had lasted only 12 years, so that Erhard still had qualified people familiar with the rules of a market system's functioning at his disposal. The only change required in this sphere, which was enacted by military authorities on 17 June 1948, was to establish the *Bank Deutscher Laender*, responsible for the issuance of Deutschemarks and currency reform.

Erhard also inherited a 'demonopolized' economy. Allied forces demonopolized the German chemical industry (centralized in IG Farben); the coal and steel industries (centralized in Holding Montana); and the banking system. IG Farben was divided into four independent firms, Holding Montana into 28 independent firms, and the banking system into 33 regional banks which were again subordinated to the *Bank Deutscher Laender* in 1948. In 1947 the Allied forces introduced Law No. 56, the anti-cartel law, which dissolved 1100 monopolistic agreements.

Erhard also had the provisions of two legal acts which could be introduced step by step in a planned manner during the following months, or even years. The first, which was enacted by military authority, prepared the way for stabilization policy; the second created the basis for broader system reforms. Erhard also had at his disposal a new currency which was printed in the United States in the autumn of 1947.

Poland 1990

Stabilization changes

The Solidarity government headed by Tadeusz Mazowiecki inherited an economy in a state of hyper-inflation and chaos. The economy was partly market governed and partly centrally planned, and was essentially beyond control. The government's economic programme, announced in October 1989 and entitled 'The Economic Programme and Its Main Foundations and Directions', had three key components: an anti-inflationary stabilization programme, an economy liberalization programme, and a privatization plan.

In the last months of 1989, the economic situation forced the government to concentrate on stabilization, though preparations were also being made to introduce a programme to liberalize the economy. The stabilization programme which was accepted by the Ministry of Finance in consultation with the International Monetary Fund aimed at stifling high inflation and eliminating shortages. This programme comprised four main elements: restrictive monetary policy, elimination of the budget deficit, restrictive income policy and exchange rate stability. Controlled incomes and a controlled exchange rate would play the role of economic anchors.

Restrictive monetary policy was accomplished through a radical reduction in the money supply (net domestic assets) and the establishment of a high prime interest rate that exceeded inflation in real terms. This move was accompanied by a law regulating credit operations by introducing interest rate adjustments in all prior credit agreements. The law also restricted so-called preferential credit.

The policy to eliminate the budget deficit proceeded primarily through the removal of tax credits and radical reductions in subsidies for food, raw materials, production input and energy carriers.

Control over incomes was achieved through the elimination of the wage indexation that had been introduced in July 1989 as a result of a round-table discussion. In its place severe tax penalties were placed on wage increases, so that only a modest growth of wages was allowed with respect to price increases (0.3 in January, 0.2 in February–April, 0.6 in May, 1.0 in July and

0.6 since August). Wages which exceeded 140 per cent of the average wage obligated the recipient to pay a 500 per cent tax on the differential.

The final reform measure set a unified exchange rate of 9500 zloties per US dollar on 1 January 1990, as a stable convertible rate for all of Poland's international trade with the West. This represented a devaluation from 6500 zloties per dollar at the end of 1989. The fixed exchange rate provided an effective nominal anchor, stabilizing the prices of traded goods in zloty terms.

Liberalization changes

The objectives of the liberalization changes were to open the economy to foreign competition, to deregulate the majority of commodity markets, to liberalize the structure of prices and to bring the economy closer to a free market. The operation was intended to create a macroeconomic basis for a final restructuring of the economic system. The liberalization policy comprised four elements. First was the liberalization of prices: over 90 per cent of prices were to be determined by the market. The prices that remained under administrative control, among them energy, transportation, housing and pharmaceuticals, were significantly increased to ration the available supply. Second was liberalization of domestic trade; for example, farmers were allowed to bring food directly to the market themselves, thereby bypassing the monopolized food-processing industry. The third element was the removal of restrictions on the private sector, including the registration of new firms and restriction on their activities. Fourth was the liberalization of foreign trade by introducing a customs law corresponding to EEC standards and reducing import and export quantity barriers.

Institutional changes

The most challenging task the new government faced in 1990 was the introduction of institutional changes. These involved the complete redefinition of property rights and wealthholding, as well as the introduction of a capital market and financial institutions. The institutional sphere is the most difficult aspect of reform because of the resistance of existing structures and popular conservatism rooted in a lack of basic knowledge about the functioning of these institutions.

By 1990 the Polish government had achieved the following:

1. The introduction of a new anti-monopoly office. This led to the break up of some of the government-owned enterprises in a number of industries.
2. Improved procedures governing the tax collection system. The 1990 changes in the tax system were generally cosmetic; a value added tax went into effect on 1 January 1992.

3. Privatization of state-owned enterprises under alternative plans. Five large firms were privatized at the end of 1990 by public stock offers.

Poland started its reforms on the basis of its old communist financial system, with outdated accounting and trade codes. It was a matter of good fortune that the trade code remained intact during the 40 years of communist rule (in this respect the other Central European countries are less fortunate). Thus the stock exchange and a securities and exchange commission were able to materialize in April 1991. New accounting codes intended to be comparable to those of the West remain under study.

A comparison of the German and Polish reform programmes

Reform of the monetary system – within a broader reform of the economy – was necessary in both countries to improve the economic situation. Both Erhard and Balcerowicz were faced with excessive monetary overhangs of an unknown total amount. In Germany this overhang resulted from preservation of the 'Price-stop' policy imposed in 1938 and from excessive budgetary spending. In Poland it was the consequence of large wage increases, central price controls, swollen budget deficits, populistic tendencies and cheap credit from the central bank.

The three methods available for reducing the monetary overhang have already been noted. In principle, both Erhard and Balcerowicz had free choice; practically, however, the manoeuvring field in both countries was limited. In Germany, the severity of the situation, the political circumstances of the time, and probably Germany's own experience with hyper-inflation after World War I caused currency reform (Option 1) to be selected as the appropriate approach. Also, this was the option that had been proposed in the Colm–Dodge–Goldsmith plan and accepted by American and British allied powers.[3]

Balcerowicz also had a limited choice. Option 1, as he pointed out in a private discussion (Warsaw, 27 May 1990), was excluded as less favourable than corrective inflation (Option 2).[4] In his opinion, the price structure did not reflect demand and supply conditions as in Germany.[5] He further thought that inflation was the only method for price structure correction. He also pointed out that when he assumed his position as Deputy Prime Minister in September 1989, the inflation rate had already amounted to 600 per cent (in December, close to 900 per cent) and that the oversupply of money had already been drained, so that at the beginning of January 1990 a balanced-price policy would be possible.

This general comparison shows that Erhard and Balcerowicz applied similar cures to a similar disease for different reasons. Erhard administered currency reform; Balcerowicz administered corrective inflation.

Polish liberalization measures seem to be more substantial than those of Germany. In January 1990 Poland freed approximately 90 per cent of its prices, while Erhard released only one-third of Germany's prices in June 1948. After strong political pressure, he was then forced to reimpose price control for some goods which were freed earlier. Similarly, imposition of the law on price control (*Gesetz Gegen die Preis-treiberei – Preiswuchergesetz*) on 20 August 1948 and a promise to establish a Central Price Board were backwards steps. These concessions developed in response to both a vote of 'no confidence' for the Director of Verwaltung fuer Wirtschaft and threats of a general strike. Although these concessions were ignored in the course of following actions, they reflect the political meanderings of the architects of German reform.

When compared with German reforms, Polish reforms appear more inclusive. At present Poles continue their policy of control of transportation tariffs and housing rents, but agriculture is subject to the market. These aspects of the Polish situation cause difficult political problems for Balcerowicz.

Summarizing, it can be said that in spite of the fact that Erhard and Balcerowicz introduced different stabilization measures, they achieved similar results. Their measures were swiftly and methodically carried out and had positive results. In this author's opinion, the liberalization measures introduced by Balcerowicz went further than the changes made by Erhard during his first year of tenure. It is relevant that the network of market institutions existing in Germany in 1948 was more advanced than the networks existing in Poland in 1990. In this respect, Leszek Balcerowicz had to start from scratch. The more than 50 year interruption in the functioning of the market system in Poland eliminated basic market institutions and qualified specialists, along with entrepreneurial attitudes and a Western-style work ethic. All are essential for successful day-to-day business activities.

Areas of comparable achievement
The effectiveness of the German and Polish reforms will be evaluated in a comparative fashion according to the following headings: results that are comparable; results in which German achievements were considerably greater than those of Poland, and results in which Poland's economy is outperforming Germany's.

The most impressive effect of reform in both countries was the removal of black markets and their replacement by street trade. (A comparable phenomenon is currently observable in the GDR after monetary union with the Federal Republic.) If black markets provide scarce goods at much higher prices, the street markets offer goods available at regular department stores at much lower prices. For example, in West Germany liqueur and cognac at regular markets were sold for 45–50 DM; on street markets they were available for 10–15 DM ('Nach der Waehrungsreform', 1948). In Poland the street market prices were, on average, 10 per cent lower than in regular department stores. Reform in both countries accomplished the suppression of inflation, though with different degrees of success. The price index in Poland grew faster than the same index in Germany, specifically by more than 120 points.

As seen in Figure 7.1a and b, consumption goods prices in Poland during the first 12 months after reforms increased by 250 per cent and by 112 per cent in Germany. The difference can be explained by the difference in methods applied to fight inflation. Moreover, only 11 product groups were under control in Poland during this period. In Germany, price control covered almost two-thirds of all consumption goods produced, and supplies of food, agricultural products and most raw materials were rationed.

A comparison of consumption goods and investment goods prices in both countries exhibits a surprisingly similar pattern, as is evident from Figure 7.1a and b. The faster growth of investment and consumption goods prices during the first two months occurred because on 20 June 1948 energy and coal prices were raised significantly. Prices rose in Germany by three times, and in Poland by five times. This probably had an initial impact on the faster growth of investment product prices.

Price changes in both countries within the consumption area are also similar (See Figures 7.2a and b). Food prices grew more slowly than other prices. Slower growth was especially observable in Germany, where they increased by only 47.2 per cent; in Poland they increased by 215.9 per cent. This was a result of the remaining obligatory price control and rationing of food in Germany. For example, the rationing of sugar was not lifted until March 1950.

The pattern of monthly price index changes is also very similar, with a very sharp increase in the price index in the first month after the introduction of reforms, between 20 per cent (food) and 110 per cent (investment goods), followed by a fast decline in the rate of price growth in the next two months. After the third month following reforms, price growth is steady in both countries at a very similar average of 5 per cent. This outcome suggests that inflation was either too large in Germany or relatively too small in Poland. This probably resulted from an underestimation of the amount and velocity of money in circulation in Germany and overestimation of the amount of money in Poland.

The lower than expected inflation index growth in Poland is the result of two factors: the high inflation rate in 1989 which had already absorbed a big part of the money excess, and the very consequent monetary policy of 1990. The price index in Poland in June 1990 was about 15 times higher than in

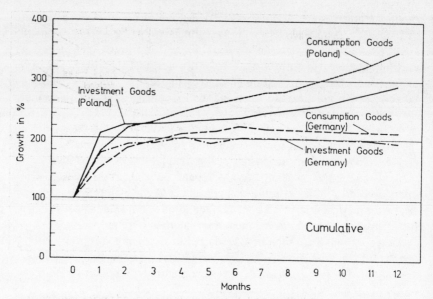

Figure 7.1a: *Cumulative price index growth in Germany and in Poland during the first twelve months after reforms*

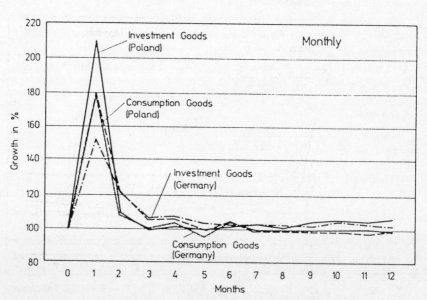

Figure 7.1b: *Monthly price index growth in Germany and in Poland during the first twelve months after reforms*

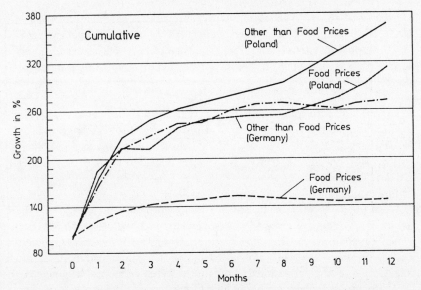

Figure 7.2a: Cumulative growth of consumption goods price indices in Germany and in Poland during the first twelve months after reforms

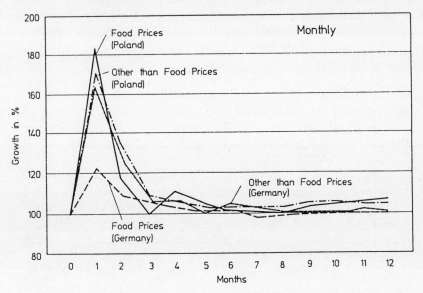

Figure 7.2b: Monthly growth of consumption goods price indices in Germany and in Poland during the first twelve months after reforms

December 1988, but most of this increase reflects events that happened in 1989. The 1990 price index changes reflect the last stage of monetary recovery. In Germany, on the contrary, the second half of 1948 reflects the *beginning* of this process. The other reason for Polish success is in its tight monetary policy.

Areas of better results in Germany
Reform in both cases brought about a lowering of the real wage indices. What is surprising is that this decline was deeper in Germany than in Poland. In Germany during this period, real wages declined by 42.6 per cent; in Poland they declined 33 points (see Figures 7.3a and b). Strong wage controls prevailed in both countries.

Wage increases were controlled in Poland during this period through the tax on excessive wage growth. Wages were allowed to grow by 60 per cent, which equalled the inflation growth. Wages were truly frozen in Germany until November 1948. Thus, Poland's inflation index increased more rapidly than Germany's, which resulted in the lower decline in the real wage index.

While anti-inflationary programmes worked very similarly in Germany and Poland, the production and labour market effects differ remarkably. The most striking phenomenon is the difference in industrial production output. During the first two months, a 29 per cent increase in the production index is observable in Germany, as is evident from Figures 7.4a and b. Very similar tendencies are evident in the production of coal. During the first 12 months, German production increased by 42.6 per cent while in Poland coal production fell 5.6 points.

Asymmetry is also apparent in the structure of production. Reform in Germany revived the light industry sector which specialized in the manufacture of consumption goods. By contrast, in Poland this sector of the economy experienced the fastest decrease. The German textile and clothing industry similarly enjoyed a growth of 56 per cent (Office, 1949, p. 144); while the overall production of textiles and clothing in Poland dropped 38 per cent (*Informacja*, 1990, p. 37). This caused a most severe crisis in the Polish textile industry centres in Lodz, Bielsko, Biala and Bialystok.

There is no doubt that German reforms revitalized the economy; in Poland, to the contrary, reform has prolonged the crisis. The only positive aspect is that the severe limitation of the domestic market is not as restrictive in the private sector. Its production increased 8 per cent in the year 1990.

Opposite tendencies are also apparent in the labour market. Erhard's reform in Germany caused employment to become stabilized at the June 1948 level; in Poland there was a fall in employment of about 11.5 per cent (See Figures 7.5a and b).

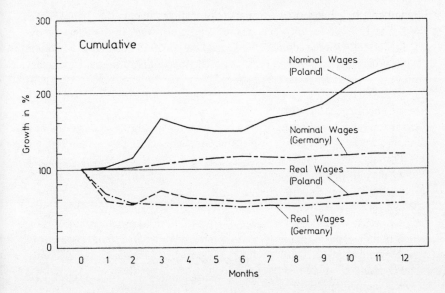

Figure 7.3a: *Cumulative nominal and real wages indices in Germany and in Poland during the first twelve months after reforms*

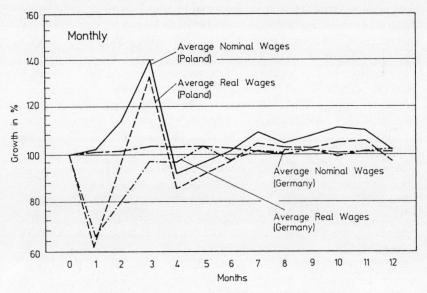

Figure 7.3b: *Monthly nominal and real wages indices in Germany and in Poland during the first twelve months after reforms*

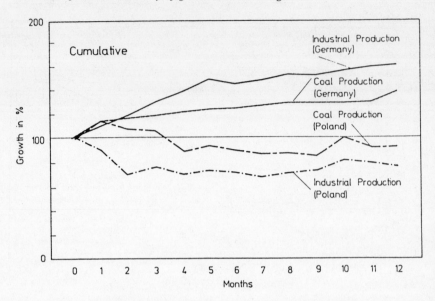

Figure 7.4a: Cumulative industrial production indices in Germany and in Poland during the first twelve months after reforms

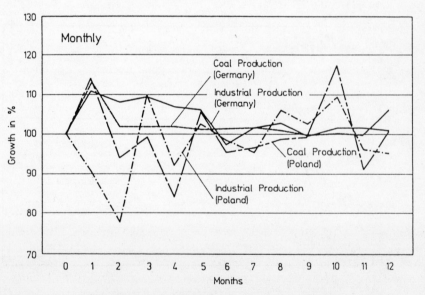

Figure 7.4b: Monthly industrial production indices in Germany and in Poland during the first twelve months after reforms

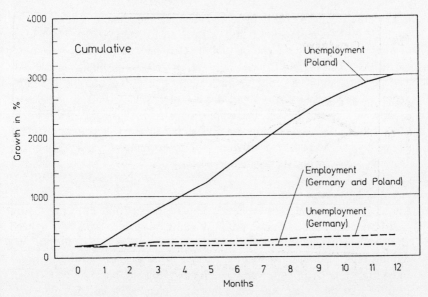

Figure 7.5a: Cumulative employment and unemployment indices in Germany and in Poland during the first twelve months after reforms

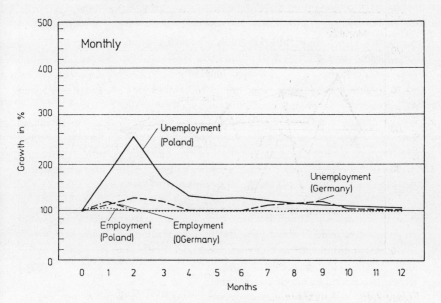

Figure 7.5b: Monthly employment and unemployment indices in Germany and in Poland during the first twelve months after reforms

Unemployment in Poland increased about 16 times and reached the level of 1,125,000 unemployed (40,000 in December, 1989), with the predicted number of 400,000 at the end of 1990. In Germany the unemployment level increased 2.7 times and reached the level of 760,000 unemployed. Moreover, the situation in the 1948 German labour market was abnormal with an influx of large groups of refugees from East Germany, Poland, the Soviet Union and Czechoslovakia. The employment index shows different tendencies; stabilization in Germany and decline in Poland. This pattern confirms the prior observation of a positive reform impact on the revitalization of the German economy and its negative impact in Poland.

Areas of better results in Poland
Foreign trade is an area of economic activity in which the Polish economy did substantially better than Germany. Figures 7.6a and b display the indices showing export and import activities in both countries during the first 12 months after reform as well as the balance of trade. Clearly reform stimulated foreign trade in both countries. Figures 7.6a and b show that German exports grew by 56 per cent, while those in Poland grew by 165.5 per cent. Imports grew by 25.9 per cent and 123 per cent respectively. The basic difference is evident in the balance of trade. In the case of Poland this balance was positive all year, except in January. In Germany the balance was positive all year with the exception of the last two months. Poland accumulated a $4.6 billion foreign trade surplus in trade with Western countries and 4.3 billion transferable rubles in trade with post-communist countries. In the comparable time, Germany accumulated a $970 million trade deficit, which was equalized by an international help programme. The main reason for such different tendencies was the different policies of the Erhard and Balcerowicz governments concerning the exchange rate.

The architects of German monetary reform believed that the exchange rate of the new currency against other currencies would, in principle, reflect relative prices prevailing at the time of the currency reform. Purchasing power parity of the Reichsmark at existing (official) prices was estimated at 3 RM per US dollar in 1937. Allowing for some likely increases in the price level after currency reform, the exchange rate of the Deutschemark was set at 3.33 DM per US dollar. Because of inflation, the exchange rate appeared to be too low, which caused pressure for a devaluation of 21 per cent which occurred 16 months after reform in November 1949. The rate was set at 4.2 DM per US dollar (at the same time the DM was revalued upwards against the British pound by about 14 per cent).

The overpriced Deutschmark supported larger imports and damaged German exports. During the first 12 months after reform, exports amounted to 1.0 billion dollars and imports amounted to 1.9 billion dollars with a deficit

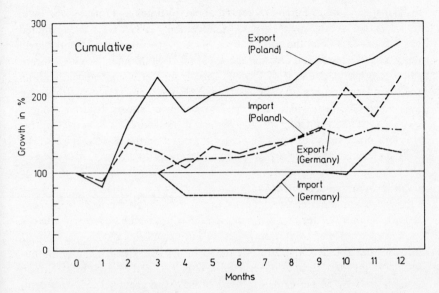

Figure 7.6a: Cumulative export and import results in Germany and in
Poland during the first twelve months after reforms

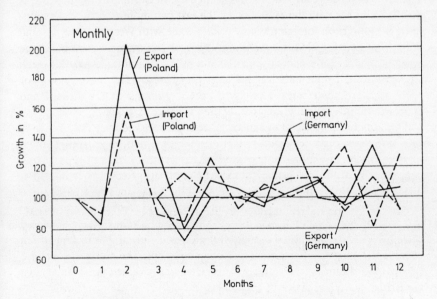

Figure 7.6b: Monthly export and import results in Germany and in
Poland during the first twelve months after reforms

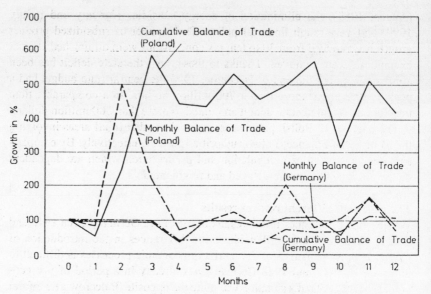

*Figure 7.7:   Cumulative and monthly balances of foreign trade in Ger-
many and in Poland during the first twelve months after
reforms*

of 900 million dollars. One year later, exports amounted to 1.4 billion
dollars while imports amounted to 2.3 billion with a repeated deficit of 900
million dollars (Salomon, 1954, p. 15). This deficit was covered by the allied
powers, most notably the United States within the framework of the GARIOA
(Government And Relief in Occupied Areas) programme and the Marshall
plan. The bulk of this financial support for the reconstruction of Germany
was transformed into non-repayable grants under the London debt agreement of 1953 which also dealt with the remaining debts of the Reich.

The effect of Balcerowicz's policy was quite the opposite. The fast devaluation of zloty in the last quarter of 1989 resulted in an overpriced dollar
and an underpriced zloty. The very high exchange rate of 9 500 zloties per
US dollar led the overly indebted Polish economy to a surplus in international trade. Within 12 months Poland accumulated a 4.6 billion dollar
surplus. (The amount predicted for the whole year was a deficit of about
$800 million.) In trade with post-communist countries, Poland achieved a
surplus of 4.3 billion in transferable rubles. The successes in stabilizing the
exchange rate of the zloty and international trade in Poland is thus comparable with the successes in the fight against inflation.

The Polish government's achievements in eliminating the state deficit is
also remarkable. This outcome required the elimination of food subsidies

(August 1989), the elimination of energy subsidies (January and 3 July 1990) and very tough financial policy. The number of subsidized product groups was reduced from 30 to ten; tax concessions were diminished and tax exemptions were removed. Thanks to these cuts, the state deficit has been eliminated, and at the end of December 1990 the central state budget had a positive balance of more than 1 700 million dollars. In a comparable time the German bi-zonal state deficit amounted to more than 500 million dollars.

The analysis of Polish policies seems to show that in all areas involving the Ministry of Finance, Polish authorities perform effectively. By comparison, decisions such as deregulation and privatization which are dependent on the political system are delayed and fragmented.

The causes of different reform results
Whether the differences in the results of reform in Germany circa 1946 and Poland circa 1990 are attributable to the differences in the introduction of the market mechanism or to the inertia of economic processes is difficult to interpret. In 1947 and 1948 Germany was already in a period of fast economic growth. Poland's situation was quite the opposite. Balcerowicz's reform started during a period of decline in both production and real wages. The official data for 1989 show that the production index for December 1989 was 11 per cent lower, employment 6 per cent lower, and coal production more than 20 per cent lower than the preceding year ('Z Materialow', No. 4, No. 29, 1990). Erhard's reform coincided with the all-European trend of post-war recovery growth, while the Balcerowicz reform arrived at the moment of a second wave of Polish crises. There is, of course, the further matter of data reliability. While the positive effects of Erhard's reform in 1948 were slightly overestimated, to some degree Poland's economic decline in the first half of 1990 is also overestimated.

It must also be remembered that the introduction of currency reform in Germany was widely anticipated: an 'open secret'. The only unknown was the day when it would happen. For example, Russian-sponsored presses in Berlin were publishing details about coming reform a fortnight before 20 June 1948, despite strict official secrecy on American and British sides ('Soviet', 1948). Expecting currency exchange, businesses hoarded large amounts of attractive goods. The *Schaufenstereffekt* (shop-window effect) of reform was a result of this hoarding. There were no such reserves of goods in the Polish economy at the end of 1989. Quite the opposite, the Soviets, because of their difficulties, had reduced their export of goods to Poland by about 50 per cent, which deepened the difficulties in the Polish supply situation.

Lessons from the German and Polish reforms

Lessons from Erhard's reform

The German experience suggests that currency reform alone does not guarantee success in making the transition to a market economy. Indeed, numerous monetary reforms in Central Europe between 1946 and 1953 had comparable results. Polish monetary reform in November 1950, although also modelled after the West German original, did not solve underlying problems and brought about renewed inflation two years later. Economic reform is therefore far more than an exchange of new money for old money at an arbitrarily determined exchange rate. It also implies a freezing of prices, a lowering of taxes on income, corporations, wealth and inheritances, and a liberalization of the business environment.

Any currency reform that involves a substantial and sudden reduction of monetary assets in the private sector essentially amounts to a partial or complete default by the public sector. This has far-reaching implications for the relationship between creditors and debtors in the economy at large. Therefore, measures are needed to compensate those who have suffered social hardship as a result of currency reform. The establishment of a 'burden equalization fund', or a promise of one, helps to gain social support for reform.

The German experience also demonstrates that international financial support for reconstruction is needed during the early years. This support, either in the form of credits or of non-repayable grants, helps in the comprehensive restructuring of the economy (Sachs and Lipton, 1990, p. 66).

The German experience also suggests that reform is a very slow-working recovery mechanism. At a minimum, a half-year period is necessary in order to observe the first positive economic results. It was Christmas in Germany when Erhard and his colleagues noted that imported geese were not selling; because other prices had started to fall ('Weihnachtsgeschaeft', 1948) consumers were saving instead of spending. Yet six months after reform the first beneficial effects were observable in Germany: there was a fall in the cost of living, declining inflation and a restoration of confidence in money.

The German experience shows also that money exchange does not automatically solve the inflation problem. Corrective inflation is unavoidable as a tool for reconstruction of a healthy price structure. The German example further shows that successful reform requires a prepared, thoroughly organized action plan. The German programme was thoroughly planned, well orchestrated, and carefully implemented within a broader programme for the country's economic restructuring. Reformers' implementation should depend on the political situation.

The German experience also shows that the introduction of reform is a political, as well as an economic endeavour. When reformers are confronted with political obstacles, even while possessing strategic goals, they have to make some political concession to the opposition to achieve the main goal. Such concessions were made in the reimposition of price control, promises granted in establishing the central price board, and in labelling the new system a 'social market economy' in spite of the fact that it introduced measures that had a monetaristic character.

Lessons from Balcerowicz's reform

Poland's actions show that it is easier to stabilize the financial situation and liberalize the economy than it is to make institutional changes. In other words, it is easier to restrain inflation than it is to demonopolize and privatize the state sector. The Polish experience also shows that the implementation of a healthy and convertible currency does not automatically solve restructuring problems. The clearly visible insufficiency of a market mechanism to institute system changes leads to a paradoxical situation where the central state administration forcibly introduces a market, but at the same time tries to refrain from force and from intervention in market processes. This, like socialist 'democratic centralism', is contradictory and requires a search for a delicate balance between directive and liberal actions.

The Polish case also reveals that reform requires strong social support. This support in Poland is guaranteed through the support of government actions by strong independent trade union movements (Erhard also received support from Theodor Blank and Hugo Karpf, Chairmen of the strongest trade union organizations in Germany). Paradoxically, this support (contrary to Germany) is not coming from organized groups of private producers such as farmers or craftsmen, who have already experienced operating in the market-place and who could especially benefit from a free market economy. Thanks to bureaucratic restrictions, these groups enjoy a privileged monopolistic position (strong barriers for new entrants and no competition), and real markets present them with new challenges.

The review of the 1948 events and the following years in Germany and the first 12 months of reforms in Poland illustrates that the stabilization of the economy by currency reform or by corrective inflation through price, wage and trade liberalization is only one stepping stone – albeit a very important one – to economic recovery. Another important factor is the presence of a population desperate for economic and political reconstruction. The last, but not least, factor is the presence of strong governments and strong personalities with a great vision, and with the power and courage to make decisions which may be unpopular with the public but prove effective in the long term.

Notes

1. This paper has been underwritten by the International Fellowship Programme for Advanced Soviet and East European Studies from Bundesinstitut fuer Ostwissentschaftliche und Internationale Studien in Koeln, West Germany, whose support is gratefully acknowledged. The author offers special thanks to Dr Alfred Schueller from Forschungsstelle zum Vergleich wirtschaftlicher Lenkungssysteme in Philipps University Marburg/Lahn, and Dr Helmut Wagner from Freie Universitaet Berlin for encouragement during this project and their support during research. The author wants also to express his gratitude to Dr Marek Dabrowski of the Polish Academy of Science (at that time Deputy Prime Minister of Finance), as well as to Dr Jane Thompson Follis from the University of Southern Indiana for comments and help in the preparation of this paper.
2. This package of laws contained the following: the law on employment and the law on termination of employment contracts, the law on economic activity with the participation of foreign parties (foreign investment law), the law on small business activity with the participation of foreign parties, the foreign exchange law, the customs law, the law on turnover tax, the law on taxation obligations, and the law on credit policy. Two of the laws passed concerned employment, four pertained to international relations, and five were connected to the new tax system. All related primarily to the financial side of state activity.
3. Hans Moeller (1961, p. 17) also discusses the option of overhang removal through a radical tax policy, increases in productivity, and excessive imports. Because of its slowness and low effectiveness, this option, though theoretically possible, was never considered in both analyses cases, and is not discussed here.
4. Option 3 was not taken into consideration because of its limited scope and political limitations (resistance of the employees in the state enterprises). On the contrary, the social-democratic-oriented local state governments were in the process of enacting nationalization decrees attempting to nationalize the heavy and coal mining industries. For example, such a nationalization of the coal mining industry in Ruhrgebiet was embarked upon by the government of Nordheim-Westfalen on 6 August 1948. These decrees from the allied powers' authorities were later regarded as invalid and their fulfilment was halted.
5. At that time Deputy Minister Marek Dabrowski seemed to share my opinion. In his 1990 paper in the weekly *Polityka*, when summarizing the first four months of reforms, he says 'Inflation was more quickly suppressed than it was commonly expected', in the first sentence.

Bibliography

Abelshauser, W. (1975), *Wirtschaft in Westdeutschland 1945–1948. Rekonstruktion und Wachstumbedingungen in der Amerikanischen und Britischen Zonen*, Stuttgart: Deutsche Verlags-Anstalt.

Abelshauser, W. (1983), *Wirtschaftsgeschichte der Bundesrepublik Deutschland (1945–1980)*, Frankfurt/Main: Suhrkamp.

Dabrowski, M. (1989), 'Coraz dalej od normalnosci', *Lad*, No. 17, April 17, p. 1.

Dabrowski M. (1990), "Trzeba jeszcze wytrwac." *Polityka*, No. 21, May 21, p. 1.

'Die Ruhlkohle wird sozialisiert', *Allgemeine Zeitung*, No. 129, August 7/8.

'Drittes Waehrungsgesetz der Militaerregierungen (Umstellungsgesetz)', *Frankfurter Rundschau*, June 26, 1948, p. 1.

Erhard, L. *Bundestagsreden*, Bonn: Hrsg. von Rainer Barzel, AZ Studio.

'Erstes Waehrungsgesetz der Militaerregierungen', *Frankfurter Rundschau*, (Gesetz No. 61), June 19, 1948, p. 1.

Hamel H. (1989), 'Ordnungspolitische Gestaltung der Wirtschaftssysteme', in: *Soziale Marktwirtschaft – Sozialistische Planwirtschaft*, 5th edn, Muenchen: Verlag Franz Wahlen, 25–58.

Informacja o przebiegu procesow gospodarczych w listopadzie 1990 r. Zespol Komitetu

Ekonomicznego Rady Ministrow ds. Monitorowania Gospodarki, Warszawa, December 15, 1990.

'Kohlengruben-Subventionen', *Frankfurter Rundschau*, No. 215, December 18, 1948, p. 5.

Laitenberger, W. (1986), *Ludwig Erhard. Der Nationaloekonom als Politiker*, Goettingen, Zuerich: Verlag Fisher.

'Lebenshaltungskosten Seit 1938 um 64 Prozent Gestiegen', *Frankfurter Rundschau*, July 1949, p. 2.

Mayer, T. and Thumann, G. (1990), 'Radical Currency Reform: Germany, 1948', *Finance & Development*, March 6–8.

'Moeglichkeiten und Grenzen einer liberalen Wirtschaftspolitik', *Neue Zuercher Zeitung*, No. 2672, December 14, 1948.

Moeller, H. (1961), *Zur Vorgeschichte der Deutschen Mark. Die Vaehrungsreformplaene 1945–1948*, Basel: Kyklos-Verlag Basel.

'Nach der Waehrungsreform in Westdeutschland. Die Merkmale der Uebergangsphase', *Neue Zuercher Zeitung*, July 7, 1948.

Office of Military Government for Germany (US), *Monthly Report*, No. 49, Statistical Annex: 1949.

'Privatization Law. Balcerowicz's Giant Leap', *The Warsaw Voice*, No. 91, July 22, 1990, p. 1.

'Robienie jajka z jajecznicy', Interview with Vice-Prime Minister Leszek Balcerowicz, *Gazeta Wyborcza*, February 19, 1990.

Roepke, W. (1948), 'Die Krise der Zahlungsbilanzen', *Neue Zuercher Zeitung*, August 7, No. 1402, 1–2.

'Rzad oglosil programme gospodarczy. Glowne zalozenia i kierunki', *Rzeczpospolita*, No. 239, October 13, 1989.

Sachs, J. and Lipton, D. (1990), 'Poland's Economic Reform', *Foreign Affairs*, Summer, **69**, (3), 47–66.

Salomon, R. (1954), *Begriff und Problematik der Wirtschaftlichen Engpaesse*, Kiel: Verlag Wirtschaft.

Schueller, A. (1975), 'Die Wirtschaftsordnung der Republik Deutschland und Ihre Strukturbedingungen', *Wirtschaftspolitische Chronik*, Heft 2, Kiel: Institut fuer Wirtschaftspolitik an der Universitaet Kiel.

Schueller, A. (1988), 'Die Verschuldungskrise als Ordnungsproblem. Plaedeoyer fuer eine vertrauensbildende Entwicklungspolitik', *Neue Zuercher Zeitung*, No. 158, July 10–11.

'Soviet "Isolates" Berlin From Western Zone After Currency Reform Announcement', *The Christian Science Monitor*, June 19, Boston, 1948.

'Weihnachtsgeschaeft leicht enttaeuschend', *Frankfurter Rundschau*, December 24, 1948.

Wiederaufbau im Zeichen des Marschallplanes 1948–1952, Bundesministerium fuer den Marschallplan. Bonn, 1953.

Wuensche, H. G. (1986), *Ludwig Erhards Gesellschafts- und Wirtschaftskonzeptionen*, Bonn: Verlag Bonn Actuell.

'Z materialow GUS', *Zycie Gospodarcze*, No. 4, January 28, 1990 and No. 29, July 22, 1990.

'Z materialow GUS i NBP', *Zycie Gospodarcze*, No. 21, May 27, 1990.

8 The political economy of transitions to market economies

*Mark Knell**

Introduction

The most important element in the transition between a centrally planned and a market-oriented economy is the creation of a 'goal-adequate' enabling environment. If the object of the transition is to introduce a new structure of production that provides a higher standard of living, then an appropriate social structure and macroeconomic environment are necessary for the transition to the new regime. For many of the governments in Eastern Europe and the IMF this has meant austere monetary, fiscal and exchange rate policies, and a reduction in the role of the state. Unambiguous evidence proving that this type of an enabling environment is appropriate for the transition process, however, is lacking. While there has been some improvement in the industrial structure of many of these economies, 'creative' market responses have not been as widespread as expected. This paper argues that an important reason why the economic environment is inadequate for the transition process is the political economy of development adopted by the IMF and applied in the standby arrangements made with the Eastern European countries and the former Soviet Union.

Many believe there is a 'consensus' that the IMF (and World Bank) view of the development process is the only one that promotes stability and growth. Some, including J. Sachs and R. Dornbusch, have even described deviations from policy recommendations of the IMF as 'populist experiments' – a rather unfortunate term that implies that policies that deviate from this 'new orthodoxy' are unsound and simply reflect the inability of the population to decide what is best for it. While many of the 'populist experiments' do not have sound economic theory supporting them, some do. This paper will take a similar view as the WIDER study in development economics led by L. Taylor (1988) but will emphasize the importance of a political economy of transition. Because the rapidly rising unemployment in Eastern European economies reflects a number of different factors, 'heterodox' stabilization policies that place more emphasis on Keynesian economics would work better than the IMF policy recommendations based on the new classical-monetarist view of the economy. This, however, requires a new view of political economy that can handle the problems transition economies face.

This paper also takes the position that the IMF is the most important influence on the transition economies. This does not mean that personalities such as J. Sachs, L. Balcerowicz, V. Klaus and so on have not played an important role in determining the transition programme, but that IMF conditionality requirements dominate whether it is compatible with the programmes or not. The paper progresses in the following way. The first two sections outline the conditionality requirements of the IMF and the subsequent results. Section 4 takes a critical view of this approach using China as an example. Section 5 stresses the need for a 'goal-adequate' macroeconomic environment restructuring the transition economies. Section 6 provides an alternative political economy of transition to the IMF approach. Finally, Section 7 stresses the need for an industrial policy in Eastern Europe.

IMF conditionality in Eastern Europe

The IMF was able to assert itself in Eastern Europe because of an urgent need for financial and technical assistance. However, to obtain assistance these countries must sign a 'stand-by' agreement that stipulates the conditions to obtain credit. On the surface these conditions simply reflect the need for the Fund to remain solvent. In reality the underlying theoretical framework applied in the various member countries created a tendency towards the uniformity of transition strategies and general economic decline.

The tendency towards conformity of transition strategies reflects the inflexibility of the stand-by arrangements. While most economists prefer to classify transition strategies according to whether they are 'shock therapy' or 'gradualist', there is a convergence of transition strategies between different Eastern European countries in sequencing the transition. Agreements signed with Poland and Hungary in early 1990, for example, call for similar austere measures to reduce internal and external balances and to speed up the process of restructuring, reforming and liberalizing the economy. Differences exist, of course, but they are at the starting point of the transition process: Hungary has had a history of restructuring, reforming and liberalizing the economy since 1968, while Poland continued to preserve the centrally planned economy. By 1991, price liberalization was 90 per cent complete in Poland and 92 per cent complete in Hungary.

The reason there is a conformity of transition strategies is that a typical Eastern European stand-by arrangement calls for a rapid and comprehensive transformation of the centrally planned economy into a market-oriented one. The IMF has an almost unmitigated belief in the ability of the market mechanism to solve all economic problems. It relies heavily on the spontaneity of market forces, and views the potential collapse of state enterprises as part of the 'purifying' (or *Reinigung* as Hayek called it) process of competition. Indeed, Caselli and Pastrello (1991) may have been right to argue that the kernel of the 'shock therapy' strategy overemphasizes 'the spontaneity of market forces in overwhelming depression'. The repeated praise for the transition strategy by 'the group of 24' in the IMF affirms the toughness of this belief in the market mechanism amidst depression.

At the same time there is an irony in the Eastern European IMF programmes. The rapid transition strategy is supposed to create a macroeconomic environment in which markets clear more or less continuously, and prices provide all the necessary information for a rational allocation of resources. By creating this environment, the expectation is that behaviours and motivations change in such a way that these economies will gravitate naturally towards a stable, full employment path of economic growth, and that there will be a rapid diffusion of innovation through foreign and domestic investment. At the same time, the IMF stabilization programmes *assumed* that the Eastern European economies already had markets that function in this way. In reality there was a lack of market mechanisms, knowledge of available technologies, flexibility in production, and competition. Moreover, credit markets are rudimentary and capital markets do not exist. And even if there was complete price liberalization, most markets would be monopolistic or oligopolistic. In other words, the IMF assumes things that do not exist and they strive for things that cannot exist.

The IMF clearly puts stabilization before growth. While growth is important to the IMF, the objective of a stabilization programme is to *prepare* the macroeconomic environment for structural change. It is for this reason that the IMF views rapid deregulation of domestic and export sector prices and privatization (as much as feasibly possible) as first priority in the transition strategy. However, because chronic shortages of consumer and producer goods and lengthened construction periods of plant and equipment were characteristic of the macroeconomic environment before the collapse of communism, there was a considerable amount of unabsorbed excess demand (and excess money overhang). This required a stabilization programme to absorb excess effective demand released during rapid price liberalization. In Poland, for example, prices initially rose because of the chronic shortages, but later cascaded throughout the system because of distribution conflict and the pricing behaviour of enterprises. To the government and the IMF the 'hyper-inflation' occurred because of an excess supply of money created by the central bank.

The monetarist–new classical view provides theoretical justification for policy recommendations by the IMF. Because of misperceived expectations, monetarists argue that inflation is the primary cause of economic disturbances, including falling output and rising unemployment. Because the quantity theory of money holds, an increase in the money supply leads only to proportionately higher prices and complete crowding-out of private investment by government spending if expectations are fulfilled. Unemployment may appear when there is poor information about vacancies, a high wage rate, or other obstructions in the labour market, but in the long run it does not exist. Policy recommendations, therefore, discourage fiscal policy to stimulate the economy and encourage the use of monetary policy to create an optimal economic environment for structural change.

The IMF stabilization effort is focused on controlling the growth rate of the money supply, balancing the fiscal budget and reducing government expenditures. The severity of the austere policies depends, however, to a large extent on the inflation rate. This is the main reason why the Polish stabilization programme appears more austere than the Hungarian one. It is also for this reason that the IMF emphasized money supply restrictions in Poland and the budget deficit in Hungary. In both cases, however, the objective is to reduce inflation through the constriction of demand. However, as demand constricted, a highly unstable, goal-inadequate macroeconomic environment was created in Eastern Europe.

IMF conditionality and cumulative decline in Eastern Europe

The austere stand-by agreements of the IMF created a macroeconomic environment that led to cumulative decline. These developments were very different from those expected. During the first year of the stabilization programme in Poland, industrial output fell 23.3 per cent and the unemployment rate rose to 6.1 per cent. This was a considerable difference from the 5 per cent decline in industrial output and 2 per cent unemployment rate expected. The 585 per cent inflation rate was five times the expected rate (Kolodko, 1991).

Table 8.1: Output and investment growth in Eastern Europe: 1989–1991

	Industrial output			Gross fixed investment		
	1989	1990	1991	1989	1990	1991
Bulgaria	2.2	−14.1	−27.3	−10.1	−12.0	−49.3
Czechoslovakia	0.8	−3.7	−23.1	1.6	3.0	−36.0
ex-GDR *Länder*	2.3	−28.0	−50*	0.9	−5.7	6.1*
Hungary	−2.5	−5.0	−19.1	0.5	−8.7	−11.0
Poland	−0.5	−23.3	−11.9	−2.4	−8.0	−8.0
Romania	−2.1	−19.8	−18.7	−1.6	−35.0	−16.8
Yugoslavia	0.9	−10.3	−20.7	0.5	−7.0	−

*Based on first six months.
Source: United Nations, *Economic Survey of Europe in 1991–1992*, pp. 61 and 64.

Table 8.1 shows these cumulative declines. Indeed, the United Nations (1992) was right to point out that economic events in Eastern Europe are leading to another 'Great Depression'. However, even during the 1930s, output and employment levels did not fall in Western Europe and North America as rapidly as they have in Eastern Europe during the last year and a half. In 1990 industrial output fell in Eastern Europe by 17.5 per cent on average, and in 1991 it declined another 19.1 per cent (ibid., p. 59). The consequence is a rapidly rising unemployment rate: as of January 1992 the rate was 15.2 per cent in the ex-GDR Länder, 11.9 per cent in Poland, 6.9 per cent in Czechoslovakia and 9.2 per cent in Hungary. The reason unemployment rates have not risen as rapidly as the industrial decline is partly due to the appearance of part-time labour, enterprises continuing to finance redundant labour, informal credit markets, and the appearance of a new secondary market hidden from statistics. Nevertheless, at the end of 1991 the ratio of unemployment to unfilled vacancies was 29:1 in the ex-GDR Länder, 44:1 in Poland, 9:1 in Czechoslovakia and 28:1 in Hungary (ibid., pp. 68–9). This indicates that much of the unemployment in Eastern Europe may be involuntary, not simply a problem of skills mismatches as is common when technological unemployment exists. Actually, both demand and structural factors are playing a role in the determination of unemployment in Eastern Europe, but in a way different from Western experience.

Perhaps the most alarming statistic is the rapid decline in gross investment. Granted that the accumulation ratio was unreasonably high in the shortage economy, a transition of the magnitude described requires large infusions of new capital and therefore investment. However, in Eastern Europe, gross fixed investment declined 13.7 per cent in 1990 and 22.7 per cent in 1991 (ibid., p. 59). These declines indicate that the macroeconomic environment is not goal-adequate. Although a stable macroeconomic environment is crucial for a successful transition from a centrally planned economy to a market-oriented one, it is difficult to sustain that these declines in output and investment simply reflect the structural change necessary to create a competitive economy, as economists advocating 'austerity' measures often argue.

Data also indicate a decline in real wages, labour productivity and profitability. Table 8.2 shows that real wages declined in Poland by almost 30 per cent during the first quarter of 1990, and with the exception of the fourth quarter of 1991, continued to decline through 1991 and the first half of 1992.[1] Investment also declined perhaps because of declining effective demand and profitability. Similar declines are observed in Hungary, though more gradual and not as deep. Even if these trends reverse during 1992 as the IMF suggests, the precipitous declines of the previous two and a half years will make it all the more difficult to increase the standard of living of eastern Europeans to that of western Europeans.

Table 8.2: Main indicators in Poland (percentage change against preceding quarter)

		average real wage	Investment[a]	Average profit rate[b]	Consumer prices
1990	I	–29.7	–8.8	36.0	149.2
	II	2.1	–13.0	33.0	23.0
	III	6.0	–13.0	31.6	10.5
	IV	20.0	–10.1	29.4	15.3
1991	I	–9.4	–13.4	8.3	23.0
	II	–8.3	–12.6	6.7	11.7
	III	–1.3	–10.0	6.0	6.1
	IV	4.8	–4.4	4.8	9.8
1992	I	–9.0	–	3.5	12.1
	II	–2.0	–1.6	3.3	9.1

[a] corresponding quarter of previous year.
[b] based on cost of production in 1990 and cost of total income in 1991.

Source: Biuletyn statystyczny, July 1991 and July 1992.

It is also difficult to sustain that IMF policies have been entirely successful in stabilizing prices in the Eastern European economies. In particular, the IMF makes the claim on the basis of the monetarist–new classical view that a 'low' inflation rate is necessary to the transition process. However, inflation rates continued to be high in many Eastern European countries throughout 1991. According to the United Nations (1992, p. 93) the average annual inflation rate in 1991 was 70.3 per cent in Poland, 57.9 per cent in Czechoslovakia, and 35 per cent in Hungary. Perhaps the institutional framework underlying these economies can support this inflation, but given that these economies have experienced very little inflation since 1949, this is highly improbable. Ironically, the only discernible result of the IMF strategy is the rapid elimination of shortages.

An excuse the IMF and some shock therapy advocates give for why the economy has moved less smoothly than anticipated is the inability to privatize state enterprises quickly. They argue that it is impossible to create appropriate motivations and behaviours if the enterprises remain owned by the state. However, the real problem behind the monetarist-new classical view is that there is a relatively rigid set of institutional and behavioural assumptions with continuous market clearing. It is highly doubtful that these assumptions are realistic in view of the rigidities of modern industrial structures and the diversity of individual motivations, expectations and behaviours. If this doubt should prove to be appropriate, then policies intended to reshape the environment may lead to certain undesired structural changes.

The macroeconomic environment in China

While many Eastern European economies following IMF policy recommendations converted from a resource-constrained economy to a demand-constrained economy almost overnight, the Chinese economy has been moving in this direction gradually. What makes the Chinese case interesting is that excess effective demand was essential to the macroeconomic environment. Instead of eliminating excess demand through an austerity programme, the Chinese used an existing law which permitted limited private ownership to encourage the creation of a second economy. The results were remarkable. The growth rate approached 12 per cent and was never negative. Between 1985 and 1989, the rate of growth of investment ranged from 39 per cent in 1985 to −7 per cent in 1989. Most of this growth is attributed to the second economy (Knell and Yang, 1992).

Ironically, the case against 'gradualism' was made by Lipton and Sachs because of the existence of legal and illegal second economies. According to Lipton and Sachs (1990, p. 90), second economies are created in a shortage economy by 'arbitrageurs who buy output at the official price and sell it at a 'grey' (legal) or 'black' (illegal) market price'. Moreover, they believe that the queue of buyers in a shortage economy is made up of these arbitrageurs.

Entrepreneurs, namely, individuals or villages and township collectives creating new enterprises *producing* goods for which individuals normally queue, dominate the second economy in China. Even if there are no queues or price-distorting subsidies, these entrepreneurs often enter a market because they have lower costs or better products. Although there are arbitrage activities, especially among new private urban enterprises, the majority engage in production.

The key to understanding the nature of the second economy, irrespective of whether enterprises are legal or not, is to distinguish between two types of second economy. On the one hand, a second economy can be created to engage primarily in arbitraging activities through which certain demands can be satisfied by reallocating existing resources. On the other hand, second economies can also be created to engage in production that absorbs the slack in a shortage economy. In other words, it becomes a question of whether price or quantity is the primary adjustment mechanism in a shortage economy. For Lipton and Sachs (1990, p. 92) 'excess demand is dissipated by waiting in lines, and overall utility is reduced accordingly'. This amounts to saying that people are able and willing to purchase goods in the second economy at higher prices because it reduces the time spent in queues, *provided* this time has a monetary value. Indeed, Lipton and Sachs neglect some important differences in price and quantity adjustment mechanisms and what Baumol (1990) described as productive and unproductive entrepreneurial activity.

The classical economists understood the distinction between price and quantity well. Adam Smith (1776, pp. 74–5) observed:

> The quantity of every commodity brought to market naturally suits itself to the effectual demand....[if] the quantity brought to market should at any time fall short of the effectual demand, some of the component parts of its price must rise above their natural rate.... If it is wages or profit, the interest of all other labourers and dealers will soon prompt them to employ more labour and stock in preparing and bringing it to market. The quantity brought thither will soon be sufficient to supply the effectual demand.

An application of this insight to the dual economy of China would require the inclusion of three prices: the market price, the administered price and the natural price. Because there are chronic shortages, the market price will normally be above the administered price. Under these circumstances, even if the administered price is above the natural price, there is an incentive to enter the market provided there are no significant barriers to entry, inclusive of the right to own private property. Because the market price is above the natural price, private entrepreneurs will increase total supply, gradually forcing the market price downwards. If the administered price is above the natural price, then planners will lower the price. If the administered price is below the natural price, then a shortage gap and budget gap will create an incentive to raise the price. Eventually, all three prices will converge, forcing state enterprises to compete in the market. In China, the ratio of free market prices to state prices has narrowed from 270 to 112 between 1962 and 1989, and approximately 65 per cent of agricultural commodity prices and 55 per cent of consumer good prices were market-determined in 1991.[2] Moreover, in 1991 the share of industrial output provided by state enterprises fell to 45.6 per cent.[3] The consequence has been a gradual gravitation towards the natural price through the second economy.

A key element in this strategy is the maintenance of excess effective demand. By having this excess demand, there is an incentive to enter the industry and sell goods at a price higher than the natural rate, allowing the new entrepreneur to make higher than average profits. These higher than average profits encourage other entrepreneurs to enter the industry or existing ones to expand production. To ensure that entrepreneurial activity is predominantly productive, the Chinese encouraged private initiative and used quotas when necessary. This is very different from IMF policies. Instead of increasing supply, the IMF strategy essentially reduced demand before allowing the quantities brought to market to increase. This put the Eastern

European economies in cumulative decline, making it more difficult to move onto a new higher path of economic growth.

Another important element in the Chinese case is the *creation* of a private sector. Contrary to the IMF view that state enterprises must be privatized, China created a macroeconomic environment that encouraged entrepreneurship. It was in this context that individuals and collectives *learned* how to be entrepreneurs and to contrive their own creative market responses, often to the detriment of the state sector. Evidence suggests that a small private sector is emerging in Eastern Europe through the creation of small business and small-scale privatization, but not to the same extent as in China. Unfortunately for the IMF, most of these enterprises are engaging in arbitrage activities, not production.

Cumulative causation and the macroeconomic environment
The decline in output and productivity observed in Eastern Europe is a consequence of the macroeconomic environment. By contracting demand, the IMF has set into motion economic forces that strengthen the continuous process of decline in a cumulative way. As domestic and international effective demand decreases, labour productivity falls. This creates a macroeconomic environment in which there is a reduction in competitiveness, a deterrent to investment and entrepreneurship, and additional difficulties in privatizing state enterprises. The result is a further decrease in effective demand.

The notion of cumulative causation is an explanation of economic growth as a process that involves technological progress and effective demand. Looking through the principle of effective demand, N. Kaldor (1967) provided new insights on A. Smith's (1776) observation that 'the division of labour – cause of the increased productive powers of labour – is limited by the extent of the market'. Using these new insights, Kaldor has shown that it is difficult, if not impossible, to restructure an economy without sufficient effective demand. As effective demand increases, labour productivity rises, encouraging the adoption of new process and product technologies. This increases competitiveness, creating a better macroeconomic environment for the creation of new enterprises and the privatization of state enterprises. The result is a further increase in effective demand. In other words, 'the growth of markets is determined by the growth of markets', as A. Young (1928) phrased it.

Effective demand growth is necessary for the adoption of new process and product technologies. As Schmookler (1966) argued, effective demand growth induces, to a large extent, investment in new technologies, incremental investment and research and development. Effective demand, therefore, is not only a problem for employment, output and prices, but also for growth and technological change. Indeed, the tendency towards structural stagnation in

Eastern Europe is a manifestation of the cumulative declines in effective demand and associated dynamic economies of scale. Moreover, relatively cheap labour may not be sufficient to attract foreign investors in Eastern Europe. A small domestic market often deters investors, especially those looking for long-run growth and stability. This is especially true for manufacturing, where dynamic economies of scale and backward and forward linkages to other parts of the economy are strongest. A strong domestic market coupled with foreign demand has been crucial for East Asian growth and development. Under current conditions in Eastern Europe, it is doubtful that there is sufficient domestic demand such as in East Asia, given the low wage levels.

Economic growth is also a learning process. From this perspective economic growth appears as an 'evolutionary' process of 'creative destruction' in which old technologies are discarded and replaced with new ones. This process tends to be cumulative as it depends on market demand and previous knowledge. Thus, technological change is a learning process that emanates from the interaction between users and producers in an appropriate macroeconomic environment. In this environment, creative entrepreneurial activities give rise to 'incremental and cumulative changes to products, processes and organizations' (Kozul-Wright, 1992, see also Dosi, 1988).

In the transition economies the learning process is complicated further by the need to reform the institutional (or social) structure. Because the centrally planned economy impaired 'the kinds of institutional routines and linkages required to support interactive learning', developing institutions conducive to innovation and entrepreneurship will be difficult and time-consuming (Kozul-Wright, 1992). A. Wood (1990) expressed a similar thought in a commentary on China:

> It is necessary to distinguish between nominal reform, meaning official policy initiatives, and real reform, meaning changes in how the economy actually works. Nominal reform can contribute to real reform (price decontrol being an example), but does not do so if it outstrips microeconomic learning capacity. In other words, the real pace of reform may be limited by how rapidly people and institutions can learn to play new economic roles.

The essence of this remark is that legislative (nominal) reforms may surpass the learning capacity of individuals. This indicates that the social structure may act as an important constraint on the transition process. In China, for example, there has been no significant legislative reform since 1985, but real reform continued because individuals were unable to translate legislative reforms into real reforms quickly: the creation of the Shanghai stock market in 1990 is but one example. Hence, there is reason to expect that behaviour will be similar in Eastern Europe.

Towards a political economy of transition

The notion of cumulative causation suggests that there is a need for an applicable political economy of transition. While the IMF and World Bank can be commended for not simply treating the transition process as a technical issue, their emphasis on a new classical–monetarist basis for political economy is not commendable. As already mentioned above, the problem behind this approach is that there is a relatively rigid set of institutional and behavioural assumptions with continuous market clearing. Adolph Lowe criticized these rigid assumptions many years ago and suggested an alternative political economy that can, together with economic theory, address these problems.

The best way to think of the transition from a centrally planned to a market-oriented economy is as a *traverse* from one growth path to another. From this perspective, the instrumental–deductive method of Lowe (1965) provides the best methodological foundation for a political economy of transition. In Lowe's view, public controls are necessary for the attainment of democratically selected macro-goals and the maintenance of social, political and economic freedom. Instrumental analysis, therefore, formalizes the design of public controls to establish an 'environment' in which behaviours and motivations are consistent with the desired growth path or macro-goal. This analysis identifies a 'goal-adequate' transition path that optimizes the use of available technology, subject to certain social, cultural and technical constraints. Thus, both public control and freedom are complementary and necessary conditions for transitions from centrally planned to market economies.

The object of instrumental analysis is to *'search for the economic means suitable for the attainment of any stipulated end'* (Lowe, 1976, pp. 11–12). Instrumental analysis inverts the new classical–monetarist approach to political economy by treating the desired future structure as given and treating some of the known data as unknown. The instrumental approach presupposes three kinds of data: (1) the initial state of the economic system; (2) the macro-goal or terminal state of the economic system (specified either by stipulating numerical values for target variables or by stipulating qualitative interrelations among the target variables); and (3) certain laws, rules and empirical generalizations. Given these data, the following unknowns can be determined: '(1) the *path* or the succession of macro-states of the system suitable to transform a given initial state into a stipulated terminal state; (2) *patterns of micro-behaviour* appropriate to keeping the system to the suitable path; (3) *micro-motivations* capable of generating suitable behaviour; and (4) *a state of the environment* including possibly, though not necessarily, political controls designed to stimulate suitable motivations' (Lowe, 1987, p. 176).

The reversal of the means–ends nexus creates a distinction between the structural and behavioural components of an economic system. Unlike in new classical–monetarist political economy, this distinction allows for structural analysis *before* behavioural or 'force' analysis. This does not mean that behavioural analysis can be ignored. It simply means that it is important to define the social and technical context before introducing behavioural aspects that may cloud the problem.

Structural relations operate as constraints on the motion of economic systems and the range of feasible paths between economic systems. Because the technical relations of production are the same in all economic systems, it becomes necessary to make a distinction between social and technical relations. The 'technical structure' describes the production of commodities by means of commodities. In other words, the technical structure refers to the existing technology and feasible technological possibilities of adapting the economy's capital stock to the requirements of the desired terminal state. For Lowe, the existing capital stock is the main structural barrier to short-term adjustments in the path of growth. A change in the path of growth can result from a change in technology. This requires the liquidation of part of the old capital stock and the formation of a new capital stock, as well as time and financing. As this process takes place, technological unemployment and sectoral imbalances will appear in the short period, and may persist in the long period unless an appropriate economic environment that will lead to full employment of labour and capital exists.

Underlying the technical structure of production is a 'receipt–expenditure structure' that relates aggregate monetary demand with aggregate monetary supply (Lowe, 1976, p. 86). Embodying the principle of effective demand, the interdependence of the production–receipt–expenditure relationship defines the relationship between physical and monetary flows. However, physical relations are conceptually different from monetary relations because 'the validity of these physical relations transcends the socio-political differences of economic systems' (ibid., p. 42). Likewise, monetary relations, such as those between wages and profits, are dependent upon the supporting social structure of the economic system.

The 'social structure' refers to the institutional framework in which decision-making processes take place. The institutional framework consists of the following components: (1) the industrial organization (including market forms and labour organizations); (2) the financial intermediaries (including instruments of money, credit and capital markets); (3) the legal system (including property rights and other legal codes); (4) the social system (including the health care system, the educational system and the welfare system); and (5) the historical context (including cultural and ethical-religious traditions). While it is possible to assess a growth path without reference to

the institutional arrangements, institutions may act as an important constraint to the transition path. In other words, a goal-adequate structural
adjustment path must be both technically and socially feasible.

A goal-adequate traverse requires knowledge of the patterns of micro-
behaviour, motivations and the state of the environment (which includes,
inter alia, monetary, fiscal, industrial and environmental policy instruments)
which sustain the economic system. For Lowe (1976, p. 17), 'these patterns
themselves are closely related to the prevailing social structure that defines
the institutional framework within which economic activity is to operate'.
Economic policies that intend to overcome unemployment and sectoral imbalances must, therefore, engender appropriate behavioural and motivational
responses.

The institutional arrangements play a particularly important role in transition economies. There is no difference between centrally planned and market
economies in structural analysis at the technical level. It is the social structure
that engenders different motivations and behavioural patterns. The institutional
framework is of particular importance in transition economies because of the
perception that the existing social structure is a constraint on the growth
path. Evidence that the Soviet Union was unable to sustain an intensive
growth path supports this perception (Knell and Rider, 1992).

It is possible to calculate the requirements necessary to maintain a prevailing structure or to achieve a different one without making assumptions about
motivations, expectations or other behavioural responses. Inclusion of the
institutional framework identifies the set of feasible adjustment paths. The
analysis is further extended by asking what is the most appropriate institutional
framework for the optimal structural adjustment path. An analysis of this
type expands the set of feasible adjustment paths, but may require additional
time for behaviours and motivations to respond to the institutional reforms.
Indeed, an important element in restructuring the centrally planned economies is to introduce a new range of feasible growth paths by rewriting laws
and introducing new institutions.

A traverse from one growth path to another necessarily requires an analysis of speed, sequencing and restructuring – all crucial issues for the transition
economies. However, unlike the analysis by Lipton and Sachs (1990), speci-
fication of the future structure of the economy required in this approach to
political economy that institutional changes be viewed as *instrumental* to the
achievement of clearly specified macro-goals. This is not simply a matter of
setting a goal of increasing the living standards of all Eastern Europeans, but
a matter of determining what types of public controls and institutions are
necessary to achieve this goal. In other words, what kind of economy do
Eastern Europeans want? Indeed, the steps towards establishing the necessary

institutional arrangements for such a controlled market system should be made at an early stage of the transformation process.

After determining the desired terminal state, the structural path of adjustment progresses through a sequence of macro-states. In this context an important question is whether privatization of state industries is a necessary perquisite for restructuring or vice versa. An analysis of this type would require knowledge of motivations and behaviours in their social contexts. Given the complexity of the situation, incentive patterns will probably not improve very much with privatization, especially if the enterprise is large. Moreover, rapid privatization might encourage what Baumol (1990) described as 'destructive entrepreneurship'. As the case of China illustrates, the creation of new enterprises is what is important, not the privatization of existing state enterprises. Indeed, the Chinese case also illustrates that it is possible to implement a set of public controls that channels excess demand generated by chronic shortages towards the private sector.

The need for industrial policy in Eastern Europe

Restructuring the formerly centrally planned economies is the ultimate goal of the transition process. Because of the enormous magnitude of the restructuring process in Eastern Europe, effective demand and public controls become crucial. This requires changing the nature of the state to embrace incentive-based planning instead of directive-based planning, and democracy instead of despotism. In other words, the state must play a new role in creating a new 'national system of innovation'.

Restructuring the transition economies requires a massive infusion of new capital and knowledge. As McKinnon (1991) has shown, much of the capital stock in these economies is not viable at any world market price, especially in manufacturing. On this basis it is easy to jump to the conclusion that these economies do not have a comparative advantage in these industries. However, it is possible to determine which industries have a potential comparative advantage and the time needed to upgrade the technology, given the technical and social constraints. This may require softening the 'budget' constraint to make available credit, subsidies, and so on for investment.

The IMF believes that the state should play a diminishing role in the transformation of the new structure. The Fund does not, however, adequately take into account that manufacturing is more conducive to dynamic economies of scale, and that the learning process may be long and arduous. This implies that the state must play an active role in the transition economies through the creation of an industrial policy. There are many examples in East Asia where the state was essential in creating new industries, providing investment subsidies and in promoting entrepreneurship both in the public and private spheres.

The introduction of comprehensive industrial and strategic trade policies is part of the national system of innovation, and thus the macroeconomic environment. Because the macroeconomic environment is critical for the transition process, industrial and strategic trade policies must be co-ordinated with fiscal, monetary and incomes policies. Assuming that all of the economies in transition want to be on a growth path leading to a higher standard of living than the previous growth path was capable of, then an appropriate macroeconomic environment must encourage technological change. To do this, however, there must be motivation to invest in these technologies and learn how to use them. Moreover, because the transition economies are going through a transition from autarky to free trade, then comparative advantage becomes important to the choice of technique problem.

The speeding up of the cumulative decline of the Eastern European economies can be blamed to a large extent on policies emanating from monetarist and new classical economics. The austere economic policies implemented throughout Eastern Europe neglect effective demand problems and the need to set up comprehensive industrial and strategic trade policies. As a consequence, they have neglected two of the most important determinants of economic growth. Indeed, it is the opinion of the IMF and the World Bank that austere stabilization policies be implemented in Eastern Europe *before* structural reform can be implemented. Unfortunately, there will be little structural change after the austerity programme.

In Lowe's political economy radical 'social decontrol and economic *laissez-faire*' would not be a solution to the cumulative declines observed in Eastern Europe. Instead, it is a question of balancing freedom and order. While it is clear that the communist state was unable to balance freedom and order, it is highly unlikely that the rapid movement towards the free market proposed by the IMF would bring much improvement. Adopting a theory which presumes an automatic gravitation towards the full employment of labour and capital is one mistake, and the unwillingness of the IMF to recognize different attitudes and behaviours is another. The idea of balancing freedom and order requires an active role for the state in guiding the transition from a centrally planned economy to a market-oriented one. Otherwise the transition economies are sure to be an economic system in travail for a long time to come.

Notes

* This paper was written while a visiting scholar at the University of Graz, Austria and was presented at the Vienna Institute for Comparative Economic Studies in July 1992. Tables were updated in November 1992. Comments from Christian Gehrke, Heinz Kurz, Ingrid Rima, Gunther Tichy, Wenyan Yang and the Vienna Institute are gratefully acknowledged.
1. Similarly labour productivity fell 20.8 per cent during the first quarter 1990 and fell 13.4

and 10.2 per cent during the first two quarters of 1991 indicating significant labour hoarding.
2. *Statistical Yearbook of China*, 1990 and *US News and World Report*, 27 May 1991, respectively.
3. The *Financial Times*, 7 January 1992.

Bibliography

Baumol, W.J. (1990), 'Entrepreneurship: Productive, Unproductive, and Destructive', *Journal of Political Economy*, **98**, 893–921.
Caselli, G.P. and Pastrello, G. (1991), 'Poland: From Plan to Market Through Crash?', in P. Havlik (ed.), *Dismantling the Command Economy in Eastern Europe*, Boulder: Westview Press.
Dosi, G. et al. (1988), *Technical Change and Economic Theory*, London: Pinter Publishers.
Gehrke, C. and Knell, M. (1992), 'Transitions from Centrally Planned to Market Economies', in Knell and Rider (1992).
Hagemann, H. and Kurz, H. (1990), 'Balancing Freedom and Order: On Adolph Lowe's Political Economics', *Social Research*, **57**, 733–53.
International Monetary Fund, *IMF Survey*, various issues.
Kaldor, N. (1967), *Strategic Factors in Economic Development*, Ithaca: Cornell University Press.
Knell, M. and Rider, C. (1992), *Socialist Economies in Transition: Appraisals of the Market Mechanism*, Aldershot: Edward Elgar.
Knell, M. and Yang, W. (1992), 'Lessons from China on a Strategy for the Socialist Economies in Transition', in Knell and Rider (1992).
Kolodko, G. (1991), 'Transition from Socialism and Stabilization Policies: The Polish Experience', *Rivista di Economia Politica*, June.
Kozul-Wright, R. (1992), 'Entrepreneurship and Institutional Reform in the Transition Economies', unpublished paper.
Lipton, D. and Sachs, J. (1990), 'Creating a Market Economy in Eastern Europe: The Case of Poland', *Brookings Papers on Economic Activity*, 75–133.
Lowe, A. (1965), *On Economic Knowledge: Toward a Science of Political Economics*, White Plains: ME Sharpe, 2nd edn, 1977.
Lowe, A. (1976), *The Path of Economic Growth*, Cambridge: Cambridge University Press.
Lowe, A. (1987), *Essays in Political Economics: Public Control in a Democratic Society*, New York: New York University Press.
McKinnon, R. (1991), *The Order of Economic Liberalization*, Baltimore: Johns Hopkins University Press.
Schmookler, J. (1966), *Invention and Economic Growth*, Cambridge: Harvard University Press.
Smith, A. (1776), *An Inquiry into the Nature and Causes of the Wealth of Nations*, Oxford: Oxford University Press, 1976.
Taylor, L. (1988), *Varieties of Stabilization Experience*, Oxford: Oxford University Press.
United Nations (1992), Economic Survey of Europe in 1991–1992, New York.
Wood, A. (1990), 'China's Economic Reform: Nominal Pause, but a Degree of Real Progress', *Financial Times*, October 4.
World Bank (1991), *World Development Report 1991*, Oxford: Oxford University Press.
Young, A. (1928), 'Increasing Returns and Economic Progress', *Economic Journal*, **38**, 527–42.

9 Structural change, productivity and employment: perspectives from a unified Germany

Harald Hagemann and Stephan Seiter*

The background of the 'economic, monetary and social union'

In November 1989 powerful demonstrations forced the Stalinist regime ruling the German Democratic Republic (GDR) to give up. People were allowed to travel to the Western part of Germany. In December the Berlin Wall crumbled. March 1990 saw the first free and democratic elections in the GDR, which were won by a conservative coalition. Thousands of people, especially younger ones, left the GDR in search of better jobs. Both the Federal Republic of Germany (FRG) and the GDR were concerned with halting this flood. East Germany lost many of its qualified and innovative people, while West Germany had to provide housing for them. The initial enthusiasm about the newly won freedom and unity was soon followed by disillusionment.

The idea of 'economic, monetary and social union' has to be viewed against this background. One economy, one currency and one social system for both parts of Germany were the aims of this union. The FRG and GDR remained separate states but formed an economic and monetary union. The first *Staatsvertrag* came into effect on 1 July 1990 and the West German Mark (DM) became legal tender in East Germany. All payments were subsequently made in DM, though all transactions were not treated equally. Prices, wages, pensions and rents were converted at par, while debts were settled at a rate of 1 DM against 2 East German Marks (M).[1] It took only a short time to complete national unity once the monetary union had been attained. On 3 October, the five newly founded *Länder* declared their *Beitritt*, that is, they joined the FRG according to Article 23 of its constitution.

The numerous proposals of the '*Staatsvertrag*' were discussed among economists, the Bundesbank, politicians, unions and businessmen concerning the best procedure for introducing the DM into East Germany and the consequences of this monetary reform. Many specialists warned against too early a change. The German Council of Economic Advisers (*Sachverständigenrat*), for example, declared its concerns in a public letter to Chancellor Kohl[2] which demanded time for the East German people to adjust. It expressed the fear that quick substitution of the DM for the East German Mark would reveal the weakness of 40 years of central administration.

The members of the Council identified the differences in the income levels between the two states as a major difficulty. Furthermore, they predicted the need for tax increases as well as the substitution of East German consumption goods which would affect East Germany's output, and consequently its labour market. The data for the second half of 1990 show that the sceptics were right. Almost every sector of the economy was affected by the monetary reform. In particular, there was a sharp breakdown in production. Compared to July 1989, as shown in Figure 9.1, East Germany produced 42.1 per cent less in July 1990, the month after the monetary reform. In the third quarter of 1990, as is seen in Figure 9.2, manufacturing industry produced only 54.9 per cent as compared to the second quarter.[3] This development is without precedent in Germany. Even after World War I in 1919, Germany still produced 57 per cent of its 1913 output. The downswing of the Great Depression between 1928 and 1932 led to a decline of 'only' 41 per cent.[4]

What happened? East Germany had suddenly become an open economy endowed with a convertible currency. Under central planning, resources

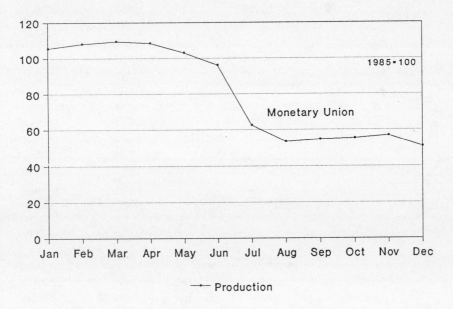

Source: Deutsche Bundesbank 1991a.

Figure 9.1: Industrial production in East Germany 1990

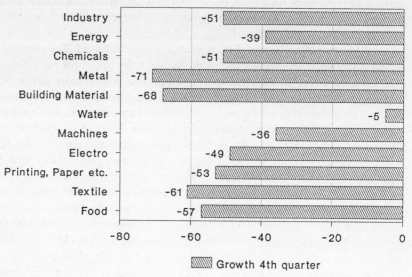

Source: DIW 1990a.

Figure 9.2:   Development of industrial production IV/89 to IV/90 (in per cent)

were allocated by central administration which left the economy with industries that were not competitive with the West. The attempt of the Council for
Mutual Economic Assistance (CMEA), the East European counterpart of the
EC, to reach self-sufficiency resulted in a very specialized industrial structure different from that which would have developed if the GDR had taken
part in the world-wide division of labour. There were no external competitors
for the combinates. The main export markets were located among the former
partners in the CMEA. By no means did produced goods match peoples'
wants.[5]

The monetary union opened East German markets to Western competitors. New products, better advertising and new brands appeared. East German
consumers could now buy Western products, and did so on a large scale.
Even though it is true that many of the goods supplied by East German firms
were not competitive (in price or in quality) with Western products, some
irritating substitution processes took place. Often consumers preferred Western products which were more expensive but not always of better quality.
Hence, East German companies lost substantial parts of their former markets.[6]

The introduction of the DM also had particular consequences for the
foreign trade of East Germany. Products became expensive relative to their

quality because they were now being evaluated in terms of a scarce hard currency. Traditionally, exports and imports were charged in *'Transferroubel'*. After 1 July the *'Transferroubel'* was devalued from 4.67 M to 2.34 DM, so that East German companies' foreign trade revenues dropped. The resulting leakage was financed by the state.[7] But this is not the end of the story. On 1 January 1991, the *'Transferroubel'* system broke down: most payments within the CMEA were now made in convertible currencies.[8] This reform is leading to substitution processes in East European countries, since these nations are suffering a shortfall in foreign reserves. The great magnitude of foreign debt is complicating the problem, since export revenues are needed for discharging these debts. This has led to a tremendous fall in the export of East German goods.[9] The loss of demand, particularly from the Soviet Union, will have important consequences for the East German economy. Some 600,000 jobs depended at least indirectly on trade with the former leader of Eastern Europe.[10] As is evident from Figure 9.3 unemployment increased from 272,000 in July 1990 to 1,068,600 in July 1991. In July 1990, 650,000 persons were classified as short-time workers; in July 1991 this number was estimated to be about 1.6 million.[11] In this context short-time work implies an average loss of working time of about 56 per cent per worker.[12] The 'real'

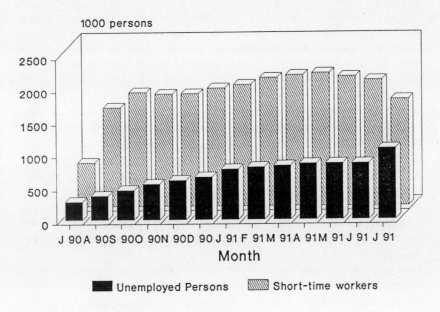

Source: DIW 1991b, BBk 1991b, Iwd 1991b, c.

Figure 9.3:   The East German labour market

number of unemployed workers became much higher when the special rule for short-time work expired at the end of 1991.[13] At the end of 1991 the 'real' level of unemployment amounted to nearly three million, which constitutes an unemployment rate in excess of 30 per cent – a level that is comparable to that of the Great Depression of the early 1930s.

The economic situation of East Germany

Productivity and GNP

East Germany's economy was, and still is, less efficient than that of West Germany. Estimates of the *Deutsches Institut für Wirtschaftsforschung* (DIW) indicate that the level of labour productivity has been less than 40 per cent of that of West Germany. This result is certainly a consequence of hidden unemployment in the former GDR. High rates of idle time, absentee rates and poor logistics further contributed to low productivity.

The social and political tasks (kindergartens, libraries, meetings and so on) which companies had to fulfil also contributed to low efficiency. In addition, terminating employment was very complicated. There were no incentives for 'saving' labour. On the contrary, the hoarding of labour was normal in order to reach plan standards easily.[14] Thus it was possible to increase productivity whilst reducing labour input without affecting output. However, as the development in the first months after the monetary reform made clear, companies started by closing down or separating out parts of their operations not directly necessary for production.[15] Although many workers were displaced in this period, productivity did not increase; it even decreased because lay-offs were accompanied by a sharp reduction in production. East Germany's GNP amounted to 242.3 billions in 1990 (see Table 9.1). Looking at Figure 9.4 which shows the composition of GNP and its development provides further interesting hints. Investment was reduced by about 5.7 per cent compared to 1989. Imports increased dramatically: comparison of 1990 with 1989 shows an increase of 66.9 per cent. Imports increased by 109.1 per cent in the second half of 1990 compared to the same period the year before.[16]

Even though these data are preliminary, it is obvious that East Germany consumes more goods than it is producing. As a separate state, East Germany could not afford such a process very long. All this will lead to new problems, and not only for the new part of the FRG. To fill the gap, West Germany's enterprises are utilizing their capacities at a high level. However, not all the goods needed can be produced in West Germany. As a consequence, there will be a deficit in the current account for the first time since 1979, a very unusual situation for Germany.[17]

Table 9.1:   General data for West and East Germany

	West Germany	East Germany
Population (thousands)	61 832	16 247
Area skm	248 678	108 333
GNP 1990 (billion DM)	2 425.5	242.3
Gainful employment 1990 (thousands)	28 410	8 665
Productivity 1990 (DM per hour)	39.46	14.87
Productivity 1990 (DM per employee)	64 210	26 633

Source: Sachverständigenrat 1990, DIW 1991a, *Wirtschaft und Statistik* 1990, Bach *et al.* 1990.

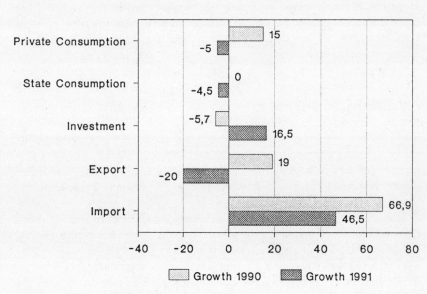

Source: Ifo 1991, 1991 estimation.

Figure 9.4:   Development of GNP composition (in per cent)

The sectoral pattern of the East German economy

With the former centrally administered economy and an international division of labour mainly limited to the Comecon countries, it is not surprising to find a very different sectoral configuration in the East German economy than that in West Germany. A closer look at this pattern, as is apparent from Figures 9.5a and b, shows that East Germany is still over-industrialized and has an agricultural sector larger than other developed economies. In 1989 about 37 per cent of the employees worked in the industrial sector and 10.4 per cent worked in agriculture. West Germany shows a very different pattern: 31.5 per cent in the industrial sector and 3.7 per cent in agriculture.[18] Services are more important in West Germany than they are in East Germany.[19] It becomes clear from this sectoral pattern that the East German economy must change substantially. This change will take some time, and it is necessary to differentiate between the short and the long run. Let us first concentrate on the short run.

Certainly, the great hope for structural change is in the service sector. This part of the economy is thought of as having the potential to attract a large share of the labour force. But to fulfil this possibility, the service sector must first undergo a difficult transformation process. As was pointed out above, monetary reform has led to an unbelievable breakdown in the industrial sector. Less production, or even no production, means less demand for services connected with production. Additionally, when people lose their jobs, they face a lower income. As a consequence they are more constrained in their demand both for goods and for services. Experience shows that demand patterns have changed in favour of consumer durables.

Companies do not only experience demand constraints, but also supply problems. Until 1 July 1990, in accordance with the aims of the former system, the service sector was divided into two parts. Social services such as medicine and child care were well developed in contrast to privately consumed services, for which the demand could not be satisfied. The development of the service sector is further hampered by the same problems other sectors confront. There are, for example, few new shops because of the unsolved question of ownership.

Two industries have expanded considerably since the introduction of the DM; specifically banking and insurance, which are at the centre of any capitalist economy and require substantial advising activity. Success in these industries requires a capability to supply a variety of 'products' unknown in the former socialist economy. As a consequence, most qualified employees available to fill the new jobs, especially in banking, are Germans from the West rather than from the East. Insurance companies have not created many new jobs in the first year after the monetary reform. It can be expected that

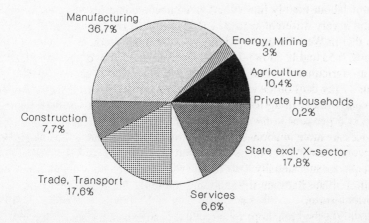

Source: Rudolph 1990, own calculations

Figure 9.5a: Sectoral structure of East German labour-force (1989)

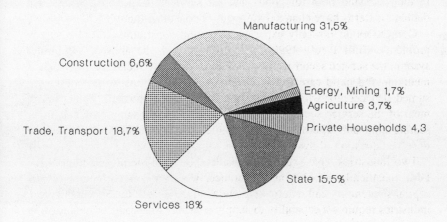

Source: SVR 1990, own calculations.

Figure 9.5b: Sectoral structure of West German labour-force (1989)

part-time work will become more common in this industry; a phenomenon already well known in West Germany.[20] In the short run, therefore, experience seems to indicate that the service sector will not be able to absorb all the employees set free in other sectors.[21]

The question of ownership
Investment plans are hampered by the question of the ownership of many of the assets that had been dispossessed by the partition of Germany. With reunification the present problem is to determine who should be considered their legitimate owners. The problem is likely to be in the German courts for many years to come. One of the major issues is whether the former owner – if ever found – will have a right to property once owned, or whether there will be only financial compensation. The first solution is likely to discourage a substantial amount of investment. Investors will not be willing to stake capital in East Germany if they confront the risk of loss because of a court's decision. So the second solution of sale and privatization with subsequent compensation is often advocated.

The problem of infrastructure
The East German economy suffers from two other main problems. First, its infrastructure has completely deteriorated. The few existing highways are in poor condition and the railway system, of which two-thirds was single-track, is obsolete. Since three-quarters of transportation within the former GDR was by train, this obsolescence is an important reason for the low efficiency of the East German economy. Additionally, the building materials used were of poor quality, so that only low speed was possible. Slow transportation resulted in low productivity.

Automobile and air transportation have been of subordinate importance. Berlin-Schönefeld, for example, was the hub of East Germany's air traffic, some 85 per cent of all flights starting and ending there. Car traffic has been of minor importance, for the road network is only half as dense as in West Germany.

Modern communication systems, perhaps the most important component of the infrastructure of a business economy, remained in their infancy. Only 1.8 million telephone connections have been installed, so that nine or ten persons have to share one telephone. Like the railway and road systems, the telephone lines were old-fashioned. Modern electronic communication systems such as E-Mail or Telefax were almost unknown.[22] This deficit compromises modern methods of production.

Firms using just-in-time production need telephone and telefax services and so on. Modern roads and other transport systems are equally relevant, for poor streets and railway systems hamper and lengthen the distribution process. Just-in-time production also requires a diversified system of suppliers. Even if the infrastructure is adequate there will be little production without an adequate material supply system. Thus firms need a network of small suppliers to fulfil specific demands. In the absence of an advanced internal division of labour, East Germany's economy suffers from a lack of companies with this capability. This fact could prevent West German investors from building new facilities in the new *Länder*.[23] Improving the infrastructure will increase productivity because it reduces costs and saves time, making modern production systems possible and worthwhile.

Employment of women
Another important difference between East and West Germany concerns the participation rate of women. In the former GDR this was one of the highest in the world, with 89.6 per cent of women in the age group 16 to 60 in employment, as compared to 63.4 per cent in the West (a rate which still is quite low by international standards).[24] There are several reasons for this difference, which is displayed in Figure 9.6a. First, labour was scarce in the GDR because of low productivity. But low productivity had yet another consequence: it resulted in low real income, so women had to work to

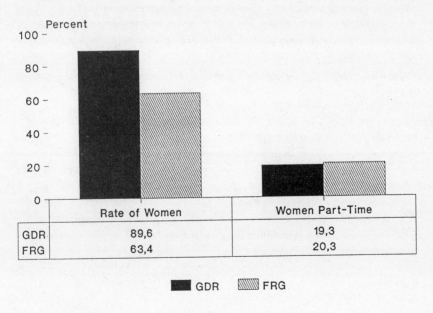

	Rate of Women	Women Part-Time
GDR	89,6	19,3
FRG	63,4	20,3

■ GDR   ▨ FRG

Source: DIW 1991f.

Figure 9.6:   Rates of employment in East and West Germany

achieve higher family incomes. A second reason is that working was not only a right, but often a social requirement for the citizens in the GDR.

In Western societies it is usually not easy for women, especially mothers of young children, to find a job. In the GDR the state provided care for children and the elderly. Hence, companies could afford to provide social facilities.[25]

What will happen to female labour-force participation in the new Germany? As has been argued above, companies are likely to retrench their social services. Two solutions are conceivable. The public solution will require state and city administrations to establish and finance adequate facilities. If, for any reason, this is not possible the private sector, especially families, must carry out these tasks.

Empty public treasuries are an important barrier to a public solution. East German cities confront many problems and inadequate financial options. The housing problem in particular will influence the financial requirements of the city administrations. As the new owners, they are responsible for renovating old, dilapidated buildings. Substantial amounts of money are necessary for this task. On the other hand, tax revenues are expected to increase by less than the allocation out of the *Fond Deutsche Einheit* (German unity fund) decreases in the next several years, thereby intensifying financial problems.[26] As a consequence, women will often be forced to leave their jobs and stay at home to care for children. Looking for new jobs, women are more likely to rely on the service sector for employment, where part-time work is more common.[27] Men could do so as well, but experience shows that normally women are the ones who are attracted to part-time work.

Even after a successful restructuring of the East German economy, the number of jobs will probably be far fewer than the 9.5 million that were available in the former GDR. This is partly the consequence of greater mobility, that is, the possibility of finding work in the West German labour market.[28] It can be predicted that the participation rate of women will be 'harmonized' down to the West German level. Women will thus be among the major losers of the transition process.

In the short run there will be no quick recovery in East Germany's economy. The shock of a new economic system is hard to withstand. Growth and structural change will take time. Some possible paths of long run development will be discussed in the next section.

Future perspectives of the East German economy

Output, productivity, wages and employment
The dominant prediction for the future development of the East German economy might best be represented by the 'J' curve idea. That is, output and employment fall in the first phase of the traverse process from a centrally planned to a market economy. But it will strongly increase in the medium and longer run.[29] There can be no doubt that the period immediately following the currency union was accompanied by a strong decline in output and employment. Revaluation and international competition have brought to light the inefficiencies and technological backwardness of the former socialist economy. Furthermore, with the dissolution of the CMEA, most Eastern European markets have been lost. Devaluation cannot soften the adjustment shocks for firms when there is a currency union. Thus, hidden unemployment becomes open unemployment and/or short-time work.

A recent joint economic forecast by the five leading economic research institutes (Kiel, Hamburg, Berlin, Munich and Essen) predicted annual increases in real GNP of 2.5 per cent for the West German economy, and declines in excess of 17.5 per cent for the East German economy.[30]

The transition to a market economy has also changed the perspectives for sectoral development of the East German economy – away from the old capital-intensive industries using many raw materials towards consumption industries and, especially, towards the service sector. The sectoral structure of the former GDR was biased in favour of manufacturing, agriculture and the public sector, and against the private service sector.[31] Recent studies show that most of the new employment opportunities in the West German economy in the 1980s were created in the service sector.[32] The service sector, which was the stepchild of the old socialist economy, will emerge as the great hope for the East German economy in the 1990s.

Whereas the service sector will have a high growth potential in the longer run, the first half year after the currency union witnessed a dramatic overall decline.[33] This unfavourable short-run development is the consequence of a substantial increase in service prices, noticeable budget constraints on private households, and the accumulated backlog demand for high class durable consumer goods which has led to a lower share of services in overall consumption expenditures since the fall of the Berlin Wall. It has to be expected that this negative development in the first phase of the transition process will soon be reversed as investment barriers are overcome and the economic situation improves.

One of the most important and intensively discussed topics is the relation between wages, productivity and employment. Besides the political suppression of the old Stalinist regime, differences in income (and consumption) opportunities were the most important cause of heavy migration to the West. These income differentials reflected differences in productivity. Labour productivity in the GDR prior to the currency union was estimated at about one-third that of the West German level.

With the new collective wage agreements made in the first months of 1991, it has become clear that wage increases will run far ahead of productivity increases. Wages in major sectors of the East German economy were recently increased from about one-third to 60 per cent of the West German level. Further increases of up to 100 per cent of the West German level are scheduled for the years until 1993–94.[34] As a consequence, the competitive position of the East German economy will deteriorate further and employment problems will be aggravated. The creation of profitable new jobs will limp behind the destruction of old jobs which have become unprofitable. Long-term unemployment will develop.

What is the rationale for the narrowing of wage differentials between East and West as quickly as possible? Why did the recommendations of economic experts such as the German Council of Economic Advisers, that wages should be differentiated according to the efficiency levels of sectors and firms and, in general, be increased with productivity, not materialize? One reason is that the mobility of workers limits the extent of wage differentiation. With the fall of the Berlin Wall, conditions for greater uniformity of the labour market have developed. Since workers now have the exit option, the attempt to stabilize prevailing wage differentials would cause new waves of migration, thus aggravating the housing problems already existing in West Germany.

But the outcome of the current reinforced displacement of workers, besides causing social unrest, may be the same. So we face a classical dilemma. There is widespread agreement that modernization of the infrastructure, breaking down of investment barriers and the establishment of qualification programmes for workers will help in the long run.

But what can be done in the short run? One controversial proposal is the introduction of wage subsidies[35] to bridge the gap between real wage and productivity levels in the early years of the transition process. This has the advantage of inducing labour demand directly. But wage subsidies must be temporary and declining, so that the potential drawback of hampering structural change, which would be far more costly in the long run, will not materialize. The low productivity level in the former GDR is the core of the problem. Whereas the currently prevailing productivity differences signal the potential gain in productivity in the former GDR in the longer run (when a successful restructuring may lead to an approximation of the West German level), it is clear that labour productivity can only be raised by an enormous capital accumulation. This holds for private investment as well as for public investment. A well-functioning infrastructure is the necessary precondition for the realization of many private investments, and thereby of economic growth and productivity increases.

Since major parts of the capital stock and public infrastructure in the former GDR are obsolete, the scope for productivity increases is currently severely limited. 'The capital stock in industry is largely obsolete both from the production and the demand side. Outdated technologies are used, and output is not competitive'.[36] This means that Germany must direct a great share of its investment towards East Germany for many years. Insofar as capital is channelled into traditional paths such as housing and roads, this will probably cause a loss of international competitiveness compared to countries like Japan where more can be invested into research and modern technology.

Analogy to West Germany after 1948: true or false?
An analogy is often drawn between the East German situation after July 1990 and the West German development after the currency reform of June 1948. Both cases seem to be characterized by an abundance of qualified labour and a shortage of capital. With capital accumulation, privatization and institutional changes going on in East Germany, a rich potential for productivity increases and higher growth rates of production should develop.

Although there is some truth to the catching-up hypothesis, from our point of view the East German economy will not arise as quickly as some politicians have promised and many economists have expected. The current situation in East Germany differs from that of West Germany in 1948 in important aspects. Whereas the index of industrial production went up by 50 per cent in the first five months after the West German currency reform in 1948, in East Germany just the opposite has happened, namely, as already noted, a total breakdown in industrial production.

Eastern European countries today have to undergo a far greater process of structural change than did the FRG after 1948. This holds also for the capital stock which, in West Germany in 1948, was not so obsolete from the technological point of view. Despite the destruction following the bombing of World War II, the capital stock in 1948 was about as great as in 1939.[37] So with investment starting again after the currency reform of June 1948, the marginal productivity of capital was extremely high at first, due to the effects of repair investment in factories and public infrastructure, such as the rebuilding of major bridges. Engineers and workers coming back from the war had not lost their technological knowledge. Forty years later the situation is totally different. Not only does a modern capital stock have to be built up from scratch, but far greater institutional changes are needed. As the development in the first year after the currency reform has shown, these institutional and psychological changes require much more time than originally expected.

East Germany will probably be the first country to be successful in completing the transition process from a socialist to a market economy. Having a big and rich brother in the West offers a number of advantages. But as the wage example shows, advantages very often go hand in hand with disadvantages. With respect to the development of real wages, there is a striking difference between East Germany and countries such as Hungary and Poland, where real wages decreased considerably during the first stage of the transition process. This option is blocked in East Germany because mobility barriers on the labour market have broken down. Although the old East German industries are hopelessly uncompetitive, wages are still rising. As a consequence, employment figures are far more negative than in Hungary or Poland. So one might say that, in this respect, being part of the larger united Germany is a crucial disadvantage – in the short and medium run.

West Germans, on the other hand, are not only suffering the burden of unification, that is higher taxes, higher interest rates and a noticeable increase in the inflation rate, but they also are benefiting from the shift and massive diversion of spending away from Eastern towards Western goods. This has led to a better economic development in the old FRG in the years 1990 and 1991 than in most other OECD countries. Far greater is the split in the growth rates between the economies in the old and the new *Länder.* One of the labour market consequences is an increasing number of commuters from East to West Germany. If one looks at this totally different development, one indeed might be tempted to conclude: 'History doesn't know justice, the second economic miracle (*'Wirtschaftswunder'*) will take place in the West of Germany as well'.[38]

The Former GDR: a new Mezzogiorno?

It has been noted that, in general, a currency union offers opportunity for Calabria as well as California.[39] Surely, it is true that a currency union as such is no guarantee for successful economic development. The Italian example after 1861 with the *Mezzogiorno*, and the American example of the southern states (lagging for a long time after the civil war ended in 1865) have shown this.

Predictions about the future perspectives for the East German economy range from the pessimistic scenario of a vicious circle, Germany's *Mezzanotte* as the equivalent to Italy's *Mezzogiorno*,[40] to the totally different Schumpeterian scenario of new frontiers and the associated opportunities for innovators and investors. Of course, there are countervailing tendencies, as can be seen, for example, with respect to the capital stock. On the one hand, the former socialist economies such as East Germany need far more capital to close the current productivity gap than the West German economy did after 1948. On the other hand, there is an opportunity to build a new and highly modern capital stock within the next decade.

Unification implies the integration of the new and the old *Länder,* that is two economies with great differences in factor endowment: the East German one with its abundance of qualified labour and the West German one with all its capital and technological knowledge. After some time this will lead to gains from trade and an adjustment of per capita income. This development will probably be associated with greater regional imbalances, in the same way they have developed between the south and the north of the FRG over the last two decades, between the south and the north of England, and the north and the south of Italy. Greater parts of the new five *Länder* (Mecklenburg West-Pommerania, Brandenburg, Saxony, Saxony-Anhalt and Thuringia) will catch up with the backward regions in the old *Länder.* But the recent decision in favour of Berlin as the capital means that there will be at least one major centre with more knowledge-based economic activities and a higher rate of growth which will act as a magnet for the surrounding parts of East Germany.

Notes

We would like to thank Michael Landesmann, Ingrid Rima and Christof Rühl for helpful discussions and valuable comments. This chapter includes data that were available up to September 1991.

1. See Deutsche Bundesbank (BBk) (1990).
2. See Sachverständigenrat (SVR) (1990, pp. 306–308).
3. See Deutsche Bundesbank (1991a, p. 74) and DIW (1991a, p. 55).
4. See Konjunkturgruppe (1991, p. 39).
5. See for this for example Sachverständigenrat (1990) or Bode and Krieger-Boden (1990, pp. 84–97).
6. Those substitution processes seem to be of a short term nature. Almost one year after the beginning of the monetary union, East German products, especially food, are in demand again. Some kind of backswing can be experienced. See, for example, DIW (1991e, p. 368).
7. See DIW (1991c, p. 128).
8. Meanwhile, the CMEA has been dissolved by a meeting of its members in June 1991.
9. The Soviet Union debts, for example, are estimated at 43.4 billion US dollars in 1990. See IWD (1991a, pp. 4–5).
10. See DIW (1991c, p. 127).
11. See Figure 9.3. The number of short-time workers decreased by 283,000 in July. This was paralleled with a roughly equivalent rise in the level of unemployment by 226,000 to reach 12.1 per cent of the labour force in East Germany. The monthly rise in unemployment was particularly pronounced among women, where the increase was 15 per cent against a rise of 10 per cent for men.
12. This rate was estimated for the second quarter of 1991. See DIW (1991e, p. 369).
13. See Sachverständigenrat (1991, p. 23).
14. For a more detailed analysis see Vogler-Ludwig (1990).
15. See DIW (1991c, p. 128).
16. These data are based on prices of the second half of 1990. See DIW (1991e, p. 382) and

Arbeitsgemeinschaft deutscher wirtschaftswissenschaftlicher Forschungsinstitute (1991, p. A29).

17. Experts of DIW estimate that there will be a swing of about 100 billion DM in the balance of current account (1991e, p. 372). DM will tend to lose value compared to other currencies, and its position in the EC will be weakened. But it is not quite clear in which direction the exchange rate will develop because increasing interest rates attract foreign capital which, as a consequence, will raise the exchange rate.

18. Comparing sectoral structures of East and West Germany involves many problems. Since the statistical systems of both states were different, different values could be found in different studies. See for example IWD (1990) and Heinze *et al.* (1991). The sectoral structure of East Germany shows one speciality, the so-called *x-sector*. This sector includes military activities, *STASI*, secret services, customs, parties and so on. There was no publication of these data in the former GDR.

19. See Figures 9.5a and 9.5b. East Germany's structure is about that of West Germany's in the 1960s.

20. In these industries part-time work is already familiar in West Germany. See DIW (1991c, p. 136).

21. Recent studies show that even in the service sector the number of old jobs being lost outnumbers the new ones being installed. See DIW (1991d, p. 327).

22. See Sachverständigenrat (1990, pp. 81–2).

23. A survey by the Ifo-Institute (Munich) revealed that telecommunication is the most essential part of infrastructure for West German companies. 81 per cent of the persons interviewed were of the opinion that improvements in this field are very urgent; 50 per cent ranked improving and extending the road network as among the highest priorities. See Nerb and Städtler (1990).

24. See DIW (1991f) and also DIW (1990a, b).

25. See Brander (1990).

26. See DIW (1991c, p. 141).

27 See for this Brander (1990).

28. It is estimated that about 350,000 people were commuting from East to West Germany in May 1991. (See *Konjunktur aktuell* 1991, p. 77.) A further increase in the number of commuters as well as a further migration to the West will probably dampen the predicted increase in the level of unemployment.

29. See, for example, Siebert (1990 a, b).

30 Projections for GNP in East Germany anticipate decline at a rate of 21.5 per cent p.a.. Experts have become more pessimistic. See DIW (1991e, p. 382).

31. See Figures 9.5a and 9.5b.

32 See Gerstenberger *et al.* (1990, p. 7).

33 See DIW (1991c, p. 132).

34 The most important wage settlement in the metal industry assigns such an increase in the three years from April 1991 to April 1994. In the public sector a similar agreement has been made.

35. See, for example, Akerlof *et al.* (1991) and Klodt (1990, p. 620).

36 Siebert (1990b, p. 5).

37. See the results of the United States Strategic Bombing Survey, Krengel's important 1958 study, and recently Schmieding (1990).

38. Spahn (1991, p. 79).

39. See Siebert (1990c, p. 58).

40. See Kurz (1991, p. 12).

Bibliography

Akerlof, George A., Rose, Andrew K., Yellen, Janet L. and Hessenius, Helga (1991), 'East Germany in from the Cold: The Economic Aftermath of Currency Union', *Brookings Papers on Economic Activity*, No. 1, 1–105.

Arbeitsgemeinschaft deutscher wirtschaftswissenschaftlicher Forschungsinstitute e.V. (1991),

'Die Lage der Weltwirtschaft und der deutschen Wirtschaft im Frühjahr 1991', *Wirtschaftskonjunktur*, No. 4, A1–A32.

Bach, H.K *et al.* (1990), 'Zur Arbeitsmarktentwicklung 1990/91 im vereinten Deutschland', *Mitteilungen aus der Arbeitsmarkt- und Berufsforschung*, **23**, (4), 455–73.

Bode, Eckhardt and Krieger-Boden, Christiane (1990), 'Sektorale Strukturprobleme und regionale Anpassungserfordernisse der Wirtschaft in den neuen Bundesländern', *Die Weltwirtschaft*, No. 2, 84–97.

Brander, Sylvia (1990), 'Beschäftigungsperspektiven für Frauen in den neuen Bundesländern', ifo-schnelldienst, Nos 35–36, 32–9.

Deutsche Bundesbank (BBk) (1990), 'Die Währungsunion mit der Deutschen Demokratischen Republik', *Monatsberichte* 7/1990, 14–29.

Deutsche Bundesbank (BBk) (1991a), *Monatsberichte*, 3/1991.

Deutsche Bundesbank (BBk) (1991b), *Monatsberichte*, 6/1991.

Deutsches Institut für Wirtschaftsforschung (DIW) (1990a), 'Erwerbstätigkeit und Einkommen von Frauen in der DDR', *DIW-Wochenbericht*, No. 19, 263–7.

Deutsches Institut für Wirtschaftsforschung (DIW) (1990b), 'Vereintes Deutschland–geteilte Frauengesellschaft?', *DIW-Wochenbericht*, No. 41, 575–582.

Deutsches Institut für Wirtschaftsforschung (DIW) (1991a), 'Die wirtschaftliche Entwicklung in Deutschland im vierten Quartal 1990', *DIW-Wochenbericht*, No. 7, 47–56.

Deutsches Institut für Wirtschaftsforschung (DIW) (1991b), 'Arbeitsmarkt im Sog des wirtschaftlichen Gefälles zwischen Ost- und Westdeutschland', *DIW-Wochenbericht*, No. 7, 57–62.

Deutsches Institut für Wirtschaftsforschung (DIW) (1991c), 'Gesamtwirtschaftliche und unternehmerische Anpassungsprozesse in Ostdeutschland', 1. Bericht, *DIW-Wochenbericht*, No. 12, 123–43.

Deutsches Institut für Wirtschaftsforschung (DIW) (1991d), 'Gesamtwirtschaftliche und unternehmerische Anpassungsprozesse in Ostdeutschland', 2. Bericht, *DIW-Wochenbericht*, No. 24, 323–46.

Deutsches Institut für Wirtschaftsforschung (DIW) (1991e), 'Deutschland im Umbruch', *DIW-Wochenbericht*, Nos 26–27, 365–84.

Deutsches Institut für Wirtschaftsforschung (DIW) (1991f), 'Frauenpolitische Aspekte der Arbeitsmarktentwicklung in Ost- und Westdeutschland', *DIW-Wochenbericht*, No. 30, 421–6.

Gerstenberger, Wolfgang *et al.* (1990), *'Grenzen fallen - Märket öffnen sich. Die Chancen der deutschen Wirtschaft am Beginn einer neuen Ära'*, Strukturberichterstattung 1990, Schriftenreihe des Ifo-Instituts für Wirtschaftsforschung No. 127, Berlin/München.

Heinze, Angela *et al.* (1991), 'Erwerbstätigenstruktur und Produktivitätsgefälle im Vergleich zwischen Ost- und Westdeutschland – Ausgewählte Probleme', in Kurt Vogler-Ludwig (ed.), *Perspektiven für den Arbeitsmarkt in den neuen Bundesländern*, ifo-studien zur Arbeitsmarktforschung 7, München.

Institut der Deutschen Wirtschaft (IWD) (1990), 'Weit im Rückstand', *Informationsdienst des Instituts der Deutschen Wirtschaft*, **16**, (35), 4–5.

Institut der Deutschen Wirtschaft (IWD) (1991a), 'Roßkur für den RGW', *Informationsdienst des Instituts der Deutschen Wirtschaft*, **17**, (16), 4–5.

Institut der Deutschen Wirtschaft (IWD) (1991b), 'Der Arbeitsmarkt', *Informationsdienst des Instituts der Deutschen Wirtschaft*, **17**, (28), 3

Institut der Deutschen Wirtschaft (IWD) (1991c), 'Der Arbeitsmarkt', *Informationsdienst des Instituts der Deutschen Wirtschaft*, **17**, (33), 3.

Klodt, Henning (1990), 'Wirtschaftshilfen für die neuen Bundesländer', *Wirtschaftsdienst*, No. 12, 617–22.

Konjunktur aktuell (1991), 'Der Arbeitsmarkt', June, p. 77.

Konjunkturgruppe der Abt. Gesamtwirtschaftliche Analysen und öffentliche Finanzen (1991), 'Tiefer Produktionseinbruch in der ostdeutschen Industrie', *ifo-schnelldienst*, Nos 16–17, 39–45.

Krengel, Rolf (1958), *'Anlagevermögen, Produktion und Beschäftigung in der Industrie im Gebiet der Bundesrepublik 1924–1956'*, Berlin.

Kurz, Heinz D. (1991), 'From the Frying Pan to The Fire: The Case of the Eastern German Economy', manuscript, New York.

Nerb, G. and Städtler, A. (1990), 'Infrastrukturengpässe in den neuen Bundesländern', *ifo-schnelldienst*, No. 3, 3–4.

Rudolph, Helmut (1990), 'Beschäftigungsstrukturen in der DDR vor der Wende. Eine Typisierung von Kreisen und Arbeitsämtern', *Mitteilungen aus der Arbeitsmarkt- und Berufsforschung*, **23**, (4), 474–503.

Sachverständigenrat (SVR) (1990), Jahresgutachten 1990/1, Bundestagsdrucksache 11/8472, Bonn.

Sachverständigenrat (SVR) (1991), 'Marktwirtschaftlichen Kurs halten. Zur Wirtschaftspolitik für die neuen Bundesländer', Wiesbaden.

Schmieding, Holger (1990), 'Der Übergang zur Marktwirtschaft: Gemeinsamkeiten und Unterschiede zwischen Westdeutschland 1948 und Mittel- und Osteuropa heute', *Die Weltwirtschaft*, No. 2, 149–60.

Siebert, Horst (1990a), 'The Economic Integration of Germany', *Kieler Diskussionsbeiträge* 160, Institut für Weltwirtschaft, Kiel, April.

Siebert, Horst (1990b), 'The Economic Integration of Germany – An Update', *Kieler Diskussionsbeiträge* 160a, Institut für Weltwirtschaft, Kiel, September.

Siebert, Horst (1990c), 'Lang- und kurzfristige Perspektiven der deutschen Integration', *Die Weltwirtschaft*, No. 1, 49–59.

Spahn, Heinz-Peter (1991), 'Das erste und das zweite deutsche Wirtschaftswunder', *Wirtschaftsdienst*, No. 2, 73–9.

United States Strategic Bombing Survey (1945), 'Overall Economic Effects Division', *The Effects of Strategic Bombing on the German War Economy.*

Vogler-Ludwig, Kurt (1990), 'Verdeckte Arbeitslosigkeit in der DDR', *ifo- schnelldienst*, No. 24, 3–10.

Wirtschaft und Statistik (1990), No. 12.

10 Paradise gained, paradise lost?

Heinz D. Kurz *

Introduction

On 3 October 1990, in line with Article 23 of the West German constitution, East Germany declared itself part of the Federal Republic of Germany. Anticipating complete German unification, on 1 July 1990, a monetary, economic and social union became effective between the two German states. The Deutschemark (DM) replaced the Eastmark. Legal trade barriers and barriers to capital and labour movements between the FRG and the GDR were abolished, and the legal, tax and social insurance system of West Germany was extended to East Germany. Only two years ago, observers looked to this bold step with considerable unease, fearing that a larger German economy would dominate Europe even more decisively than had West Germany by itself. They did not foresee that unification would bring not economic success, but difficulties of immense complexity and potential seriousness.

This paper focuses on the short and long-run economic consequences of German unification. A major concern is with the distributive aspects of unification policy which, it will be argued, contradicts not only principles of economic justice, but is also utterly detrimental to a quick economic recovery and restructuring in the new states of the federal republic, that is, the so-called new *Länder*.

The structure of the paper is as follows. In Section 2 a brief account of the distributive consequences of unification policy will be given. Emphasis is on the depreciation of East German human capital, broadly understood, and the redistribution of the 'property of the people' away from the people as a consequence of: (1) the terms of the currency conversion, and (2) the decided route to privatization. It should come as no surprise that the East Germans are keen to make good with massive wage increases and transfer payments what they lost with collective material wealth. Section 3 deals with the problem of competitiveness of the East German capital stock that holds the key to the short-run employment possibilities in the new *Länder*. The argument is that the rapid adjustment of East German wages to West German levels and the increase in interest rates due to the debt financing of unification by the German government, renders obsolescent large parts of the East German plant and equipment and thus destroys jobs, which only massive subsidies financed by West Germany can preserve. With a smaller volume of employment in East Germany, total income generated will be smaller too; this in turn provides fewer resources for capital accumulation and growth and thus slows down the restructuring of the East German economy. Section 4 focuses on the medium and long run. Since unemployment benefits are proportional to terminal wages earned by workers, rapidly rising East German wages imply high levels of 'unproductive consumption'; the unemployment benefits will require massive transfer payments from West to East Germany and will put a considerable strain on the West German taxpayer. Correspondingly, capacity saving will fall. Rapidly rising East German wages will thus reduce the pace of capital accumulation and the creation of new jobs. In the long run a lower rate of capital accumulation will reflect in a lower rate of productivity growth. The final section draws some conclusions.

Distributive aspects of German unification
German unification involved a massive depreciation of received 'socialist' knowledge and moral (and its associated codes of behaviour); or, in economic terms, a substantial loss of human capital. It also involved the redistribution of the material wealth of a 'nation': the so-called 'property of the people' of the former GDR. Ironically, the majority of Germans both in the East and in the West were initially unaware of this implication of the adopted policy of unification. Otherwise it would be difficult to understand why the problem of the distribution and redistribution of wealth did not play a more important role in political discussions in Germany. Indeed, it ranked below some fervently debated issues such as preserving the East German abortion law in early discussions.

Depreciation of parts of the East German human capital
A lack of understanding of the important issues may explain the remarkably little interest East Germans devoted to the issue of wealth and property. Because private ownership of the means of production and the profit motive were considered despicable and odious, the East German population had difficulty in becoming adjusted to the new social and moral norms, some of which are the exact opposite of what they used to be. Hence, a major problem of German unification and of other transformation processes in Eastern Europe seems to be the difference between the speed at which new rules are introduced and the ability to learn these rules.[1] When the surprised East Germans began to understand what had happened, it was too late for substantial modifications. This appears also to be the reason why a growing number of East Germans express the feeling of having been cheated and deceived by West German politicians. Indeed, many East Germans feel that West Germans ruthlessly exploit their lack of familiarity with the new legal

system and modes of thought and behaviour. Moral hazard problems are prevalent on a nation-wide scale. The emergence of mass unemployment and social distress have pulverized the naive conception that a change of regime would come at no cost and bring exclusively benefits to the East Germans.

For more than four decades in the GDR, private self-interested initiatives were discouraged and solutions to social problems were sought in an 'etatist' way. East Germans were trapped in a position of 'learned helplessness' as they tried to adjust from this social climate to the 'revaluation of values'. There is a lack of entrepreneurial spirit and an overabundance of entitlement mentality. What is at stake is the re-education of an entire population. Compared to it the necessary retraining of large portions of the East German labour force appears to be a minor task.

Monetary union

Monetary union entitled East German children under 15 years, adults under 60 years and pensioners to exchange up to 2 000, 4 000 and 6 000 Eastmarks, respectively, on a 1:1 basis. The exchange or conversion rate applied to most other stocks of money and financial claims, including household savings and company debt, was 1:2. The conversion rate of wage and price contracts and pension claims was 1:1. The average rate of exchange of DM for Eastmarks was approximately 1:1.8.

When the monetary union became effective, many observers believed that the terms of currency conversion involved substantial gains in purchasing power by the East German population. Compared with the black market exchange rates of 1:7 before the opening of the Berlin Wall and 1:11 afterwards, the conversion rates looked extraordinarily favourable. Hence, many feared that monetary union would fail to siphon off excess money balances, (a characteristic feature of any socialist economy) and that rapid inflation would ensue once the administration of prices ended. The Deutsche Bundesbank argued this point most forcefully.

The fears did not come true. Contrary to widespread opinion, currency conversion did not entail purchasing power gains but losses to the East Germans. While purchasing power comparisons between vastly different economies such as the FRG and the former GDR are difficult, there exist clear indications that the purchasing power parity between the two currencies was close to 1:1.[2] The distinction between traded and non-traded goods, and the substantial subsidies put up by the East German state to keep prices of necessary goods low, explains this rather astounding result. Hence all financial claims, in particular private savings, that were changed at rates of 2:1 or 3:1 implied real losses. This was the first act of 'expropriation' to which the East Germans were exposed. Because of their insufficient initial endowment with financial claims, East Germans were weak compared with the West Germans and foreigners bidding for enterprises and real estates to be privatized.

The policy of privatization

A major problem for the economies in transition is the privatization of industry and land. The unification treaty clearly distinguishes expropriations before and after 1949: those before 1949 are exempt from privatization and compensation, while those afterwards are nullified. Hence everything expropriated since the founding of the GDR is, in principle, to be returned to its legitimate owner(s). Approximately one-third of the total property that can be privatized belongs to this category. The number of applications for the return of, or compensation for, expropriated property exceeds one million: golden days ahead for lawyers!

The actual route to reprivatization and compensation became a major obstacle to East German economic recovery. As long as property rights are unclear and costly disputes over these rights persist, potential investors will not risk engaging in business in East Germany. To speed up the privatization process the German parliament passed a law on 15 March 1991 (specifying Article 41 of the unification treaty) which under certain circumstances allows exceptions to the reprivatization of expropriated property to render possible investment that is beneficial to the economy as a whole (the so called 'obstacle removing law'). The new law, which in principle reaffirms the maxim: 'return of property rather than compensation', until the end of 1992 allows several exceptions to this rule in favour of employment, housing or the infrastructure.

The *Treuhandanstalt*, a gigantic resolution trust in the Ministry of Finance, is privatizing the remaining two thirds of industry and other property in East Germany. *Treuhandanstalt* managers are responsible for the liquidation of about 8000 companies in East Germany. Some 20 per cent of these companies are public utility companies that, as a rule, will become communal property, whereas the remaining 80 per cent will be privatized following a procedure in two steps. First, companies will be transformed into joint stock companies or into other legal forms of enterprise; then they will be sold on international capital markets. Before the end of March 1991 the *Treuhandanstalt* shut about 300 of the companies and sold about 1000 others, mostly small enterprises.

What is at issue is the gigantic problem of selling two thirds of the productive apparatus of an entire economy. This route to privatization exhibits serious shortcomings, the following of which deserve mention (cf. Sinn, 1990).[3] First, it is very time-consuming. Secondly, it raises the problem of a mismatch between effective demand and offer, with the consequence of dramatically falling asset prices. Thirdly, it is not only inefficient but also highly problematic from the point of view of fairness and distributive justice.

The route to privatization assumes that current investment and thus savings can buy the East German capital stock. This might be a valid assumption if the savings activated for this purpose were international rather than essentially national savings. However, it seems that so far only a very small percentage of the demand for East German firms comes from foreigners, to whom investment in the new *Länder* appears at present to be too risky and uncertain. East Germans are unable to play a more important role in the acquisition of private property, in particular productive units, because of their very limited access to liquid funds. It is the West Germans who are getting by far the largest slice of the cake and are about to take over the East German industry and real estate. Hence, the route to privatization comes close to a policy of colonization – an 'expropriation' of the East German people.

The creation of an excess supply constellation is also partly responsible for the fall in asset prices. This exaggerates the poor state of the East German capital stock. West German saving, a flow magnitude, is insufficient to buy that part of the East German plant and equipment that is not subject to restitution, a stock magnitude, at 'reasonable' prices. Consequently, there is downward pressure on the prices of the objects sold by the *Treuhandanstalt*. Two additional factors reinforce the decline in prices. First, actual and expected proceeds of firms are small because of low levels of demand for East German products, and thus low degrees of capacity utilization. Secondly, the German government's reluctance to increase taxes to finance German unification entailed soaring budget deficits that put additional strain on the capital market and drove up interest rates.

It follows that both elements of privatization policy, that is, natural restitution and the attempt to sell the remaining property on the market, are major obstacles to a quick economic recovery in East Germany. Moreover, the second contradicts distributive justice. The take over of large parts of the 'property of the people' of the former GDR by West Germans may drive a wedge into German society that prevents German unity despite German unification.

The conclusions to be drawn from these observations are clear. First, to remove a major obstacle preventing private investment activity in East Germany from gaining momentum, the maxim 'return of property rather than compensation' should be replaced by the maxim 'return of property only in cases that are not controversial; compensation in all other cases'. Secondly, to speed up privatization and to avoid the unacceptable and politically dangerous distributive effects of the current policy of the *Treuhandanstalt*, this policy should be replaced by a scheme guaranteeing that at least the remaining property is given to the people in the new *Länder*; for example, with shares of firms or of the entire East German capital stock, including non-private residential buildings and real estates.

The losses of financial claims, human and physical capital and land incurred by East Germans are large, and the proportion of East Germans who believe that unification brought them benefits that outweigh the costs is decreasing. Apparently there is a widespread feeling that losses in wealth can and should be compensated with rapid increases in wages and transfer payments: Germany is caught in a massive conflict over the distribution of income.

Wages in East Germany

The state treaty on monetary union required that pre-existing wage and salary contracts be carried over with payments in Eastmark converted to DM at par. Both immediately before and after monetary union, nominal wages and salaries rose substantially. The rise in East German wages continues unabated. There are many reasons for this. West German trade unions insist on wage parity – partly in order not to undermine their political strength (there were no comparable workers' organizations in the GDR) and partly to stem what might otherwise have been an unmanageable mass migration to the West. The absence of any effective counter-organization on the employers' side greatly contributed to this result, as did the general expectation of both workers and managers that they would soon become unemployed, in which case their unemployment benefits would be based primarily on their wages and salaries at the time their jobs were terminated (see Akerlof *et al.*, 1991).

It was particularly the wage agreement for metal workers of 1 March 1991, negotiated by the strong West German metal workers' union (IG Metall), which set the pace for the catch up of East German wages. According to this agreement, standard wages of metal workers in East Germany, including standard fringe benefits, are to match the West German level by 1995. Other wage agreements followed this example. Hence, the level of hourly wages in East Germany will reach and then overtake British and, a little later, US hourly wages within a few years. This is a dramatic development that probably will not be backed by a similar growth in East German (average) labour productivity. The implication of this is that many of the currently existing jobs in the new *Länder*, most of which are barely economical even in present-day conditions, will become obsolescent. Bad times ahead for workers seeking employment in East Germany!

Capital stock obsolescence and employment: a short-run perspective
As was mentioned above, the absorption of the former East German economy into the Federal Republic of Germany added substantially to the latter's productive resources, at least in terms of labour and land. This concentration of potential economic power was looked upon with considerable unease by many observers and commentators, fearing German economic and eventually political dominance in Europe. However, so far their fears have not come true: currency union has triggered one of the deepest economic crises affecting an economy in world history. A part of the problem lies in the disastrous underestimation of the consequences monetary union would have on the competitiveness of the East German capital stock.

Plant and equipment in East Germany
According to the East German Institut für angewandte Wirtschaftsforschung (IAW) the net value of plant and equipment (exclusive of land) in the former GDR in 1989, estimated at an exchange rate of 1 DM for 1 Eastmark, equalled 1.745 billion DM (IAW, 1990). The capital stock in the producing sector was estimated at 1.250 billion DM. With produced national income (exclusive of services) amounting to 260 billion DM, the output–capital ratio in the Eastern German producing sector in 1989 was 0.149, and its inverse, the capital–output ratio, 4.8. In the FRG in 1989 the net value of plant and equipment was estimated at some 6.500 billion DM, and the net social product at market prices equalled almost 2.000 billion DM. Hence, the West German output–capital ratio and its inverse, the capital–output ratio, estimated in terms of the above two magnitudes, were 0.3 and 3.3, respectively. Accordingly, the output produced per unit of capital in the GDR was much smaller than in the FRG.[4]

However, applying West German rules of accounting to the plant and equipment in the GDR, the IAW estimated that two thirds of the East German capital stock would have to be written off because of technical and economic obsolescence, leaving a capital stock worth roughly only 580 billion DM.[5] Akerlof *et al.* (1991) estimated that only 8.2 per cent of the work-force in industry are employed in viable enterprises. In other words, 92.8 per cent of industrial workers are employed in firms that cannot even cover short-run variable costs – a still more pessimistic result.

How can an economy, praised by both the East and West for its relatively high efficiency only a few years ago, suddenly be 'unmasked' as a system with low productivity and a capital stock that is little more than a 'pile of scrap'? One of the reasons for this rather surprising finding is the economic policy the GDR carried out in the last decade or so. In this period the East German government increased consumption to appease a population which expressed ever more openly its disapproval of the oppressive conditions in the GDR. Because this required a reduction of investment, the modernization of the East German industry and capital stock decelerated, and larger and larger parts of it became obsolete.

Capital stock obsolescence

Any attempt to assess the quality and 'quantity' of the capital stock of an economy, and thus the economy's productive capacity and competitiveness, poses tremendous difficulties. The East German economy accentuates these difficulties because it is in a state of fundamental disarray. Certain aspects of this disarray deserve mention. First, the extant capital stock reflects the former needs of the GDR and the CMEA. Since the CMEA has disintegrated and the East German economy has moved to the Western trading bloc through monetary union, the composition of its capital stock is no longer appropriate: compared with the new needs its primary and manufacturing sectors, and thus the respective capital stocks, are too large. With often prohibitively high costs preventing the transfer of durable items of capital to other productive uses, a large portion of the superfluous parts of the capital stock is rendered worthless and has to be scrapped.

Secondly, many East German firms lack competitiveness because of the low quality or outmoded character of the products they produce. In so far as these products are produced by means of capital goods that are specific to their production and thus cannot be utilized otherwise, these capital goods will have to be wholly jettisoned. Others may be used in different lines of production if it is profitable. Thirdly, many production lines, although competitive in terms of product quality, will not survive; because of low labour productivity and a high capital–output ratio, the costs of production per unit of output exceed world market product prices. The unprofitability of these firms is reflected in a negative capital value. Finally, there are those firms that are able to cover production costs, but will flounder because of inadequate marketing and product distribution. All of these factors work in the same direction, that is, they contribute to the dramatic fall in asset values.

After monetary union, prices of tradeables quickly adjusted to the going world market levels. The change from Eastmark prices to DM prices entailed remarkable changes in absolute and relative prices. While consumer prices, expressed in terms of the East German consumer price index, were fairly constant until the beginning of 1991 (when subsidies on basic consumer goods such as energy and transportation were eliminated or reduced), producer prices, expressed in terms of the price index of manufactured goods, fell by almost 50 per cent in a single month. In July 1990 the East German economy was not simply opened to the world market: it was rather exposed to international competition on terms defined by the German monetary union, which were equivalent to a huge revaluation of its currency.

Before monetary union the East German Ministry of Trade calculated, for internal purposes, the so-called 'currency yield coefficient' (*Devisenertragskoeffizient*), which is the amount of DM received per unit of Eastmark employed in the production of export goods. In 1989 this coefficient was 0.23, that is the GDR imported goods worth 0.23 DM in exchange for goods exported worth one Eastmark. Hence currency union implied a revaluation of approximately 4:1 relative to the previously used internal exchange rate. Since the conversion rate for wage contracts was 1:1, the wage rate in terms of export goods increased by roughly 400 per cent. It should come as no surprise that East German export industries went into rapid decline. No open economy can absorb such a shock without serious damage.

Immediately after currency union, output in East Germany fell sharply. The main reason for this was, of course, the swift and massive diversion of spending away from the East towards the West. Whereas in the past trade relationships among socialist countries were essentially politically decided, the former trading partners of East German firms now have to pay for their imports in hard currency that is scarce. Because of the low quality of East German goods, the former Comecon countries will probably buy from other sources including Western Europe, the United States and the Far East. Whether effective demand for East German goods increases in the future depends, in part, on the world economic situation. With the major trading partners of Germany in a recession, prospects for a quick recovery in East Germany are dim.

Incremental investment

While the above argument is able to explain, in an elementary way, the economic 'destruction' of real capital and employment after monetary union, several qualifications will be added. First, the above argument assumes that the pattern of operation and utilization of plant and equipment in East Germany is constant, despite the gradual introduction of a market system and the exposure of the East German economy to international competition. This change of regime will probably eliminate redundant labour and increase the intensity of work. In short, the process of production will probably become more efficient because of competitive pressure.

Secondly, in some cases investment of a relatively small magnitude, or incremental investment, is able to markedly improve efficiency and labour productivity. Very often the task of such investment is simply to overcome existing bottlenecks, with the effect that productive capacity rises substantially. While there can be no doubt that the restructuring of the East German economy requires massive capital accumulation over many years, the efficiency of the existing process of production can be improved if there is some incremental investment.

Finally, only parts of the output of the East German economy, and thus only parts of its productive apparatus, are subject to full international competition. In this context the distinction between traded and non-traded goods becomes all-important. While monetary union exposed the East German export sector to the world market, a rather large group of non-tradeables were affected only indirectly by international competition. It follows that the above argument applies essentially to the capital stock employed in the production of traded goods only, whereas the capital stock employed in the production of non-traded goods is largely exempt from it.

Tight capital markets

The magnitude of the capital stock needed in East Germany will put a substantial strain on capital markets and raise interest rates. Currently, the tightness of the German capital markets is predominantly due to the soaring budget deficits of the Federal state and its *Länder*. When the German government propagated the remarkable opinion that German unification and the restructuring of the Eastern German economy do not require a substantial rise in taxes, capital markets had to cope with massive increases of public credit demand to finance transfer payments to the East German population and investment in the infrastructure of the new *Länder*. The effect was a marked increase in the level of nominal and real interest rates (where the real interest rate is the nominal rate minus the rate of inflation). By summer 1991 the real interest rate paid on long-term public obligations in Germany was well above 6 per cent, and thus substantially higher than in the United States. Given the immense demand for liquid funds to rebuild the East German economy, real interest rate differentials between Germany and its major trading partners will probably prevail: Germany, once the world's most important capital exporting nation, may become a major capital importer.

By January 1991 the German trade balance, known to be persistently positive, showed a deficit. That is, private savings were no longer able to finance private investment and the sky-rocketing budget deficit. Negative trade balances might well become a characteristic feature of Germany's near future. The implication of this is that Germany's net foreign investment position will gradually be eroded. Since Germany comes second to Japan in terms of its net foreign wealth, that is its cumulated foreign net investments, Germany can easily afford to run trade deficits and import capital. While fears that Germany might become a net debtor are, of course, unwarranted in the short and medium run, they cannot be dismissed out of hand in the long run. All depends on the economic success, or lack thereof, of German unification. What is clear, however, is that the net amount of capital owned by Germans abroad, which was estimated at half a trillion DM in 1990, does not match the sum of private capital needed to rebuild the productive capacity of East Germany: depending on the amount of the capital stock in existence that is or will soon become economically obsolescent, the East German capital need might be in the range of one to one and a half trillion DM. Hence the opinion occasionally expressed in political discussions that repatriation of German capital can accomplish the task of restructuring the East German economy is unsustainable.

Capital accumulation and productivity growth: a long-run perspective
A rapid adjustment of East German wages to West German levels is not only detrimental to the survival of the old capital stock. Under given conditions it is also detrimental to the formation of new capital by depressing the potential for accumulation. The main reason for this is the social union, which extended the West German labour law and unemployment benefits scheme with small modifications to East Germany. Accordingly, unemployment benefits amount to 65 per cent of former net wages. With large numbers of East Germans becoming unemployed at substantially increased terminal wages, a larger proportion of the German net national income will go into consumption. Consequently, the share of capacity saving will go down and capital accumulation can be expected to decelerate.

'Unproductive' consumption and capacity saving
A simple macroeconomic model can illustrate the negative impact of high real wages in East Germany on full capacity saving, that is saving associated with the full utilization of profitable productive capacity, and thus potential investment.[6] Let v designate the given and constant capital–capacity ratio and a the given labour-capacity ratio, or labour coefficient; assume for simplicity that capital does not deteriorate. g is the rate of capacity saving, or the potential rate of capital accumulation. Let ω be the real wage per unit of labour, and α the percentage of the real wage paid as unemployment benefits. There is no saving out of wages or unemployment benefits; they are both consumed. In this simple economy, total output Y equals investment plus consumption:

$$gYv + C = Y. \tag{1}$$

Consumption equals consumption by workers that are employed and by workers on the dole. Hence:

$$C = \omega L + \alpha \omega N (0 < \alpha < 1), \tag{2}$$

where L is the amount of employment and N the amount of registered unemployment. Applying a similar distinction found in classical economics, albeit in a somewhat different context, ωL is 'productive consumption' and $\alpha \omega N$ *is* 'unproductive consumption'. Since $L = aY$, equation (2) can be written as:

$$C = \omega aY(1+\alpha\theta), \text{ where } \theta = \frac{N}{L} \tag{3}$$

θ gives the ratio of 'unproductive' (in the sense of not productively employed) to 'productive', that is, employed, workers. In this model, θ is higher, the higher the East German real wage rate because of capital and thus job obsolescence. That is:

$$\theta = f(\omega), \text{ where } f'(\omega) > 0. \tag{4}$$

Substituting equation (4) in (3) and the latter in (1), and solving for g gives:

$$g = \frac{1 - \omega\alpha[1+\alpha f(\omega)]}{v}. \tag{5}$$

From equation (5) it follows that a higher level of real wages, by increasing the proportion N/L and at the same time the unemployment benefit $\alpha\omega$, reduces the rate of capacity saving, that is the maximum rate of accumulation attainable. Since there is no reason to expect that under the conditions characterizing the present situation in Germany the actual rate of accumulation will move contrary to the potential or maximum rate, we may conclude that rapidly rising real wages in East Germany will retard the process of capital formation and thus the restructuring of the economy of the new *Länder*.

Capital accumulation and productivity growth
Adam Smith begins the *Wealth of Nations* (1776) by pointing out that a nation's real income per capita, and its growth, depends on two factors: (1) 'the skill, dexterity, and judgement with which its labour is generally applied', and (2) 'the proportion between the number of those who are employed in useful labour, and that of those who are not so employed'. While united Germany gets high marks regarding the first aspect, it performs rather poorly with regard to the second.

Let Y be net national income, P total population, F the total work-force, L the number of productive workers and N the number of 'unproductive' workers (which in our case is identified with the number of unemployed workers). Obviously:

$$\frac{Y}{P} = \frac{Y}{L}\frac{F}{P}\frac{N}{F}\frac{L}{N}.$$ (6)

With $z = Y/P$ as income per head, $y = Y/L$ as labour productivity, $p = F/P$ as the participation rate, and $e = L/F$ as the rate of employment, we have:

$$z = ype,$$ (7)

or, in terms of proportional rates of growth,

$$\hat{z} = \hat{y} + \hat{p} + \hat{e}.$$ (8)

The predominant effect of German unification so far has been a reduction in the overall rate of employment, e. The unemployment rate rose significantly faster among females in East Germany. A related effect is the reduction in the participation rate, p. Again, the female rate fell faster in East Germany, which before unification amounted to 48 per cent.[7] Further, if the rate of growth of labour productivity is positively correlated with the rate of capital accumulation, the slowdown of the latter will probably be reflected in a smaller growth of output per worker, $\hat{y}$. Hence all factors contributing to the growth of income per capita in Germany are pointing downwards.

Conclusion

Unemployment in East Germany is predominantly 'classical' unemployment, that is, unemployment due to a massive shortage of plant and equipment. To overcome this shortage the quick formation of new, fresh capital is needed. Yet, as this paper has argued, the terms of German unification entailed a huge conflict over the distribution of wealth and income that is detrimental to social cohesion in Germany as a whole and to the quick recovery and restructuring of the East German economy. A major error of unification policy was to deprive a large part of the new *Länder* population of the 'property of the people'. Understandably, East Germans now try to compensate this loss with rapid wage increases and substantial transfer payments. Moreover, the East German workers were supported by the West German trade unions which, for good reasons, feared that large wage differentials between West and East Germany would serve as an incentive for massive migration from the new to the old *Länder*. This would increase competition among workers in Western Germany and exert a downward pressure on wages, thereby eroding the bargaining position and political power of the trade unions relative to the employers' associations. Yet, with East German wages rising rapidly to the West German level, ever-larger parts of the East German capital stock and the jobs associated with it are rendered obsolete.

Rising levels of unemployment in an environment characterized by the West German labour law and its relatively favourable unemployment benefits scheme, involves a substantial strain on the German social budget and the diversion of resources away from investment towards consumption. Hence, the process of fresh capital formation, desperately needed to overcome the economic malaise in the new *Länder*, is seriously hampered.

Unless there is a reversal of the unification policy, in particular the adopted policy of privatization, there is little hope that Germany will be economically and socially balanced and politically stable, in short: a united Germany. There is still the possibility of changing direction and minimizing damage. However, time is running out.

Notes

*   The present paper is essentially an extract of two papers written by the author in Summer 1991 (cf. Kurz, 1992 and 1993). I should like to thank Mark Knell and Ingrid Rima for valuable comments on an earlier draft of the paper. It goes without saying that any remaining errors are my responsibility.

1.   This is also the main reason why I am sceptical that the so-called 'shock therapy' is superior to a more gradual approach to the transition process, as maintained by many commentators and quite a few Western advisers to Eastern European governments (see in particular Lipton and Sachs, 1990).

2.   According to the Ifo-Institut für Wirtschaftsforschung the parity was 1 Eastmark to 0.98 DM (cf. Ifo-Schnelldienst No. 43 of 7 May 1990, 13/1990), whereas the Deutsches Institut für Wirtschaftsforschung, using another approach, found out that the purchasing power of 1 Eastmark equalled that of even 1.20 DM (cf. DIW, Wochenbericht 21/1990 of 25 May 1990).

3.   After the two papers on which the present contribution is based had been written, G. Sinn and H.-W. Sinn published a careful study of the multifaceted problem of German unification (cf. Sinn and Sinn, 1991). In this study the earlier criticism put forward by H.-W. Sinn against the decided route to privatization is expounded in great detail and some novel arguments are put forward.

4.   A lower output–capital ratio need not involve a lower rate of profits (or rate of interest), given the real wage rate, since it could be associated with a higher output–labour ratio or (average) labour productivity. However, labour productivity in East Germany was estimated to be around 30 per cent of the level in West Germany only.

5.   Siebert (1990) in an early attempt to assess the East German capital stock assumed that half of it has to be scrapped. See also Siebert (1991).

6.   The concept of capacity savings does not imply the full employment of labour. It gives potential saving forthcoming at the level of production and income associated with the full utilization of profitable plant and equipment.

7.   The female participation rate in West Germany was 38 per cent.

Bibliography

Akerlof, G.A., Rose A.K., Yellen J.L. and Hessenius, H. (1991), 'East Germany In From The Cold: The Economic Aftermath of Currency Union', *Brookings Papers for Economic Activity*, No. 1.

Deutsche Bundesbank (1990 and 1991), *Monatsberichte der Deutschen Bundesbank*, various issues: Frankfurt am Main.

Deutsches Institut für Wirtschaftsforschung (DIW) (1990 and 1991), *Wochenberichte*, various issues: Berlin.

Ifo Institut (1990 and 1991), *Ifo Schnelldienst*, various issues: Munich.

Institut für angewandte Wirtschaftsforschung (1990), 'Die ostdeutsche Wirtschaft 1990/1991', 22 October 1990.

Kurz, H.D. (1992), 'Whatever Happened to the East German Economy?', in M. Knell and C. Rider (eds), *Socialist Economies in Transition: Appraisals of the Market Mechanism*, Aldershot: Edward Elgar Publishing.

Kurz, H.D. (1993), 'Distributive Aspects of German Unification', in H.D. Kurz (ed.), *United Germany and the New Europe*, Aldershot: Edward Elgar Publishing.

Lipschitz, L. and McDonald, D. (eds) (1990), *German Unification: Economic Issues*, Occasional Paper no. 75, Washington, DC: International Monetary Fund.

Lipton, D. and Sachs, J. (1990), 'Creating a Market Economy in Eastern Europe: The Case of Poland', *Brookings Papers on Economic Activity*, no. 1.

Siebert, H. (1990), 'The Economic Integration of Germany', *Kieler Diskussionsbeiträge*, no. 160, Kiel: Institute of World Economics.

Siebert, H. (1991), 'The Integration of Germany: Real Economic Adjustment', *European Economic Review*, **35**, 591–602.

Sinn, G. and Sinn, H.-W. (1991), *Kaltstart. Volkswirtschaftliche Aspekte der Deutschen Vereinigung*, Tübingen: J.C.B. Mohr (Paul Siebeck).

Sinn, H.-W. (1990), 'Macroeconomic Aspects of German Unification', *Münchener Wirtschaftswissenschaftliche Beiträge*, Discussion paper no. 90-31.

The New York Times, New York (1990 and 1991), various issues.

The Week in Germany, New York (1990 and 1991), various issues.

11 Accountability and interregional income transfers in the former USSR

Volodimir N. Bandera

Introduction

As Gorbachev's economic reforms unfolded, one Soviet republic after another intensified its demands for sovereignty and, hence, for accountability in interrepublic transactions. The pressure also mounted on Moscow to become fiscally accountable. During the process of *perestroika* or restructuring, the principle of economic accounting or *khozraschet* at the microeconomic level of enterprise was extended to embrace the accountability and self-financing of the republics at the macro level. Not surprisingly, their quest for substantive economic sovereignty reinforced the drive for political independence, not only in the three Baltic states, but also in Russia, Ukraine, Georgia and the other republics. With the dissolution of the USSR in December 1991 the former Soviet republics have become separate economies. This establishes the need for evaluating their potential as trading partners.

The purpose of this paper is to interpret the fiscal and trading balances of Ukraine as a separate Soviet republic in relation to the rest of the USSR just before its dissolution. This involves macroeconomic disaggregation of the Soviet imperial economy from which member republics were in the process of separating themselves. The parliament of Ukraine proclaimed its independence on 24 August 1991, and this action was confirmed overwhelmingly by a referendum on 1 December 1991. The task is to estimate Ukraine's balance-of-payments account and interpret it in relation to the budgetary and national income accounts.[1] Our focus on 1988 is fortuitous because more complete data were released for that year. Also, the stringent fiscal and trade structures that linked the republic to the union were still intact, and not yet overwhelmed by inflation or deliberately hindered by Russia and the other successor states.

We intend to supplement the more common budgetary studies of the former Soviet republics with a comprehensive Western-style balance-of-payments analysis. This analytical approach can offer valuable insights about the potential this, and by extension other, former Soviet republics are likely to have as trading partners. One wonders in particular if this new country has the capacity to balance its external accounts while trying to establish its own independent currency. Steps were being taken in this direction as early as

1991, when Ukraine's central bank began to form a separate monetary system and applied for membership of the IMF.

Interregional income transfers ordained by Moscow

The former USSR was characterized by huge interrepublic income transfers. Their magnitude was revealed in a comprehensive study by A.G. Granberg and his team of econometricians at the Novosibirsk Economic Institute. Granberg summarized the territorial transfers of output in the USSR as follows (Granberg, 1973, p. 156):

> Regional balances of inflow and outflow of the gross output are comprehensive indicators of territorial economic interdependence. Counting external exports and imports, only the developed South (Ukraine plus Moldovia) and the Ural regions make a substantive credit contribution to the country's economy. These two regions show a credit balance in their income accounts. If external exports and imports are not counted, also the West (Belorussia plus the three Baltic states) would show a credit balance.

Specifically, the magnitude of contributed net exports (+) and received net imports (–) as a percentage of gross domestic product in the seven macro-regions in the early 1970s was as follows: the South (Ukraine plus Moldovia) 7.5 per cent; the Ural region 3.2 per cent; the West (Belorussia plus Baltic states) 0.0 per cent; the Centre –4.2 per cent; Western Siberia –0.5 per cent; Eastern Siberia –9.1 per cent; and the Far East –7.3 per cent.[2] It is clear that the more developed European regions have been losing current output for the benefit of the sparsely populated Eastern Asian regions. This pattern reflects a geopolitical development strategy which, according to Holubnychy (1975) had its origins in the imperial tsarist Russia.

For many decades, the proclaimed official Soviet policy was the equalization of the standard of living and the overall pace of economic development of the 15 Soviet republics. Under that pretext, the central planners enforced massive and protracted interregional shifts of labour and capital resources. Objective economists questioned these burdensome and ineffective policies timidly at first but, more recently, have been quite vocal, especially those who were spokesmen for various republics. The issue became widely discussed in both professional and popular Soviet publications. However, since reliable statistics are lacking, it was rightly asserted that:

> The question of economic relations of union republics is complex in two senses. First, at the present time there is no information about what republics give to the all-union fund and what they receive. Second, today there are no precise criteria regarding the justification of these flaws. The situation could be clarified by detailed interrepublic balances of production and distribution in physical and value terms, as well as the resulting magnitudes – the republics' contributions to

the all-union budget and subsidies from the budget (Koroteeva *et al.*, 1989, p. 44).

Western efforts to construct and analyse national income and balance-of-payments accounts for individual Soviet republics were frustrated by the lack of reliable data and methodological problems. However, studies by Bahry (1987), Bandera (1977), Gillula (1979), Holubnychy (1975) and Melnyk (1977) agree that Soviet interregional transfers of capital and other resources were large and protracted over many decades.[3] Schroeder (1991), Hogan (1991) and Bahry (1991) explain how Moscow's unwillingness to decentralize, to reduce and share its vast powers over the allocation of resources, and to become otherwise accountable to the constituent republics contributed to the dissolution of the USSR and the rise of independent successor nations.

Western Sovietologists traditionally de-emphasized or even ignored the regional aspects of the Soviet economy. In a 1991 symposium on economic transition in the Soviet Union and Eastern Europe, more than a dozen experts did not even consider the possibility of fragmentation of the USSR or the disbanding of the Moscow-dominated Council for Mutual Economic Assistance.[4]

Efforts to analyse interregional economic relations prove difficult since Soviet publications typically provide only fragmentary empirical evidence and conceal essential primary data. We demonstrate the advantages of applying the Western-style balance of payments and the income-absorption concepts in the analysis of former Soviet republics, now the successor states. The discipline of these macroeconomic accounts would compel the statisticians and the economists to address the underlying thorny methodological problems of empirical estimation and analytical interpretation of macroeconomic data generated in non-market economic systems typified by arbitrary prices and other distortions.

Insights from the balance of payments of the republic

In order to extend our understanding of the evolving positions of the constituent republics *vis-à-vis* the union, an attempt is made here to construct and interpret a comprehensive balance-of-payments account for a specific republic. Ukraine in 1988 is chosen as an example because the experience of this particular republic has been previously interpreted in econometric studies and several Western publications (Koropeckyj, 1981, 1992).

Since it is necessary to identify the peculiar fiscal and trading interaction between an administrative entity and the centrally managed USSR, the balance of payments of a Soviet republic can be patterned after a now conventional scheme previously devised for Puerto Rico (Isard, 1960, pp. 173–8).

Table 11.1:   Balance of payments of the Ukrainian SSR, 1988 (million rubles)

	Credit entries (+) entailing in-payments	Debt entries (–) entailing out-payments
A. CURRENT ACCOUNT[a]		
(exports (+), imports (–))		
1. external trade[b]		
1.1 With socialist countries	6 253	5 968
1.2 With capitalist countries	3 533	2 981
2. Trade with Soviet republics, union government excluded[c]	40 060	36 430
3. Transactions with union government		
3.1 Defence expenditures in Ukraine[d]	13 200	
3.2 Administration and other	4 500	
Balance of current account	22 167	
B. CAPITAL & UNILATERAL TRANSFERS ACCOUNT[e]		
4. Transfers of taxes to union budget		
4.1 Turnover tax[f]		6 103
4.2 Taxes on population		2 914
5. Union share of enterprise profits[g]		17 985
6. Other union revenues from Ukraine		26 563
7. Union budget allocations to Ukraine		
7.1 To finance Ukraine economy[h]	17 304	
7.2 For social and cultural programmes	9 138	
7.3 For Chernobyl clean-up[j]	5 000	
Balance of capital & unilateral account		22 123
C. ERRORS AND OMISSIONS (balance)		0 044

Sources and methods of estimation:
a. Data in parts 1 and 2 exclude trade in services such as tourism.
b. External trade figures in international prices are based on *PlanEcon Report* (1990, p. 2). Ukraine's share of the union total was calculated by applying the percentages implied by data in *Vestnik Statistiki* (3/1990, p. 36); namely, exports 14.6 per cent and 13.8 per cent of the union total.
c. *Vestnik* (ibid.). Much of this intra-union trade was within union-controlled enterprises that were similar to multinational corporations in the West.
d. Ukraine's prorated share of the union total of 73 000 million rubles, as reported in *Ekonomicheskaia gazeta* (1989, p. 3).
e. In Part B, financial data are derived mainly from Ministerstvo (1989).
f. Represents 35.2 per cent of total turnover tax collected in Ukraine.
g. Ukraine's contribution was 23.5 per cent of the union total according to the method used by Melnyk (1977).
h. Ukraine's estimated share was 13.2 per cent; the same as the republic's proportion in total USSR state investment.
i. The clean-up was managed by the union Ministry of Nuclear Energy. It is assumed here that the budgeted funds for this purpose constituted a unilateral transfer of funds back to Ukraine.

As shown in Table 11.1 the intent of this account is to encompass all trade and financial transactions occurring during one year. The transacting partners of the republic are: (1) countries outside the union receiving exports and supplying imports; (2) the rest of the union which sells to, and buys from, the republic; and (3) union government engaged in direct purchases in the republic as shown in the current account, and in fiscal and banking transactions as shown in the capital account.

The logic of this type of accounting requires that total inpayments (+, credits) must equal total outpayments (–, debits); whether the payments are actual or of a bookkeeping nature is irrelevant here. The overall equality of debits and credits is assured since, conceptually, each transaction at the micro level involves a double entry. This accounting equality must remain when transactions are aggregated into convenient categories, even though the pairing of debit and credit entries for specific transactions is obscured in the process of aggregation. For example, a wheat export of 100 million rubles that is entered as a credit (or inpayment) must have, somewhere in the statement, an offsetting debit (or outpayment) entry of: (1) 100 million rubles worth of imports; or (2) 100 million rubles in cash receipts; or (3) 100 million rubles worth of 'unrequited' outpayments such as grants and tributes to foreigners; or (4) 100 rubles loaned to foreigners; or (5) some combination of these. When bookkeeping inconsistencies result in a statistical discrepancy between total credits and debits, the required accounting equality between the two is assured by a correcting entry, 'Errors and Omissions'.

Four methodological issues emerge from the exercise of constructing the balance of payments for Ukraine as in Table 11.1. First, contrary to expectation, the data on the republic's transactions with the rest of the union were incomplete in spite of *glasnost*. Disaggregated data show Ukraine to be a net exporter of food, machinery and metals, and a net importer of fuels, lumber and consumer products (Goskomstat, 1990, p. 40). But although such fragmentary statistics on the output and destination of producers' goods abound, corresponding aggregate data in value terms are unreliable. As explained in the notes to Table 11.1, the estimates of Ukraine's trade and financial transfers were pieced together from various sources.

Secondly, it is deemed essential to estimate current account transactions of the republic with the union government as a separate entity. This would be straightforward if the sale of goods and services to the union government (or subsequently to the Commonwealth administration) only involved exports outside the republic's boundaries, so that such trade would be part of the entry 'the rest of the union'. However, sizeable defence expenditures and the provisioning of the military forces stationed in Ukraine does not involve exports across the republic's boundaries. The inclusion of the union government as a separate trading partner is needed in order to identify the real counterpart of the transfers of taxes, profits and other payments to the union as shown in the financial account. To be sure, for 1988, 'normal trade' with union enterprises cannot be readily distinguished from 'trade with the union government', especially since about one-half of the republic's annual budget was financed through the union budget. But even though fuzzy statistical classifications are unavoidable here, meaningful estimates of the republic's interaction with the union government can be made by following consistent procedures.

The third problem is the lack of data relating to trade in services, an anomaly which also typifies published trade statistics for the USSR as a whole. From the republic's standpoint it is necessary to account for the export value of such activities as the services of Ukrainian specialists in developing countries, sales to foreign tourists in the republic, support of foreign students (4600 in 1967) and so on. For example, new science and technology transfers between the republics occurred free of charge, so that: '...regions and republics that were most mature in terms of science and technology have been losing colossal sums' (Koroteeva, 1989, p. 44). Thus, the omission of service transactions in Soviet sources and, hence, in Table 11.1, undoubtedly reduces the credit side of the current account, which reduces the statistical estimate of Ukraine's unrequited export balance.[5]

Fourthly, Soviet data underlying Table 11.1 do not account for the arbitrariness of prices. It is known that prices of primary producers' goods were sometimes set below the cost of production, while prices of certain types of manufactured goods were often above their production cost. Since Ukraine generated substantial export surpluses in producers' goods and agricultural produce, the price system understated the opportunity cost of these exports. A further distortion was created by zonal price differentials for agricultural staples, producers' goods and centrally distributed inputs such as energy.

As if this were not enough, serious price distortions were also created by union monopolies. These were organized vertically by sectors of production and operated throughout the union; perhaps as much as 95 per cent of Ukraine's industrial output was controlled by such monopolies. This industrial structure involved extensive intra-industry trade as well as intersectoral trade (both involving the republic's exports and imports) at internally set transfer prices or even on barter terms. Certainly, such arbitrary prices distort the aggregate values of exports and imports, so that the meaning of trade balances becomes elusive. This has allowed the recent appearance of many publications like Goskomstat (1990) and Plyshevsky (1990) which aimed to convince Soviet readers that Ukraine and most other republics were blessed with import surpluses as a result of their membership of the union. This illusion was created largely by evaluating external imports at inflated domestic prices. This practice, in fact, exploited the buyers and generated huge profits for Moscow; 50.44 billion rubles in 1988 alone (Goskomstat, 1990, p. 37). Indeed, Soviet imperial planning theories maintained that price manipulation was a legitimate method to accomplish interregional transfers of resources.

Methodological problems notwithstanding, the estimated balance-of-payments account of Ukraine offers significant insights into the political economy of a republic within the USSR just before its rapid dismemberment.

To begin with, consider the issue of the burden of uncompensated export balances of Ukraine. If one counts only the businesslike trade that crossed Ukraine's borders, then the 'balance of trade' (consisting of parts 1 and 2 of Table 11.1) amounts to a net export of 4.4 billion rubles, or a loss of about 3 per cent of the republic's gross social product; this estimate seems to correspond to the net loss of production as implied by Plyshevsky (1990, p. 54) and elaborated in the next section. But if non-defence purchases (part 3) and defence purchases (part 4) by the union government in the republic are added, then the net export balance of the entire current account was 22.2 billion rubles, representing a loss of 14 per cent of the republic's GSP.

Furthermore, it is helpful also to view the republic's net balance of transactions from the financial standpoint. In section B of Table 11.1, the 'capital and unilateral transfers' account consists mainly of grant-like transfers into and from the union budget; in Western terminology these are unilateral transfers, that is, one-way non-repayable and non-interest-bearing financial payments.

It was impossible to identify specific capital inflows and outflows, that is, the loan-type interest-bearing transactions which would add to Ukraine's external assets and liabilities. We may assume that the 'other union revenues' from Ukraine (part 6) include such capital transactions. In 1988, the union budget required substantial deficit spending that was financed to some extent by utilizing the savings of Ukraine's population, as well as by Ukraine's net repayment of 12.7 billion rubles of short and long-term credits to state banks (Ministerstvo, 1989, pp. 422–3).[6] Also, no attempt was made here to estimate Ukraine's share of Soviet external borrowing and lending, although such transactions, which intimately engaged Ukraine's economy, apparently increased the net international creditor status of the USSR in 1988.[7] But although the details of Ukraine's financial entanglement with the union are lacking, the essential insight should be underscored. The net negative financial balance of 22 billion rubles is of necessity equivalent to the net positive balance of the current account (using, of course, the corrective entry under 'Errors and Omissions' in section C of Table 11.1). Thus, the net loss to Ukraine is seen either as an unrequited real trade surplus or as an equivalent net efflux of financial resources.

Finally, an important insight from the balance-of-payments exercise per-
tains to the contributions of the republic to the balance of payments of the
USSR as a whole. This aspect was still being circumvented even at the
height of *glasnost* (Ivanov, 1989). Using our estimates, the international pattern of net trade flows involving the republic, the outside countries and the
union can be represented as in Figure 11.1 which, for simplicity, omits
transactions with the union government (part 3 of Table 11.1). As can be
seen, in addition to an export balance of 3630 million rubles with other
Soviet republics, Ukraine generated a trade surplus of 837 million rubles
with outside countries. Thus, the drainage of national output from the republic occurred both through the internal and the external trade mechanisms. The
latter involved Moscow's foreign trade monopoly that assigned export tasks
and import allotments and imposed the domestic prices on such external
transactions. Although *perestroika* allowed the enterprises to retain fractions
of foreign currency earned through exports, the governments of the republics
had to fight for similar access to foreign exchange. Moreover, the republics
encountered fierce opposition from Moscow when they tried to become
responsible for their own trade imbalances and the required financing. By
1991, Ukraine's government proclaimed that it had assumed full responsibility
for its share (about 16 per cent) of accumulated foreign debts and assets of
the former USSR.

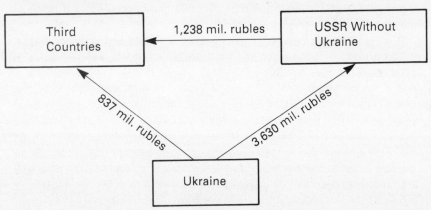

Sources: *PlanEcon* (May 25, 1990) for aggregate USSR data, and Table 11.1 in this article
for Ukraine's data.

*Figure 11.1:   Net trade flows between the republic, the 'rest of the union'
and third countries (1988)*

External balance in relation to aggregate income and absorption
The income–absorption approach to the balance of payments outlined by
Dornbusch (1980) is well suited for clarifying the relationship between
output and its utilization within the confines of a republic. This comprehensive analysis underscores the dire consequences when Ukraine was forced to
suffer unrequited export surpluses.

On the one hand, not all of the production generated in the republic (as
measured by its GSP) is being utilized internally. On the other hand, not all
goods and services absorbed or utilized by the republic originate internally.
Income and absorption may be interpreted accordingly: define income Y as the
value of the output or product generated in the republic:

$$Y = C + I + GR + GU + X \tag{1}$$

where C is the production of republic-destined consumption goods, I is re-
public-generated investment goods without the deduction for capital depreciation, GR is output paid for by the republic and local governments, GU is net
sales to union government exclusive of union enterprises, and X is external and
intra-union exports. Define absorption A in the republic as

$$A = C + I + GR + GU + M \tag{2}$$

where all variables, including imports M from other republics and outside
countries, represent the sum of goods and services utilized by the republic.

The difference between income Y (equation 1) and absorption (equation 2)
is the trade balance, B (equation 3),

$$\begin{aligned} B = \quad Y \ - \ A \ = \ X \ - \ M \\ 4.4 = 157.2 - 152.8 = 49.8 - 45.4 \end{aligned} \tag{3}$$

The figures below the variables are the estimated values in billion rubles for
Ukraine in 1988. For that year, Ukraine's income Y, as measured by GSP, was
152.2 billion rubles (roughly one-fifth of the USSR total GSP). An estimate
of aggregate absorption, A, was derived from the ratio of the indices of per
capita utilization to per capita national product in Ukraine; according to
Plyshevsky (1990, p. 54) this ratio was 87:90.

Thus, the net unrequited export balance of 4.4 billion rubles is seen as a
net loss of absorption which represents three per cent of the GSP of Ukraine.
In this interpretation, the net expenditure in the republic by the union government for administration and defence-type goods and services is not counted
in the more narrowly defined net export balance, B, although such expendi-

ture was in fact financed by the revenue extracted from the republic, and, as explained above, may be perceived as part of the loss to the region.

The fundamental insight which follows from the above analysis merits emphasis. The unrequited trade surpluses experienced by Ukraine in 1988 and other years involve equivalent losses of absorption in the form of consumption and/or investment in the republic. We can, therefore, appreciate why the issue of interrepublic income transfers became explosive in the struggle of the republics with Moscow as the arbiter of territorial redistribution of output. In the spirit of *glasnost*, national leaders embarked on a kind of *perestroika* (restructuring) that would prevent the perceived exploitation by the so-called 'centre'. National independence became their goal.

Concluding remarks
The outcry for regional accountability in the late 1980s had far-reaching consequences for the political economy of the Soviet Union, which was managed as a highly centralized imperial system. The unrequited income losses sustained by many republics could hardly be expected to continue. From Ukraine's standpoint, large income transfers ordained by central authorities constituted an unjustified form of tribute. Moscow's monopoly over foreign trade, which enabled the centre to profiteer as a middleman, was increasingly challenged. Ukraine, in particular, resolved not to participate in any kind of centre-directed economic scheme that smacked of the old system.

The suggested use of Western balance of payments and income–absorption analysis can help to identify and interpret the real content of interrepublic income transfers. With the dissolution of the USSR in December 1991, the preponderance of transactions with the union government will essentially disappear. Moreover, the direction, content and the terms of trade of individual successor countries will no longer be determined by Moscow. These changes will be of fundamental significance for Ukraine and its trading partners. To be sure, the analysis of the balance of payments will be expedited when the republics improve their own macroeconomic data, while prices will approach their equilibrium market levels.[8]

In closing, what can be expected of Ukraine's ability to balance its external accounts as an independent country? This is an important question, since the new state has ventured to form its own monetary system based on a separate currency, the *hryvna*. The prospects are fairly optimistic. After all, the new country will avoid the forfeiture of its earnings of hard currencies. It remains to be seen whether the pent-up demand for imports, once ruthlessly suppressed by Moscow, can be held in check by Ukraine's newly formed national bank as it tries to establish a stable rate of exchange with substantial convertibility. The IMF and the World Bank are watching, cognizant that there is an inherent desire to increase domestic absorption, irrespective of the need to maintain a stable exchange rate and a debt-free status *vis-à-vis* the rest of the world.

Notes

1. With a population of about 52 million and an area of 233,000 square miles, Ukraine is comparable to France. The republic produced just under a fifth of the total output of the USSR, and accounted for a similar share of Soviet foreign trade.
2. Since data aggregated into seven macro-regions combine the small republics and subdivide the huge Russian Federation RFFR, this tends to downplay the extent of income transfers; even so, they appear to be very large indeed.
3. The institutional aspects of the fiscal transfers are explained by Bahry (1987), who also evaluates the budgetary balances from the standpoint of the republics (Bahry, 1991). Holubnychy (1975) focuses on the geopolitical and military factors in the territorial development of the tsarist and Soviet empires. A summary of nine different sources by Melnyk (1977, p. 288) indicates that between 1925 and 1970 Ukraine was losing 9 to 20 per cent of its national income; the estimates differ depending on the period investigated and the method of calculation. Recall that French indemnities to victorious Prussia were 5.6 per cent of the national income during 1872–75, and that Germany's burdensome reparations to the Allies during 1924–32 amounted to 2.5 per cent.
4. See the prestigious *Journal of Economic Perspectives*, Autumn 1991, which is published by the American Economic Association. In this issue the map of the huge former Soviet geopolitical domain does not even identify the independent Baltic states or any of the other ascending successor states.
5. The burden of provisioning the military bases has been a major issue in the Baltic states and, later, in Ukraine during the separatist upheaval. The territorial aspect of the huge Soviet military budget was, of course, suppressed in Soviet statistics.
6. A significant portion of the large union budget during the late 1980s was financed by an outright emission of money. The injection of such new money through government expenditures in Ukraine constituted another method by which Moscow could acquire Ukraine's output. Moreover, the unwarranted expansion of money contributed to an actual and suppressed inflation for consumer goods, a malady over which the republic had no control.
7. Citing a specialized Leningrad periodical CHAS PIK, *PlanEcon* (25 May 1990, pp. 24–7) shows that the USSR extended substantial hard currency credits to Third World countries in the late 1980s – $8.2 billion in 1988 alone. As of 1 November 1989, the outstanding indebtedness of the Third World to the USSR was $68 billion, and of the socialist bloc 44 billion rubles. In 1989, Soviet liabilities to Western and CMEA banks rose from $36.8 billion to $44.4 billion, while Soviet deposits in these banks remained unchanged at $15.2 billion. Although Ukraine has started to participate directly in international joint investment projects and is otherwise trying to attract foreign capital, aggregate data on these transactions are only beginning to appear.
8. The head of the State Committee for Statistics, which was transformed into the Ministry of Statistics of Ukraine in 1992, reported (Borysenko, 1990) that the republic has implemented ambitious measures to collect and report comprehensive data on trade, income and other macroeconomic variables. Although some international financial and trade data have started to appear since then, a comprehensive balance-of-payments account is expected to be calculated for 1992.

References

Bahry, D. (1987), *Outside Moscow: Power, Politics and Budgetary Policy in the Soviet Republics*, New York: Columbia University Press.
Bahry, D. (1991), 'The Union Republics and Contradictions in Gorbachev's Economic Reforms', *Soviet Economy*, 7, (3), 215–55.

Bandera, V.N. (1977), 'External and Intraunion Trade and Capital Transfers', chapter in Koropeckyj (1977).
Borysenko, M. (1990), 'Dokorinna perebudova statystyki v umovakh onovlennia suspilstva' (Fundamental Reform of Statistics During the Revival of the Society), *Ekonomika Radianskoi Ukrainy*, no. 6.
Dornbusch, R. (1980), *Open Economy Macroeconomics*, New York: Basic Books.
Gillula, J.W. (1977), 'Input–Output Analysis', chapter in Koropeckyj (1977).
Gillula, J.W. (1979), 'Economic Interdependence of Soviet Republics', in *Soviet Economy In Time of Change*, Washington, DC: Joint Economic Committee.
Goskomstat SSSR (1990), *Vestnik statistiki*, no. 3.
Granberg, A.G. (1973), *Optimizatsia territorialnykh proportsii narodnogo khoziaistva* (Optimization of Territorial Proportions of the National Economy), Moscow.
Hogan, W.W. (1991), 'Economic Reforms in the Sovereign States of the Former Soviet Union', *Brookings Papers in Economic Activity*, no. 2.
Holubnychy, V. (1975), 'Teleology of the Macroregions in Soviet Union's Long-Range Plans, 1920–90', chapter in A. F. Burghardt (ed.), *Development Regions in the Soviet Union, Eastern Europe and Canada*, New York: Praeger.
Isard, W. (1960), *Methods of Regional Analysis*, New York: Wiley.
Ivanov, I. (1989), 'Problemy khoziaistvennogo rascheta vo vnesh-ekonomicheskoi deiatelnosti' (Problems of Economic Accounting in Foreign Economic Activities), *Voprosy ekonomiki*, no. 9.
Koropeckyj, I.S. (ed.) (1977), *The Ukraine Within the USSR: An Economic Balance Sheet*, New York: Praeger.
Koropeckyj, I.S. (1992), *The Ukrainian Economy: Achievements Problems, Challenges*, Cambridge, Mass.: Harvard University Press.
Koropeckyj, I.S. and Schroeder, G.E. (eds) (1981), *Economics of Soviet Regions*, New York: Praeger.
Korotéeva, V., Perepelkin, L. and Shkaratan, O. (1989), 'From Bureaucratic Centralism to Economic Integration of Sovereign Republics', *Problems of Economics*, **32**, (3).
Melnyk, Z.L. (1977), 'Capital Formation and Financial Relations', chapter in Koropeckyj (1977).
Ministerstvo finansov SSSR (1989), *Gosudarstvennyi biudzhet SSSR*, (Moscow).
PlanEcon Economic Report (1990), nos. 21–29, Washington, DC.
Plyshevsky, B. (1990), 'Narodnoe khoziaistvo v minuvshem godu: Territorialnyi aspect' (The National Economy During the Past Year: The Territorial Aspect), *Planovoe khoziaistvo*, no. 4.
Schroeder, G.E. (1991), 'Perestroyka in the Aftermath of 1990', *Soviet Economy*, **7**, (1), 3–13.

12 The role of the firm in the transition to a free market: lessons from the Japanese and American models

Zoltan J. Acs and Felix R. FitzRoy

Introduction

A deep underlying adherence to the principle that there are significant economies to be reaped from large-scale production is embedded in the socialist model. Large units of production are viewed as the most efficient means for transforming inputs into outputs, and any deviation from mass production is a socially wasteful use of resources (Kornai, 1990). This belief in the inherent potential of scale economies, dating back at least to Karl Marx, was coupled with the view that it promoted the corporate form of organization, which he expected to lead to a '... constantly diminishing number of the magnates of capital, who usurp and monopolize all advantages of transformation'. The ultimate state is one in which: '... the entire social capital would be united, either in the hands of one single capitalist, or in those of one single corporation' (Marx, 1912, 836). Lenin (1916) was likewise obsessed with the efficiencies to be gained by large scale production units. His expectations about the benefits of concentration were further enriched and developed for socialism by Stalin and those who interpreted the economics aspects of his views.

Such thinking did not diverge markedly from the doctrine common in the West, where the importance of size and economies of scale was also emphasized. The 1950s and 1960s saw the zenith of mass production in the United States. This was the world of countervailing power so aptly described by Galbraith (1967), in which virtually every major institution in society acted to reinforce the stability needed to promote mass production in giant corporations. In fact, the unprecedented growth experienced in the West during this period has been attributed less to technology than to prevailing social and political forces working to provide the market stability required for successful mass production. Thus, during the 1950s and 1960s in the West, the emphasis on large units of production and scale economies did not seem to be at odds with contemporary economic doctrines about production. In both East and West, mass production was seen as the technologically dynamic form of production (Piore and Sabel, 1984).

Mass production was housed in large, vertically integrated hierarchical organizations with strict internal planning and bureaucratic control. It derived its efficiency from extreme specialization of resources. The productive process was separated into a series of distinct tasks which were assigned piecemeal to narrowly trained workers and/or specialized capital equipment. In Eastern Europe, by way of contrast, industry made massive investments in 'command and control' planning, especially as it related to management decisions over the medium term about the level of inputs and outputs possible for the production equation. As Michael J. Piore (1991, p. 4) pointed out: 'Eastern Europe continues to be committed to this form of industrial development while Japan and the West have largely abandoned it in favor of approaches which stretch resources and make them, and the organizations in which they are housed, more flexible'.

There is much evidence to support practical lessons from Japan and the West for Eastern European firms. We start with a critical review of the fundamental institutional reform for creating efficiency in Eastern European firms under privatization. Lessons from the Japanese can be incorporated into the recent literature of institutional economics to provide a more coherent theory. Both these literatures, however, neglect the role of technology in relation to firm organization and also as to size; thus we will also discuss recent developments in these (not unrelated) areas to throw additional light on our comparative analysis of the J- (Japanese) and A- (American) firm for Eastern Europe. Policy and other conclusions are summarized in the final section.

Does privatization enforce efficiency?

The basic argument for privatization of the ubiquitous giant corporations of Eastern European is efficiency (Clague and Rausser, 1991; Murrell, 1991). The argument is compelling. During the previous four decades there were three distinguishing features of industrial policy in Eastern Europe: state ownership of economic assets, the centralization of those assets, and a system of command planning without markets to allocate their use. As Roman (1990) observed, the political power based on a monolithic one-party system rapidly appropriated the means of production on a vast and massive scale throughout the Eastern European countries. This resulted in the bulk of economic assets being controlled by the state. As Table 12.1 shows, the share of economic activity, measured either by output or employment, emanating from the state sector was substantially greater in the East than in Western countries. In Eastern Europe, the amount of national output accounted for by state-owned enterprises ranged from 97 per cent in Czechoslovakia (1986) to about 65 per cent in Hungary (1984). By contrast, even in France, which has the greatest share of assets controlled by the state of any

Table 12.1:   *Size of the state sector: comparison of Eastern and Western countries*

Countries	Share of output(%)	Share of employment (%)
Eastern Europe		
Czechoslovakia (1984)	97.0	–
East Germany (1982)	96.5	94.2
Soviet Union (1985)	96.0	–
Poland (1985)	81.7	71.5
Hungary (1984)	65.2	69.9
Western Countries		
France (1982)	16.5	14.6
Austria (1979)	14.5	13.0
Italy (1982)	14.0	15.0
Turkey (1985)	11.2	20.0
Sweden	–	10.6
Finland	–	10.0
United Kingdom (1988)	11.1	8.2
West Germany (1982)	16.7	7.8
Portugal (1976)	9.7	–
Denmark (1974)	6.3	–
Greece (1979)	6.1	–
Norway (1979)	–	6.0
Spain (1979)	4.1	8.0
Netherlands (1973)	3.6	8.0
United States (1983)	1.3	1.8

Source: Milanovic (1990), Tables 1.4 and 1.7.

Western nation, only 16.5 per cent of national output emanated from state-owned enterprises.

It is easy to see why privatization and market creation loom so large on the horizon. However, *exclusive* focus on the transition from planning to market obscures other dimensions of the Eastern European economic structure which are probably even more important for long-run efficiency.[1] Thus Eastern Europe lags far behind the West in terms of its organizational and technological development, which has very little to do with planning *per se*. This lag reflects the continued commitment to a model of industrial development based on mass production. Exemplified by Adam Smith's pin factory and Henry Ford's Model T, this involved the production of standardized products for mass consumption markets. It derived its efficiency from the extreme specialization of resources (inflexibility) (Acs and Audretsch, 1993).

It may be that the absence of a market system is responsible for the current state of affairs in Eastern Europe, but even this is a dubious proposition. In the West, the new institutional forms were largely a response to the heightened instability in the business environment of the 1970s and 1980s relative to the earlier post-war decades. The variability of energy and other raw materials pieces, exchange and interest rates, and sudden shifts in the composition of demand underlie this uncertainty. The Eastern economies were insulated from these developments by the fact that they constituted a separate trading bloc with their own energy and raw material sources (Piore, 1991).

Responsiveness to these changes in the West was, in any case, extremely varied. Managers in Japan, Germany and Central Italy began to adopt their organizational forms and modes of interaction relatively early, and have been quite successful overall in the transition. As a group, American businessmen were among the last to acknowledge the need for adjustment and have had an extremely difficult time carrying it out. The key issues here have less to do with the level of concentration, the distribution of ownership of private property and the way in which markets themselves are structured, than with the informal organizational and productive systems within the firm.

The debate over privatization in Eastern and Central Europe needs to be viewed in a larger context and recast more in terms of managerial efficiency. Refocusing the discussion to analyse the impact of privatization on managerial control moves the debate away from the ideological ground of private versus public, to the more pragmatic ground of managerial behaviour and accountability.[2] Viewed in this context, the pros and cons of privatization can, and should, be measured against the standards of good management regardless of ownership (Goodman and Loveman, 1992).

What emerges, then, is that neither public nor private managers will always be in the best interest of the public. Privatization will be effective only if private managers have incentives to act in the public interest, which includes, but is not limited to, efficiency. Profits and the public interest overlap best when the privatized asset operates in a competitive market. It takes competition from other companies to discipline managerial behaviour, something still lacking in the former Eastern European countries. When these conditions are not met, continued government involvement will likely be necessary. The simple transfer of ownership from public to private hands will not necessarily reduce the cost or enhance the quality of service.

We now turn to the evidence on the debate between the J-firm and A-firm in the West to shed important light on the changes that managers in the East need to make.

A- and J-firm organization compared

Much modern discussion of productive organization starts from what are variously referred to as mobility costs, sunk costs or firm-specific investments, typically in highly specialized equipment.[3] Skills learned on a particular job or machines installed for a certain task may be more productive currently than in their next best use.[4] When factors of production are thus partially immobilized, a surplus over opportunity cost, or quasi-rent, arises. If labour is perfectly mobile (has no specific skills or other assets), as in much classical and neoclassical theorizing, then capital owners naturally appropriate the enterprise surplus and hire labour at competitive market wages. Conflict potential increases when workers are also immobilized or specialized, so that bargaining to attain a 'fair' distribution of productivity gains is required, and workers cannot simply be paid their perhaps declining opportunity cost without destroying incentives for co-operation and specific investment.

In western industrial societies the traditional response to this dilemma has been two-fold (Leijonhufvud, 1985). Increasing division of labour and Taylorist work organization have reduced the total skill content of individual tasks, as well as specific training, which facilitates mobility and payment at market rates. On the other hand, collective bargainers have insisted on precisely defined job classifications, and pay-scales which rise with skill and seniority in order to protect older workers from unscrupulous employers and to provide job-ladders or internal promotion possibilities, at least in 'primary' employment. Detailed, formal bargaining agreements reduced the scope for *ex post* differences of interpretation, and permitted arbitration by third parties when conflict did arise. Mass production and surplus-sharing became feasible even under traditionally adversarial industrial relations.[5]

The rigidities imposed by Taylorist organization have become increasingly dysfunctional in recent years, as demand has shifted away from traditional standardized, large-scale production to customized and batch production (Piore and Sabel, 1984). Rapid technological change has reinforced the need for a more flexible and adaptable work-force, unconstrained by detailed job classifications and restrictive work rules, as we discuss below. As future tasks become less predictable, the cost of detailed, formal collective agreements rises, but so too does the scope for *ex post* opportunism and distributive conflict or mutual 'hold up' between the parties.

In their recent comparative institutional theories of the firm, Leibenstein (1987) and Tomer (1987) start essentially from the prisoners' dilemma situation in the firm, when major (potential) gains from co-operation remain unrealized in a low trust, adversarial stance.[6] However, Leibenstein and Tomer miss the crucial role of organized labour in stabilizing inefficient organization.[7] Their analysis of the J-firm agrees with Aoki's (1988) most detailed account, as well as with Dore (1987), Abbeglen and Stock (1985) and many others in broad outline, though individual emphasis of course varies.

The key features of J-firm organization on which a wide consensus has emerged would seem to be the following. First, much fewer and less detailed job classifications facilitate job rotation, and there is team-work and career development for blue collar as well as managerial employees. Firm-specific training is encouraged by long-term employment prospects for 'primary' workers; this is supported by work-sharing instead of lay-offs as well as internal reallocation in response to cyclical and structural shocks. Long-term employment also allows employers to reduce short-term monitoring of performance in favour of long-run promotion prospects. Age–earnings profiles are much steeper than in the A-firm for all classes of employee, and a substantial lump sum payment on retirement is customary, while piece rates are rare. Aoki (1988) notes that employees whose performance turns out to be consistently unsatisfactory are sometimes dismissed mid-career, so the consequent loss of seniority and retirement benefits represents a severe penalty. On the other hand, the need to accumulate private savings for retirement with very limited social security *reduces* the lifetime cost of deferred pay because less borrowing is required for optimal life-cycle consumption.

Decentralized, firm-level wage bargains seem to be more flexible in Japan than elsewhere,[8] and, of course, promotion prospects depend on firm performance. Employees of the J-firm have more to lose from bankruptcy, and Aoki (1988) argues that, essentially, all employees thus hold an equity stake in the firm.[9] Motivation and co-operation towards long-run goals are thereby encouraged, with *participative* management imposing a joint responsibility on both workers and external capital owners.

Another remarkable feature of the J-firm is a much lower ratio of administrative and supervisory employees than in A-firms, as well as a substantially smaller ratio of top salaries to production wages. This suggests that more human capital or higher skills of production workers have reduced the *marginal* productivity of the factor management, while there is direct evidence for higher labour productivity in complex manufacturing processes (Aoki, 1988). We discuss technological ramifications below but, in any case, the A–J-firm comparison does appear to correspond with the distributive conflict discussed in Section 1 above, and to provide some explanation for the slow adoption of J-type organizations in Western industry.

While cultural factors and historical accidents may support J-firm organization in Japan, as Leibenstein (1987) argues in some detail, there is also considerable – though still unsystematic – evidence for the comparative advantage of J-type organization in a Western environment. This evidence includes the success of growing numbers of Japanese subsidiaries using local labour in Europe and America (Florida and Kenney, 1991), as well as research on profit sharing and co-operative work organization.[10]

Co-determination in West Germany, Sweden and other European countries has been credited with improving labour relations compared to Anglo–American practice, though measurable benefits have not been identified.[11] The German version is dominated by powerful, centralized trade unions, and seems to have hindered rather than encouraged movement towards J-firm organization, for reasons which support our earlier observations on the role of adversarial collective bargaining in general. German labour law provides extensive powers for union and labour representatives to participate in management in the firm. In this version of representational industrial democracy, visible benefits for employed workers such as uniformly higher wages, job security and shorter hours have been the main goals.[12] Decentralization and local flexibility have been resisted by union leaders intent on maintaining their domination of a centralized, industry-wide bargaining process. Firm-level, unionized labour representatives typically co-operate with management in personnel and other areas within their province, and are also united in their opposition to substantive decentralization of internal organization. J-firm organization requires a relocation of decision-making powers from central management functions to flexible teams on the shop floor. The successful coalition between influential union functionaries and management officials is likely to lose relevance and power under *informal* labour–management co-operation and team work, so union opposition (in the face of growing market pressures for change) is a predictable special-interest group response.[13]

In their authoritative account of the 'transformation of American industrial relations', Kochan, Katz and McKersie (1986) document the increasing adoption of J-firm features (such as flexible team work with a drastically reduced number of job-classifications, and employee participation programmes) in non-union establishments. Some movement towards greater flexibility in union bargaining is also observable.

It is surprising how few of the insights from the new industrial relations have penetrated the new institutional economics. Thus Alchian and Woodward (1988) emphasize the importance of team-work in the firm without mentioning the much greater use of flexible teams in J-firms than in the traditional Taylorist organizations of Western manufacturing.[14] Similarly, Williamson's 'comparative institutional assessment' of work modes (Williamson, 1985, pp. 223–31) never mentions Japan or team work! His main concern here is to demolish a strawman – the rather obviously absurd idea that hierarchy and authority in complex organizations are dispensable. Despite his sensible injunctions to consider 'real organizational phenomena' and to 'adopt a comparative orientation' (p. 238), Williamson consistently neglects A–J-firm comparison along with the distributional conflicts retarding the spread of J-firm organization, and the competitive market pressures which are transforming American (and other Western) industrial relations (including the success of Japanese transplants in the US, with J-firm organization documented by Florida and Kenney (1991)).

Technology and flexibility in the J- and A-firm

We have argued that important lessons can be learned from the J-firm regarding organizational practices, particularly with reference to job classification and team work. Similarly, in the area of technology there is much to learn from the J-firm. The 'conventional' wisdom is that the J-firm has concentrated on process innovation, improving the quality and reducing the cost of existing products while neglecting basic research leading to radical innovation. By contrast the A-firm has created a string of successful product innovations, but has neglected process innovation.[15] An important difference is that the Japanese innovative effort is concentrated in the large (but more flexible and efficiently organized) corporation, while small enterprises and spin-offs are a (if not *the*) major force for innovation in the US.[16]

Also, as Aoki (1988, p. 251) points out in his careful study, small entrepreneurial firms, especially those set up by university scientists, are not likely to emerge in Japan, at least not in the near future. However, the co-operative agreements on non-market transactions known as 'flexible networking' between large corporations and small subcontractors have become increasingly important in Japan, and in different forms elsewhere.[17]

Institutionalists such as Williamson ignore the growing role of such co-operative arrangements that fall between the traditional 'markets and hierarchies' dichotomy. One reason that the pattern in the A-firm favours radical innovation, whereas the J-firm follows an incremental one, 'is related to the way internal labor markets are organized within the firm and the way these internal markets are related to the external markets' (Imai and Itani, 1984). In the US, where internal and external labour markets are more integrated, it is easy to assemble the best talent for radical innovation. Japan's 'closed' internal markets for labour as well as finance do not lend themselves to assembling the resources necessary for research and development for radical innovation.[18]

The success of Japanese industries in the sectors that account for most of their exports to the US is largely the consequence of success at developmental activity, rather than industrial policy as some have claimed (Audretsch and Yamawaki, 1988).[19] During most of the post-war years, the J-firm did not have to rely on basic research, since it was able to 'absorb' and develop technologies initially invented by American (but not European) firms. Through process development the J-firm has been able to achieve comparative advantage in manufacturing industries where sophisticated manufacturing skills and technology are of crucial importance. The dominant view of the innovation process in the A-firm – both large and small – focuses largely upon the earliest stages of the innovation process. It is essentially Schumpeterian in its preoccupation with discontinuities and 'creative destruction', to the neglect of cumulative, smaller incremental changes.

There is an accumulation of evidence that many recent Japanese successes are a consequence of greater *organizational* effectiveness in providing strong incentives for downstream development activities. The Japanese commonly provide for close interaction between product design and production engineering in the internal organization of their firms. They devote far more attention than do the A-firms to the refinement of the appropriate process technologies, and assign a more prominent role to the engineering department. While it has been known for a long time that the A-firm devotes about two-thirds of its R&D budget to new products and one-third to improve process technology, Mansfield (1988) finds that the proportions are reversed in the J-firm.[20] An important lesson for the A-firm is that if it were to improve its developmental skills, it would also improve its productivity.[21]

A remarkable feature of the organization of industry in Japan is the extent of decentralization in the manufacturing sector, a trend that appears to be accelerating over time.[22] The structure of Japanese manufacturing industry appears to have diverged broadly from that of the US. By the mid-1980s over three-quarters of the manufacturing labour-force was employed in enterprises with fewer than 500 employees (Yokokara, 1988). The importance of small firms in Japan cannot be understood without examining their role in the famous subcontracting system. The subcontracting system does not seem to be just a device to deliver monopolistic rent to the large contracting firm, but seems to exist for reasons of productive and informational efficiency. The shortage of capital to internalize these activities to the extent found in the A-firm is an often mentioned reason for the extent of the subcontracting system – and, therefore, the presence of small firms. However, if this were the only reason, '...and there was no intrinsic advantage in subcontracting...over more complete integration, the former would have gradually been replaced by the latter as the growth rate of the economy slowed down and the internal resources of the J-firm accumulated in the 1970s and the 1980s' (Aoki, 1988, p. 214). By subcontracting, the J-firm may have developed a comparative advantage over the A-firm by allocating scarce managerial resources to such *key* developmental activities as design, process innovation (assembly) and product innovation. This characteristic has accelerated rather than declined.

While most theories of the J- and A-firm still focus on large corporations, Piore and Sabel (1984) have argued that demand is shifting away from traditional mass production products towards more small-batch production, which is facilitated by firm flexibility.[23] According to Carlsson (1984, p. 91): '... it is clear that the economics of industrial production has been revolutionized by the cost reduction of small scale production relative to large scale and the degree of *flexibility* offered by the technology'.[24] A general outcome of these factors is that in mass production industries the greater flexibility of the new forms of automation is likely to allow the efficient survival of relatively smaller firms (as compared to the past) (Dosi, 1988).

The question of flexibility is directly linked to scale economies in the manufacturing process. Essentially, the greater the need for flexibility, the more difficult it is to utilize a highly dedicated machine designed for a large-scale production line, since the production volume is determined by both the type of product and the market, not by the manufacturer alone. Thus, in considering flexibility, it is necessary to include not just capacity utilization aspects but also strategic (management) questions relating to the organization of the firm, as well as technological (engineering) questions relating to the manufacturing processes themselves. Strategic flexibility relates to the planning curve (envelope curve) of the firm in the sense that it reflects a menu of choices and the ability of the firm to *reposition* itself in the market (Marschak and Nelson, 1962). This type of flexibility resides primarily in the *organization*; in its people, their attitudes, and their interaction with one other and the outside world (Harrigan, 1985). A truly flexible firm will exhibit strategic flexibility (dynamic) as well as operational (static) flexibility.

The shift to modern flexible technology has been much faster in both large *and* small J-firms (and in Sweden) than in the US.[25] The reason, as Aoki (1988) and Dore (1987) make clear, is that advanced skills, flexibility and co-operation of the labour-force are required attributes of the J-firm which are inhibited by Taylorist organization and formal, low-trust collective bargains in Western (A-) firms.[26] Even automation in large-scale automation production poses similar requirements and has therefore been relatively unsuccessful in the US. 'The Japanese auto companies benefit from team systems because the systems are linked to decentralized manufacturing practices, a linkage missing in the American auto companies' (Katz *et al.*, 1987, p. 709).

Zuboff (1988) argues that we need to abandon the assumption that managers are different from the people they manage. One of the conditions that made workers appear different in the past was that workers had no information about the work process. With information technologies, workers are capable of thinking and acting on the information they have. If they are also given the skills to exploit information, a very powerful organizational resource can be created.

Outside of Japan small entrepreneurial firms seem to come closest to J-type organization. This is, of course, facilitated by high education and skill levels, and relatively small firm scale.[27] Large, mature firms with organized labour are generally not conducive to innovation, partly because of more rigid work rules and job classifications under formal bargaining, and perhaps also due to rent seeking. New start-ups and spin-offs are as severely handicapped in Europe as in Japan by a limited venture capital market. Their overregulated labour markets, and the risk aversion of experienced managers who seldom leave secure jobs (FitzRoy, 1989) are other contributing factors. Last but not least, decades of misguided policy and subsidies in support of relatively inefficient large firms in Europe have raised artificial barriers (Geroski and Jacquemin, 1985).

In Eastern Europe (Amann and Cooper, 1982), the introduction of new technologies tended to be impeded by the requirement for approval and assistance by planning authorities, who are generally more preoccupied with short-term crises than with routine decisions. At least part of this technological sluggishness can be attributed to a system of bureaucratic centralized decision-making, where the incentives not to innovate may be even greater than the incentives to innovate. The diffusion of technological information tended to be retarded because there is no direct contact between purchasers and suppliers. The decision to invest in cost-cutting process innovations was invariably sacrificed to attain and exceed the output targets set by the central planning authority. Even if an enterprise developed and introduced a new product, the lack of price flexibility dampened the rewards accruing to such innovative activity.

Moreover, Eastern European countries virtually choked off any meaningful entry of new firms from abroad in order to maintain the centralization of economic assets. Like Sherlock Holmes's dog that didn't bark, the importance of entry to the centrally planned economies might have been somewhat overlooked because of entry's most significant feature, namely, its absence (Murrell, 1990, p. 66).

Finally, as the new institutional economics of the firm has made evident, some economic activities must be undertaken within organizations. Exclusive focus on markets versus planning obscures this fact. Examples of such activities are the transfer of technological information and the exchange of goods for which quality is difficult to ascertain (Williamson, 1985). Eastern Europe's isolation from multinational firms has spoken to deny it benefits that accrued to American and Western European firms from Japanese transplants. These transplants brought Japanese-style management and important technological information with them.

Some concluding observations
Because institutional economists of the firm have tended to concentrate on the large corporation, they have neglected comparisons with the very differ-

ent modes of organization that characterize the Japanese firm. We have reviewed evidence relating to the superior performance of the latter, and the ways in which its internal organization inhibits change in large corporations in Western Europe. Strong trade unions and co-determination appear to create inflexibility in both organizations and labour markets. This experience implies that if the focus is exclusively upon the transition from planning to a market economy, it will obscure problems of organization at the level of the firm in Eastern Europe which are more important for long-run efficiency, as is the introduction of rational pricing.

Eastern European economies are triply handicapped by the large bureaucratic organizations favoured by official policy, by overregulated markets, *and* by high barriers to entry which emphasize product innovation as found in the US. A persistent tradition of policies favouring large firms, based on ill-founded beliefs in economies of scale, has operated to exacerbate Eastern European problems. However, privatization alone will not alleviate the problem posed by four decades of the centralization of assets. The debate over privatization in Eastern Europe needs to be viewed in a larger context and recast more in terms of managerial efficiency. Eastern Europe must redirect its economic policies away from mass production and scale economies. Managers must create more flexible organizations in place of mass production firms by incorporating the lessons that can be learned from Japan and the US. It will take competition from other companies to discipline managerial behaviour. Policy-makers must create and maintain competition by encouraging the entry of new domestic firms as well as foreign multinationals, and also by supporting the institutions and infrastructure which facilitate non-market co-operative agreements and joint ventures between small enterprises under 'flexible networking'.

Academics and policy-makers have delayed too long in applying the microeconomic lessons from Japan which recent comparative studies have emphasized, and which progressive entrepreneurs in the United States and Western Europe have long practiced. While more attention has been paid to the more obvious macroeconomic problems (Blanchard *et al.*, 1991), further research on micro-comparisons is clearly needed.

Notes

1. The precarious political and economic state of the emerging Eastern democracies leaves little leeway for social-Darwinist experiments based on simplistic economic models of markets without hierarchies and organizations with no transition costs. In addition to the external market, institutions and incentives for internal organizational change are urgently required, and lessons from comparisons of Japan and the West should no longer be ignored.

2. Lack of attention to existing – and more desirable – modes of internal organization in Eastern firms has accompanied almost exclusive emphasis on markets to enforce efficient production. Recent experience in the US and UK show that competition can eliminate

not only individual firms but also whole industries, rather than generating the rapid switch to the efficient, J-firm organization necessary for survival (Best, 1990; Lazonick, 1990).

3. This section draws heavily on FitzRoy and Acs (1992).

4. See FitzRoy and Mueller (1977, 1984) and Williamson (1985) for further development of this point.

5. Karier (1988) shows that unions capture about half the monopoly rents in concentrated industries in the US. Even for non-unionized workers there are large and stable inter-industry wage differentials for individuals with the same personal characteristics. These differentials are, however, correlated with industry union density, concentration, firm size and capital intensity, suggesting union threat effects, or efficiency-wage, rent-sharing explanations (Dickens and Katz (1986); Krueger and Summers (1988)). Unioni-zation is also negatively related to innovation (Acs and Audretsch (1988)).

6. See Acs and FitzRoy (1989) for a review of Leibenstein and Tomer. Arrow (1974) and Fox (1974) provide early statements of essentially this situation from very different perspectives, and Hill (1981) gives a more recent sociological account of related areas.

7. Freeman and Medoff (1984) claim that unionization can raise productivity (and wages) by improving co-operation through 'collective voice'. FitzRoy and Kraft (1985, 1987a) and FitzRoy (1988) develop Duncan and Stafford's (1982) point that collective bargains seem to reduce workers' job satisfaction. Any measured productivity gains may thus come at the price of harder and more regimented work, though quit rates decline because union bargains emphasize seniority benefits. Work sharing is opposed by US unions, who favour lay-offs instead.

8. See Gordon (1982). FitzRoy and Hart (1988) show that both wages and bonus payments in Japan are highly responsive to cyclical indicators, and that bonuses are a constant fraction of labour cost at industry level. Aoki (1988) also rejects Weitzman's (1984) 'simplistic' view of bonuses as simple profit-sharing, but instead emphasizes employees 'equity stake' in their enterprise, implicitly defined through steep age – earnings profits.

9. McCormick and Marshall (1987) regard the J-firm as essentially a workers' co-opera-tive. Though there are similarities, the important distinction remains that management is not formally elected or controlled by the work-force.

10. Ouchi (1981) already found J-firm or 'Theory Z' features in the best managed A-firms. Western experiments with co-operatives and participative management are described by Bonin and Putterman (1986) and Bradley and Gelb (1983a, b). Group incentives under uncertainty and the positive effects of explicit profit-sharing are studied by FitzRoy and Kraft (1985, 1986, 1987b). However, simply adding profit-sharing for tax or related reasons to an unchanged, Taylorist work organization is unlikely to improve motivation, and Blanchflower and Oswald (1987) find no effects in a large British sample where tax incentives are likely to have played a major role. Almost all studies surveyed in Blinder (1990) find a positive association between profit sharing, team work and productivity. Also see Lazonick (1990).

11. See Benelli *et al.* (1987), Kirsch *et al.* (1984) and Streeck (1984) for detailed studies of co-determination. Nutzinger *et al.* (1987) find no change in work organization from co-determination.

12. In a dramatic comparison of US and European experience, Freeman and Medoff (1984, p. 296) shows that: 'countries with large increases in real wages ... had smaller growth in employment or total hours than countries with small wage increases'.

13. FitzRoy and Kay (1990) provide more details. It is interesting to note that co-determi-nation in Sweden, with its still more centralized and 'corporatist' bargaining structure, has helped to restrain real wage growth and supported far-reaching experiments in flexible team-work. An example of this is Volvo, which had no counterpoints among large German employers until a recently announced decision to switch all assembly to team-work at GM auto subsidiary Opel.

14. Alchian and Woodward (1988) seem to be unaware of the historical record which shows that Taylorist management and division of labour have progressively *replaced* team-work

with more easily monitored, precisely defined and simplified individual job classifications (Gordon *et al.* (1982)).

15. There are signs of change, however, and, with its negligible military budget, Japanese civilian R&D expenditure as a percentage of sales now matches the US, with major efforts in key areas such as super-computers and super-conductivity (National Science Board (1985)). Though US R&D spending is nearly three times Japan's, a third goes to defence, which no longer drives commercial innovation (Dosi (1988)).

16. A firm's relative innovative advantage is likely to be roughly proportional to the number of suitably qualified people exposed to the *knowledge base* from which innovative ideas might derive. The key feature of a particular environment constitutes what Winter (1984) terms a 'technological regime'. For a test of the Winter hypothesis see Acs and Audretsch (1988).

17. For discussion of flexible networking in several countries see Best (1990), Howard (1990), Sengenberger *et al.* (1990), FitzRoy (1991) and Van Kooij (1991).

18. If cultural and institutional factors continue to inhibit the development of radical innovations in Japan, Huppes (1987) sees a comparative advantage for the West emerging as technical change becomes increasingly important. This view, may, however, underestimate the ability of the large J-firm to decentralize and foster innovation without the problems caused by the tradition of centralized decision-making and vertical control in the A-firm.

19. See Komiya *et al.* (1988) for a detailed study of industrial policy in Japan, and Fransman (1989) who emphasizes both government and private policy.

20. In his much quoted work, Williamson (1985) devotes little space to questions of technological change. Similarly, Leibenstein (1987) also ignores the issue of technology, while Tömer (1987) at least makes an attempt to discuss the question.

21. It is widely perceived that in the US, and to a lesser extent in the UK, small-firm innovation (and small-firm entry) (Acs and Audretsch (1989)) may indeed have been a partial response to the slowdown of the innovation process during the 1970s in large firms. For rigorous evidence on small-firm innovation for the US see Acs and Audretsch (1987) and for the UK see Pavitt *et al.* (1987). See Bailey and Chakrabarti (1988) for a complete discussion on innovation and productivity.

22. Japan has not been immune from mergers and acquisition, either during the 1960s or, more recently, in the 1980s. Nonetheless, the mergers that do occur primarily involve *small firms*. Between 1960 and 1970, for example, more than 9000 mergers were recorded. Of these, however, only 57 were capitalized at a value exceeding 3 million yen, and the bulk of them were in the distribution sector (Adams and Brock (1988, p. 40)) [emphasis added]. This seems to contradict Williamson's argument that take-overs are needed to enforce efficiency, and Chandler's earlier view that the trend in modern economies is towards increasingly vertically integrated production.

23. Numerically controlled (NC) machine tools occupy an intermediate position between 'Detroit automation' (transfer machines) and conventional hand-operated machines. In the early days of numerical control, and until the beginning of the 1970s, the application of the technology was heavily orientated towards production of small batches. But in the 1970s, increasing emphasis has been put on making NC machines larger and faster, making them more competitive with transfer machines.

24. Despite growing evidence on the increased importance of small firms (Birch (1987); Brock and Evans (1986, 1989); Sengenberger *et al.* (1990)), disagreement still remains regarding both the extent of the shift in the size distribution of firms, as well as the contribution of technology as a catalyst (Carlsson (1989); Acs, Audretsch and Carlsson (1991); Geroski and Pomroy (1987)).

25. There seems to be some evidence that small and medium Japanese firms have been trying to raise their capital intensity since the 1960s (McCormick (1988)). For evidence on the diffusion of flexible technology internationally see Carlsson (1989).

26. For a review of this literature see Campbell (1991).

27. Recent evidence suggests that small-firm entry, while not only different from large-firm entry, is facilitated in those industries where the inherent scale disadvantage of small

firms has been diminishing over time and where small firms have been able to implement a strategy of innovation (Acs and Audretsch (1989)).

References

Abbeglen, J.C. and Stock, G.K. (1985), *The Japanese Corporation*, New York: Basic Books.

Acs, Z. J. and Audretsch, D.B. (1987), 'Innovation, Market Structure and Firm Size', *Review of Economics and Statistics*, **69**, November, 567–75.

Acs, Z.J. and Audretsch, D.B. (1988), 'Innovation in Large and Small Firms', *American Economic Review*, **78**, September, 678–90.

Acs, Z.J. and Audretsch, D.B. (1989), 'Small Firm Entry in US Manufacturing', *Economica*, **55**, 255–65.

Acs, Z.J. and Audretsch, D.B. (1993), *Entrepreneurship and Small Firms: An East–West Perspective*, Cambridge: Cambridge University Press.

Acs, Z.J. and FitzRoy, F.R. (1989), 'Inside the Firm and Organization Capital', *International Journal of Industrial Organization*, **7**, 299–314.

Acs, Z.J., Audretsch, D.B. and Carlsson, B. (1991), 'Flexible Technology and Firm Size', *Small Business Economics*, **3**, (4), 307–20.

Adams, Walter and Brock, James W. (1988), 'The Bigness Mystique and the Merger Policy Debate: An International Perspective', *Northwestern Journal of International Law & Business*, **9**, (1), Spring, 1–48.

Alchian, A.A. and Woodward, S. (1988), 'Review of Williamson's The Economic Institutions of Capitalism', *Journal of Economic Literature*, **26**, (1), 65–79.

Amann, R. and Cooper, J. (eds) (1982), *Industrial Innovation in the Soviet Union*, New Haven: Yale University Press.

Aoki, M. (1988), *Information, Incentives and Bargaining in the Japanese Economy*, Cambridge: Cambridge University Press.

Arrow, K.J. (1974), *The Limits of Organization*, New York: Norton.

Audretsch, D.B. and Yamawaki, H. (1988), 'R & D Rivalry, Industrial Policy, and US – Japanese Trade', *Review of Economics and Statistics*, **10**, August, 438–47.

Bailey, M.N. and Chakrabarti, A.K. (1988), *Innovation and the Productivity Crisis*, Washington, DC: Brookings Institution.

Benelli, G. *et al.* (1987), 'Labor Participation in Corporate Policy-Making Decisions: West Germany's Experience with Codetermination', *Journal of Business*, **60**, 553–76.

Best, M.H. (1990), *The New Competition: Institutions of Industrial Restructuring*, Cambridge: The MIT Press.

Birch, D.L. (1987), *Job Creation in America*, New York: The Free Press.

Blanchard, O., Dornbush, R., Krugman, P., Layard, R. and Summers, L. (1991), *Reform in Eastern Europe*, Cambridge, MA: The MIT Press.

Blanchflower, D. and Oswald, A. (1987), 'Profit-Sharing: Can It Work?', *Oxford Economic Papers*, **1**, 1–19.

Blinder, A. (ed.) (1990), *Paying for Productivity*, Washington: The Brookings Institution.

Bonin, J.P. and Putterman, L. (1986), *Economics of Cooperation and the Labor Managed Economy*, New York: Harwood Academic Publishers.

Bradley, K. and Gelb, A. (1983), *Cooperative Industrial Relations: The Mondragon Experience*, London: Maneiann.

Brock, W.A. and Evans, D.S. (1986), *The Economics of Small Business*, New York: Holmes and Meyer.

Brock, W.A. and Evans, D.S. (1989), 'Small Business Economics', *Small Business Economics*, **1**, 7–20.

Campbell, D.C. (1991), *Managing Manpower for Advanced Manufacturing Technology*, Paris: OCDE.

Carlsson, B. (1984), 'The Development and Use of Machine Tools in Historical Perspective', *Journal of Economic Behavior and Organization*, **5**, 91–114.

Carlsson, B. (1989), 'The Evolution of Manufacturing Technology and its Impact on Industrial Structure: An International Study', *Small Business Economics*, **1**, January, 21–38.

Clague, C. and Rausser, G.C. (1991), *The Emergence of Market Economies in Eastern Europe*, Cambridge, MA: Blackwell.

Dickens, W.T. and Katz, L.F. (1986), 'Inter-Industry Wage Differences and Industry Characteristics', in: K. Lang and J. Leonard (eds), *Unemployment and the Structure of Labor Markets*, London: Basil Blackwell.

Dore, R. (1987), *Taking Japan Seriously: A Confucia Perspective on Leading Economic Issues*, Stanford, CA: Stanford University Press.

Dosi, G. (1988), 'Sources, Procedures and Microeconomics Effects of Innovation', *Journal of Economic Literature*, **26**, September, 1120–71.

Duncan, G.F. and Stafford, F.P. (1982), 'Do Union Members Receive Compensating Wage Differentials?', Reply, *American Economic Review*, **72**, 868–72.

FitzRoy, F.R. (1988), 'The Modern Corporation: Efficiency, Control and Comparative Organization', *Kyklos*, **41**, (2), 239–62.

FitzRoy, F.R. (1989), 'Age Structure, Employment Problems, and Economic Policy', paper prepared for the Commission of the European Communities, April 10, Brussels.

FitzRoy, F.R. (1991), 'Firm Size, Efficiency and Employment Revisited: A Review Article', *Small Business Economics*, **3**, (4), 321–4.

FitzRoy, F.R. and Acs, Z.J. (1992), 'The New Institutional Economics of the Firm and Lessons from Japan', *Japan and the World Economy*, 129–43.

FitzRoy, F.R. and Hart, R.A. (1988), 'Wage Component Behavior in Japanese Manufacturing Industries', in H. Konig (ed.), *New Developments in Wage Determination*, Heidelberg–New York: Springer-Verlag.

FitzRoy, F.R. and Kay, N. (1990), 'The Corporation in an Uncertain World', in D. Sugarman and G. Tenbarer (eds), *Regulating Corporate Groups in Europe*, Namos, Baden-Baden, 134–56.

FitzRoy, F. R. and Kraft, K. (1985), 'Participation and Division of Labor', *Industrial Relations Journal*, **16**, Winter, 68–74.

FitzRoy, F.R. and Kraft, K. (1986), 'Profitability and Profit Sharing', *Journal of Industrial Economics*, **35**, December, 113–30.

FitzRoy, F.R. and Kraft, K. (1987a), 'Cooperation, Productivity and Profit Sharing', *Quarterly Journal of Economics*, **102**, February, 23–37.

FitzRoy, F.R. and Kraft, K. (1987b), 'Efficiency and Internal Organization: Work Councils in West German Firms', *Economica*, **54**, 493–504.

FitzRoy, F.R. and Mueller, D.C. (1977), 'Contract and the Economics of Organization', paper presented at Interlaken, Switzerland, Seminar on Analysis and Ideology.

FitzRoy, F.R. and Mueller, D.C. (1984), 'Conflict and Cooperation in Contractual Organization', *Quarterly Review of Economics and Business*, **24**, Winter, 24–49.

Florida, R. and Kenney, M. (1991), 'Transplanted Organizations: The Transfer of Japanese Industrial Organization to the US', *American Sociological Review*, **56**, 1–18.

Fox, A. (1974), *Beyond Contract: Work, Power and Trust Relations*, London: Faber and Faber.

Fransman, M. (1989), *The Market and Beyond*, Cambridge: Cambridge University Press.

Freeman, R.R. and Medoff, J.L. (1984), *What Do Unions Do?*, New York: Basic Books.

Galbraith, J.K. (1967), *American Capitalism: The Concept of Countervailing Power*, revised edn, Boston, MA: Houghton Mifflin.

Geroski, P.A. and Jacquemin, A. (1985), 'Industrial Change, Barriers to Mobility, and European Industrial Policy', *Economic Policy*, **1**, (November), 169–204.

Geroski, P.A. and Pomroy, R. (1987), 'Innovation and the Evolution of Market Structure', Working Papers Series Number 26, November, London Business School.

Goodman, J.B. and Loveman, G. (1992), 'Does Privatization Serve the Public Interest?', *Harvard Business Review*, November-December, p. 40.

Gordon, D., Edwards, R. and Reich, M. (1982), *Segmented Work, Divided Workers*, New York: Cambridge University Press.

Gordon, R.J. (1982), 'Why US Wage and Employment Behavior Differs From that In Japan', *Economic Journal*, **92**, March, 13–44.

Harrigan, K.R. (1985), *Strategic Flexibility: A Management Guide for Changing Times*, Lexington, MA: Lexington Books.

Hill, S. (1981), *Competition and Control at Work*, London: Heinemann.

Howard, R. (1990), 'Can Small Business Help Countries Compete?', *Harvard Business Review*, Nov.–Dec., 88–103.

Huppes, T. (1987), *The Western Edge*, Boston: Kluwer Academic Publishers.

Imai, K. and Itani, H. (1984), 'Inter Penetration of Organization and Markets', *International Journal of Industrial Organization*, **2**, 285–310.

Karier, T. (1988), 'New Evidence on the Effect of Unions and Imports on Monopoly Power', *Journal of Post Keynesian Economics*, **10**, Spring, 414–27.

Katz, H.C., Kochan, T.A. and Keefe, J.H. (1987), 'Industrial Relations and Productivity in the US Automobile Industry', *Brookings Paper on Economic Activity*, **3**, 685–728.

Kirsch, W., Scholl, W. and Paul, G. (1984), *Mitbestimmung in der Unternehmenspraxis* Munchen: B. Kirsch.

Kochan, T.A., Katz, H.C. and McKersie, R.B. (1986), *The Transformation of American Industrial Relations*, New York: Basic Books.

Komiya, Ryutaro, Okuno, M. and Sazumura, K. (1988), *Industrial Policy in Japan*, New York: Academic Press.

Kooij, van, Evan (1991), 'Japanese Subcontracting at a Crossroads', *Small Business Economics*, **3**, (2), 145–54.

Kornai, Janos (1990), *The Road to a Free Economy, Shifting from a Socialist System: The Example of Hungary*, New York: W. W. Norton and Company.

Krueger, A.B. and Summers, L.H. (1988), 'Efficiency Wages and the Inter-Industry Wage Structure', *Econometrica*, **56**, March, 259–94.

Lazonick, W. (1990), *Competitive Advantage on the Shop Floor*, Cambridge: Harvard University Press.

Leibenstein, H. (1987), *Inside the Firm*, Cambridge: Harvard University Press.

Leijonhufvud, A. (1985), 'Capitalism and the Factory System', in: R.N. Langlois (ed.), *Economics as a Process*, ch. 9, Cambridge: Cambridge University Press.

Lenin, V. (1916), *Imperialism as the Latest Phase of Capitalism*, New York: International Publishers.

Mansfield, E. (1988), 'Industrial R & D in Japan and the US: A Comparative Study', *American Economic Review*, **18**, May, 223–28.

Marschak, T., and Nelson, R.R. (1962), 'Flexibility, Uncertainty and Economic Theory', *Metroeconomica*, **65**, 42–58.

Marx, K. (1912), *Capital*, translated by Ernest Untermann, vol. 1, Chicago: Kerr.

McCormick, B.J. and Marshall, G.P. (1987), 'Profit-Sharing, Job Rotation and Permanent Employment: The Large Japanese Firm as a Producer's Co-op', *Industrial and Economic Democracy*, **8**, 171–82.

McCormick, K. (1988), 'Small Firms, New Technology and the Division of Labor in Japan', *New Technology, Work and Employment*, **3**, Autumn, 134–42.

Milanovic, B. (1990), 'Privatization in Post-Communist Societies', *World Bank*, Washington, DC: World Bank mimeo.

Murrell, P. (1990), *The Nature of Socialist Economies: Lessons from Eastern Europe Foreign Trade*, Princeton: Princeton University Press.

Murrell, P. (1991), 'Symposium on Economic Transition in the Soviet Union and Eastern Europe', *Journal of Economic Perspectives*, **5**, Autumn, 3–9.

National Science Board (1985), *Science Indicators: The 1985 Report*, Washington, DC: US Government Printing Office.

Nutzinger, H.P., Schasse, U. and Teichert, V. (1987), 'Mitbestimmung in zeitlicher Perspektive: Ergebnisse einer Fallstudie in einem Grossbetrieb der Autoindustrie', in: F.R. FitzRoy and K. Kraft (eds), *Mitarbeiterbeteiligung und Mitbestimmung in Unternehmen*, Berlin/New York: De Gruyter.

OECD (1991), *Managing Manpower for Advanced Manufacturing Technology*, Paris.

Ouchi, W. (1981), *Theory Z*, New York: Addison-Wesley.

Pavitt, K., Robson, M. and Townsend, J. (1987), 'The Size Distribution of Innovating Firms in the UK: 1945–1983', *Journal of Industrial Economics*, **55**, March, 291–316.

Piore, M.J. (1991), 'Eastern Europe: The Limits of the Free Market Solution', mimeo, MIT, Cambridge.

Piore, M.J. and Sabel, C.F. (1984), *The Second Industrial Divide: Possibilities for Prosperity*, New York: Basic Books.

Roman, Zoltan (1990), 'Four Decades of Public Enterprise in Hungary', in John Heath (ed.), *Public Enterprise at the Crossroads*, London: Routledge.

Schleifer, A. and Summers, L.H. (1988), 'Breach of Trust in Hostile Takeovers' in A. Auerbach (ed.), *Corporate Takeovers: Causes and Consequences*, Chicago: University of Chicago Press.

Sengenberger, W., Loveman, G. and Piore, M. (1990), *The Reemergence of Small Business*, Geneva: ILO.

Stiglitz, J.E. (1987), 'The Causes and Consequences of the Dependence of Quality on Price', *Journal of Economic Literature*, **25**, 1–48.

Streeck, W. (1984), 'Co-determination: The Fourth Decade', in: B. Wilpert and A. Sorge (eds), *International Perspectives on Organizational Democracy*, New York: Wiley.

Tomer, J.F. (1987), *Organizational Capital*, New York: Praeger.

Weitzman, M. (1984), *The Share Economy*, Cambridge: Harvard University Press.

Williamson, O.E. (1985), *The Economic Institutions of Capitalism: Firms, Markets, Relational Contracting*, New York: Free Press.

Winter, S.G. (1984), 'Schumpeterian Competition in Alternative Technological Regimes', *Journal of Economic Behavior and Organization*, **5**, 287–320.

Yokokara, T.(1988), 'Small and Medium Enterprises', in: Ryutaro Komiya, M. Okuno and K. Sazumura (eds), *Industrial Policy of Japan*, New York: Academic Press, 513–39.

Zuboff, S. (1988), *In the Age of the Smart Machine*, New York: Basic Books.

13 Third World development: global structure

Anindya Datta

Introduction

While the prospects for growth and rising living standards in the newly privatized economies of the Commonwealth of Independent States and the former German Democratic Republic (East Germany) are deemed optimistic, the case may be otherwise among the less developed countries of the Third World.

The topic is best addressed by first highlighting some key features in the dialectics of economic development as a process in the relationship between the industrialized West or North, as the case may be, and the less developed countries (LDCs) over the centuries. In received literature, the dynamics of global finance are applied to a kind of inert mass known as the LDCs. The evolutionary dynamics of LDCs themselves are all but neglected and the historical conjunctures are overlooked.

It is well known that the optimistic vision of Marx in the *Communist Manifesto*, the vision of a direct and inevitable process of capitalist expansion replacing the old modes of production (and ensuring a process of capitalist accumulation and economic development following the pattern of the original home countries of capitalism), was far from realized (Brenner, 1977). The international division of labour imposed on the Third World had some special characteristics. As Raul Prebisch put it:

> Under the schema, the specific task that fell to Latin America, as part of the periphery of the world economic system, was that of producing food and raw materials for the great industrial countries.
>
> There was no place within it for the industrialization of the new countries. It is nevertheless being forced upon them by events. Two wars in a single generation and a great economic crisis between them have shown the Latin American countries their opportunities, clearly pointing the way to industrial activity (Prebisch, 1962).

On the other side of the globe, the same story held for India. The spurts towards industrialization came, not during the prolonged periods of high-level contact with the West, but when the contact was attenuated during the two World Wars (Datta, B., 1957). In the case of India, it has also been noted by scholars that the initial imports of British goods destroyed the erstwhile complementarity in the Indian economy between agriculture and manufacture and led to the phenomenon called 'deindustrialization' (Bagchi, 1976), and, further, that the emphasis on cash crops led to a prolonged stagnation of food output (Blyn, 1966).

The post-World War II period is very much more diverse, both with regard to the nature of the circumstances and processes and with regard to the successes and failures. First, the circumstances and processes. Some less developed countries received massive military and other assistance for geopolitical reasons (for example, South Korea and Taiwan). Others, by and large, attempted to raise themselves to a greater or lesser degree by their bootstraps (for example, China and India). These variations in circumstances are, however, not of enough help to understand the reasons for the relative successes as well as the relative failures. Some understanding of these reasons is a prerequisite for any meaningful perception of the future in terms of the global restructuring and its effects on the economic development of the Third World, which may be in the offing. It is this understanding which we shall attempt in some broad and rather sweeping outlines below.

The experience of the Third World has been much more complicated and much less uniform since World War II. In any study of the developmental issues of the Third World, one must avoid the notion of a homogeneous mass, and think in terms of something like the division of the less developed economies into four 'families'. These are a family of large, labour-surplus, natural resource-poor economies such as India and China, in which domestic or closed economy characteristics dominate; a family of small, labour-surplus, natural resource-poor economies such as Taiwan and South Korea, in which foreign trade necessarily plays an important role; a family of small natural resource-rich countries such as the Philippines, Malaysia and much of Latin America, in which trade is again important; and a family of developing countries such as those in sub-Saharan Africa that still struggle with the construction of the human and physical infrastructure requirements for transition to modern growth (Fei and Ranis, 1975).

An important fact of recent decades is the economic success story of Taiwan and South Korea. (I will not mention Hong Kong and Singapore in this connection. These latter are city states, not typical less developed countries.) In the presentation of the stories of Taiwan and South Korea, however, two basic elements are often lost sight of:

First, the pre-independence and post-independence history of economic development in Taiwan and Korea is unique in several ways. Effective land reform carried out at the urging of Wolf Ladejinsky and under the authority of General MacArthur was a critical element (Walinsky, 1977). The fact that the *émigré* population from the mainland did not have vested interests in land undoubtedly made the process easier. Again, unlike most of the colonial countries elsewhere in the Third World, where food production stagnated while cash crops were encouraged, Taiwan and Korea (as colonies of Japan) had important food producing roles assigned to them by Japan in order to relieve the latter's agricultural problems. Hence the agricultural sector in Taiwan, and to a lesser degree in Korea, was not stagnant when independence came. The relatively healthy agricultural sector and egalitarian distribution of land lent a helping hand in the further development of these countries when they embarked on modern development.

Secondly, in the post-independence economic development too, both Taiwan and South Korea went through several essential phases, each leading to the other. It is quite wrong to claim (as has often been done), that in South Korea and Taiwan growth did not really start until around 1960 when, in both countries, there was redirection of economic policy in favour of reliance on market mechanisms and doing away with regulations and interventions. It is also untrue that the East and South-east Asian experience suggests that if the basic policy framework is non-interventionist, only limited sectoral policies are needed to stimulate areas of actual and potential comparative advantage. Painstaking work, mindful of historical specificities and preconditions, is the basis for the typology shown in Table 13.1 (Fei, Ohkawa and Ranis, 1985).

Table 13.1:   Development typology

Phase	Japan	Taiwan	Korea
P–0	Before 1870: isolation heritage	Before 1950: traditional export expansion	Before 1953: traditional export expansion
P–1	1870–1900: traditional export expansion coupled with mild primary import substitution	1950–62: primary import substitution	1953–64: primary import substitution
P–2	1900–20: primary export substitution	1962–70: primary export substitution	1964–72: primary export substitution
P–3	After 1920: secondary import substitution	After 1970: secondary import and export substitution	After 1972: secondary import and export substitution

The clear findings were that during the primary substitution (phase P–1), governments protect the domestic non-durable consumer goods market, and domestic consumers pay high prices due to the relative inefficiency of the import-substituting industries. During phase P–2, import protection is gradually reduced, while exports are facilitated. During the secondary import and export-substitution phases (P–3 and P–4), there is renewed pressure for temporary protection, and there is a tendency during P–3 and P–4 towards gradual consolidation followed by a lowering of tariffs.

These findings strengthened the Fei–Ranis position *vis-à-vis* that of Little, Scitovsky and Scott; that is, the static comparative advantage view of international trade, and hence the view that the emergence of the export substitution phase was essentially a correction of the mistakes of the import substitution phase (Little, Scitovsky and Scott, 1970). Fei and Ranis viewed the deliberate import substitution phase as an essential prerequisite, involving both labour reallocation and learning experience for the transition from a colonial agriculture-based exports phase to a post-colonial labour-based exports phase.

Conscious policy design and intervention propel the economy through the transition. There is an on-again off-again play with the market mechanism. The phases are distinguishable for all three countries, although for the late-comers (Taiwan and South Korea) there is considerable 'telescoping'. The post-independence development of Taiwan presents a sustained and powerful counter-example to the Kuznets inverted 'U'-hypothesis of the necessity of inequality to accentuate for a long period when economic development makes headway and the growth rate of the economy accelerates.

In development economics it has become increasingly clear that the initial conditions in agriculture shape the future course of development in an LDC in a profound way. An agricultural sector developed along egalitarian lines permits the simultaneous attainment of growth and equity in several ways. It permits high labour-absorption, both in the agricultural sector and in the industrial sector, to start with. This is because egalitarian development of agriculture moves more towards land-saving technology than labour-saving technology, thus preventing 'premature migration' from the rural sector (Fei and Ranis, 1964). It also provides a wider and deeper *home market* for the labour-intensive mass consumption products, which, in its turn, allows the industrial sector to be more labour-absorptive in the primary import substitution phase and to maintain the level of high employment even beyond that. The width and depth of the home market for mass consumption products have more importance for the 'family' of large, densely populated countries; their absence in India, for example, made her import substitution phase quite ineffectual from the point of view of the economy as a whole (Datta, A., 1986, 1987).

There is an essential general difference between a small country and a large country, so far as the effectiveness of export as an engine of growth is concerned. A large country hits the demand barrier long before per capita export reaches a significant value. So, the role of the home market as the crucial factor at the beginning is relatively even more important for a large country than for a small country.

This is very much in evidence in the somewhat contrasting cases of Taiwan and South Korea (Fei and Ranis, 1975). While in the case of Taiwan the agricultural sector provided an important 'push' for industrialization, in the case of Korea the agricultural sector was 'pulled along' by the non-agricultural sector. In the abstract, one may conceive the South Korean economy eventually operating like the 'city states' of Hong Kong and Singapore, importing almost all required agricultural goods and depending entirely on exports. However, South Korea's agricultural sector and population are too large relative to the economy to easily and smoothly permit the hinterland being 'dragged along'.

This experience suggests that a large, densely populated country (a member of another 'family') such as India, with a moribund agricultural sector inherited from the colonial times, cannot hope to succeed along the lines of the South Korean economy. There is an apparent fallacy of composition involved in generalizing the East Asian model, on the basis of the fact that the Western markets could not absorb the exports if all of the LDCs developed the same export-orientation (Cline, 1982). But in what we discussed above, we found more deep-seated reasons to recognize; first, that the so-called East Asian model is not altogether homogeneous and, secondly, that even in a general sense it is not reproducible elsewhere.

Tugan Baranovsky's 'disproportionality crisis' may need to be solved along many different lines (Kalecki, 1971).[1] Specifically, a large country such as India, with her land reforms and egalitarian economic development thwarted early in the course of her post-independence efforts, proceeds slowly towards prematurely capital-intensive, luxury goods industries, with attenuated links with agriculture and augmented foreign linkage. There is some sliding back and forth between her populist politics and jettisoning of egalitarian priorities but, on the whole, there is a trend towards bypassing or de-emphasizing the backward subsistence agricultural sector.

In the case of a country like Brazil, belonging to another 'family', the political-economic swings are sharper and more dramatic. Interestingly, this perspective of the political economy of some leading Third World countries, which emerged above on the basis of some themes in the relatively mainstream literature, will be found to have been developed in the alternative literature, too, although often enunciated in different terms. Thus, Alain de Janvry explained the political-economic swings in the 'Southern cone'

(Argentina, Brazil, Chile, and so on) in terms of 'disarticulation' and pressures for 'articulation' (de Janvry, 1985).

Upon further introspection, one can also argue that in the countries of the Third World, where the crucial desideratum of the home market has not been provided for, the quest for a development away from the path of organically combining growth with equity has generally been facilitated by the nature and functioning of globalized finance in recent times. From Adam Smith's 'vent for surplus' to Rosa Luxemburg's 'third country', there is a tradition in the field of production, and from Hilferding to Minsky there is a tradition in the field of finance. Historical evidence suggests a pattern of US banking in the 1920s; moving its concentration of lending effort from the domestic manufacturing sector to countries in Latin America and to Germany, as they were recovering from the effects of World War I, and then turning to fund speculative activities in the New York stock exchange. There is a tell-tale similarity between this chain of events and the events of the 1960s to 1980s in the US (Darity and Horn, 1988).[2] It appears, however, that in resolving the issue related to how much of the current debt crisis of the Third World owes its origin to the loan push factor and how much to the loan pull factor, the conjunctural impulse arising from the unresolved problematique of the production structures of the Third World countries may provide a missing link. The LDCs (such as Taiwan and Korea) which dealt with the problem of the home market, and hence the problem of transition from labour-intensive production to capital-intensive production, much more successfully, used the modern modalities of globalized finance to their advantage. The countries which did not entered into the mutually reinforcing cycle of lending by the advanced centre and borrowing by the periphery, ultimately teetering on the brink of disaster. In the latter category the Latin American cases are more dramatic and more publicized, but the case of India is not less instructive.

Owing to its failure to deal with the problem of the home market, in the mid-1960s the Indian economy ran into what was called a 'structural retrogression' (Shetty, 1978), marked by considerable slowing down of the basic goods industries along with some buoyancy in the luxury goods producing industries. Import liberalization and foreign finance in the 1980s stimulated higher rates of growth in the Indian economy at the cost of losing the slowly built up potential for comparative advantage in some basic industries and by expanding in high import-content luxury industries (Kelkar and Kumar, 1990). This process is already running into the heavy weather of balance-of-payments problems with no clear resolution in sight.

There has been speculation in the larger global context as to whether or not the 'fictitious capital' aspect of the newly emerging globalized finance (awash with 'Eurodollars') along with a 'managerial class' would not turn capital to world-wide rent-seeking and return it in some sense to the characteristics of early competitive capitalism bereft of any clear-cut nation-state hegemony. While such speculation may have its place in connection with the long run, the foreseeable future does not seem to hold any optimistic prospects for the Third World. The potential impact of the entry of Eastern Europe into the world's market economy is likely to be negative by and large. The findings of the 1980s show a clear trend of trade diversion that has already begun to flush out the LDCs from the markets of the North (Nambiar *et al.*, 1991; Ghosh, 1989). As things proceed, Western Europe is likely to find its own production structure easier to mesh with East and Central European countries than with the LDCs. Thus, the extraordinary conjuncture with the premature and disproportionate export orientation of many LDCs with inadequately developed home markets may abate. Instead, there may be a closer conjuncture in Eastern and Central Europe between the need which the sphere of production or physical capital has for an external market and the need which the sphere of circulation or finance capital has for security and long-term gain.

Moreover, 'fictitious capital' is still not 'fictitious' enough. Ideology and nationalism will still play their role. The recent US move to have free trade with Mexico may be perceived as a move towards a trade bloc, a response to an integrated Europe. A trade bloc of the Americas will, however, be ill-equipped at this stage to arrest the trend towards uneven development, both within the hemisphere of the Americas and within the individual countries, for reasons explained earlier. Along the same lines, globally speaking, in the fields of trade and development the tussle between strategic mercantilism and static comparative advantage will continue, at a time when individual nations are finding monetary policy as an instrument for stabilization very much undermined (Currie *et al.*, 1989).[3] Can the newly industrializing countries fill the vacuum? It all depends. While they may be in a better position, owing to their recent historical memory of economic transition, the microcosm of the structure of an individual Third World country must provide the internal dynamics of its home market in order to bring to fruition the conjunctural impulses of the sphere of production and the sphere of circulation along a long-term growth sequence (Yaghmaian, 1990).[4]

Notes
1. History is not unilinear. At every juncture of history alternative choices for the resolution of an economic crisis are thrown open.
2. All this has been very succinctly discussed by Darity and Horn (1988).
3. The central bank's control over interest rates is undermined by global capital mobility and international policy co-ordination aimed at reducing exchange rate volatility.
4. Using the ideas of globalization of capital and Marx's expanded reproduction, Yaghmaian (1990) argues that import-substituting industrialization and export-led industrialization can be two stages of the globalization of production as opposed to two alternative

strategies, and that in both cases, developing countries inherit a built-in instability in the process of accumulation.

References

Bagchi, Amiya K. (1976), 'De-industrialization in India in the Nineteenth Century', *Journal of Development Studies*, January.

Blyn, George (1966), *Agricultural Trends in India 1891–1947: Output, Availability and Productivity*, University of Pennsylvania Press.

Brenner, Robert (1977), 'The Origins of Capitalist Development: A Critique of Neo-Smithian Marxism', *New Left Review*, 25–93.

Cline, William R. (1982), 'Can the East Asian Model of Development be Generalized?', *World Development*, **10**, (2), 81–90.

Currie, D.A., Holtham, G. and Hallett, A.H. (1989), 'The Theory and Practice of International Policy Coordination: Does Coordination Pay?', in Bryan, Currie, Frenkel, Masson and Portes (eds), *Macroeconomic Policies in an Interdependent World*, International Monetary Fund, 14–46.

Darity, William and Horn, Bobbie L. (1988), *The Loan Pushers–The Role of Commercial Banks in the International Debt Crisis*, Ballinger, 1–14.

Datta, Bhabatosh (1957), *The Economics of Industrialization*, 2nd edition, World Press, 2–4, 124–5.

Datta, Anindya (1986), *Growth and Equity – A Critique of the Lewis-Kuznets Tradition*, Oxford University Press.

Datta, Anindya (1987), 'Understanding East Asian Economic Development', in *Proceedings of the Eight International Symposium on Asian Studies, 1986*, Hong Kong Asian Research Service, 775–87.

de Janvry, Alain (1985), 'Social Disarticulation in Latin American History', in Kim, Kwan S. and Ruccio, David F. (eds), *Debt and Development in Latin America*, University of Notre Dame Press, 32–73.

Fei, John C.H. and Ranis, Gustav (1964), *Development of the Labor Surplus Economy*, Richard D. Irwin.

Fei, John C.H. and Ranis, Gustav (1975a), 'Agriculture in Two Types of Open Economies', in Reynolds, L.G. (ed.), *Agriculture in Development Theory*, Yale University Press, 355–72.

Fei, John C.H. and Ranis, Gustav (1975b), 'A Model of Growth and Employment in the Open Dualistic Economy: The Cases of Korea and Taiwan', *Journal of Development Studies*, **XI**, (2), January, 32–63.

Fei, John C.H., Ohkawa, Kazushi and Ranis Gustav (1985), 'Economic Development in Historical Perspective: Japan, Korea and Taiwan', in Ohkawa and Ranis (eds), *Japan and the Developing Countries*, Basil Blackwell.

Ghosh, Jayati (1989), 'Developing Countries – Narrowing Options', review article in the *Economic and Political Weekly* (December 16), on the *Trade and Development Report 1989*, United Nations Conference on Trade and Development, Geneva, September 1989.

Kalecki, Michal (1971), 'The Problem of Effective Demand with Tugan Baranovski and Rosa Luxemburg', in Kalecki, Michal, *Selected Essays on the Dynamics of the Capitalist Economy, 1933–1970*, London: Cambridge University Press.

Kelkar, V.L. and Kumar, R. (1990): 'Industrial Growth in the Eighties - Emerging Policy Issues', *Economic and Political Weekly*, January 27.

Little, I., Scitovsky, T. and Scott, M. (1970), *Industry and Trade in Some Developing Countries – A Comparative Study*, Oxford University Press.

Nambiar, R.G., Mehta, Rajesh and Tadas, G.A. (1991), 'East European Development – Impact on Trade of Developing Countries', *Economic and Political Weekly*, May 11.

Prebisch, Raul (1962), 'The Economic Development of Latin America and Its Principal Problems', in *Economic Bulletin for Latin America*, Economic Commission for Latin America, **VII**, (1), February, 1–23.

Shetty, S.L. (1978), 'Structural Retrogression in the Indian Economy', *Economic and Political Weekly*, Annual Number, February .

Walinsky, L.J. (ed.) (1977), *Agrarian Reforms as Unfinished Business – Selected Papers of Wolf Ladejinsky*, World Bank and Oxford University Press, 39–57, 67–153.
Yaghmaian, B. (1990), 'Development Theories and Development Strategies', in *Review of Radical Political Economics*, **22**, 174–88.

Index

pollution 3
Pomroy, R. 199
population
  Byelorussia 66
  and economic growth 21
  Germany (East) 145
  Germany (West) 145
  Kazakhstan 66
  Russia 66
  Ukraine 66, 184
  Uzbekistan 66
Portugal
  'backwardness' of 38–40, 53
  colonial wars 49
  economic growth 49–50
  employment 188
  exports 39
  government 39, 49–50, 53
  gross domestic product (GDP) 39–40
  imports 39
  output gap 50
  political instability 49–50
  productivity growth 37, 43–7, 49, 53
  size of state sector 188
  unemployment 50
post-Keynesian school 23–4
potential, development of 80–81
Prebisch, Raul 204
prices
  black market 101, 108, 130
  China 131
  consumer
    Germany (East) 166
    Germany (West) 109, 111
    Poland 109, 111
    Ukraine 184
  inflexibility of
    in planned economies 89–90, 179–80, 181
    under monopoly 95, 179–80, 181
  information on 31
  investment goods
    Germany (West) 109, 110
    Poland 109, 110
  liberalization of 92, 93, 104, 106, 108, 125, 126
  producer
    Germany (East) 166
  and resource allocation 28–9, 30, 89, 92, 93, 94, 97, 126

  Ukraine 179–80, 181, 183, 184
  see also equilibrium prices; inflation; marginal cost pricing
pricing policy, firms'
  and income distribution 21, 24
  marginal cost pricing 31, 32
  under imperfect competition 31
  under perfect competition 30–31, 33
private property
  and efficient markets 28, 31, 34
  expropriation of 58, 59, 61, 87, 162
  see also privatization; property rights
privatization
  Central and Eastern Europe 61–2, 89, 92–3, 96, 129, 148, 187–9, 197
  and efficiency 187–9, 197
  Germany (East) 11, 61, 148, 159, 162–4, 172
  identification of property rights after 2, 7, 61–2, 148, 162
  instrumental analysis and 137
  Poland 102, 107, 121, 122
  and property valuation 8, 93
  societal dangers of 3, 4, 11
  see also private property; property rights
producer prices
  Germany (East) 166
production–surplus approach 19, 20
productivity, labour
  Germany (East) 10, 144, 145, 149–50, 152–3, 164, 166, 171, 172
  Germany (West) 37, 43–9, 145, 152
  growth of
    and convergence hypothesis 6–7, Ch.3
    economic growth and 37–8, 52, 53, 68, 83, 132, 171
    Germany (West) 37, 43–9
    Japan 37, 43–9
    measurement of 37, 43–4, 53
    Norway 37, 43–9
    United States 68, 83
  in J-firm 191
  Poland 128–9, 138–9
  planned economies 30
  trade uinions and 198
product life-cycles 50–51, 53, 54
profitability
  and growth 19, 20